ATLA Monograph Series

edited by Dr. Kenneth E. Rowe

1. Ronald L. Grimes. *The Divine Imagination: William Blake's Major Prophetic Visions.* 1972.

2. George D. Kelsey. *Social Ethics Among Southern Baptists, 1917-1969.* 1973.

Social Ethics Among Southern Baptists, 1917-1969

by

GEORGE D. KELSEY

ATLA Monograph Series, No. 2

The Scarecrow Press, Inc., Metuchen, N. J.
and
the American Theological Library Association
1973

Library of Congress Cataloging in Publication Data

Kelsey, George D
   Social ethics among Southern Baptists, 1917-1969.

   (ATLA monograph series, no. 2)
   A revision of the author's thesis, Yale.
   1. Church and social problems--Baptists.
2. Southern Baptist Convention. 3. Social ethics.
I. Title. II. Series: American Theological Library
Association. ATLA monograph series, no. 2.
BX6207.A48K44 1972   286'.132   72-6332
ISBN 0-8108-0538-3

EDITOR'S FOREWORD

Although most American and Canadian doctoral dissertations in religion are available to scholars on microfilm, distribution and scholarly use is limited. A number of studies are submitted each year which deserve a better fate than to remain in the drawers of library microfilm cabinets.

The American Theological Library Association has undertaken responsibility for a modest dissertation publishing program in the field of religious studies. Our aim in this monograph series is to publish in serviceable format and at reasonable cost two dissertations of quality in the field of religious studies each year. Titles are selected by the Committee on Publication from titles nominated by Graduate School Deans or Directors of Graduate Studies in Religion.

George D. Kelsey is Professor of Christian Ethics at Drew University, Madison, N. J. He holds degrees from Morehouse College, Andover Newton Theological School and Yale University and has studied at Harvard University and the London School of Economics. His most recent book, Racism and the Christian Understanding of Man, was published by Scribner in 1965. Professor Kelsey's present study of social attitudes of Southern Baptists began as his Yale doctoral dissertation. A Travel and Study Award from the Ford Foundation for the academic year 1971-72 enabled him to extend his research and writing on the social thought of the nation's largest Protestant body. We are pleased to publish this study as number two in our series.

Kenneth E. Rowe, Editor

Drew University Library
Madison, New Jersey

iii

PREFACE

The Southern Baptists are one of the largest Protestant bodies in the United States. Although their churches and even conventions have been organized in other parts of the country, they are still overwhelmingly a southern, regional body. Owning to their size, long history and influence in the region, the South can seriously be spoken of as Southern Baptist territory.

As a major American religious body, Southern Baptists enjoy another distinction, or even advantage. They are the dominant religious group in the one region of the United States in which religion is still a powerful, if not the chief ethical sanction. It is not straining a point to say that the moral aspects of Southern culture have by and large been provided by Southern Baptists. Not only have they been the dominant religious body through the generations, but their prominence in the social, political, and economic life of the South has accorded with their numbers.

The purpose of this book is to reveal the nature and quality of the moral leadership of Southern Baptists in their region through an examination of their social doctrines. Some of the ethical teaching in this book is abstract. It represents the moment of cool reflection on a moral issue within the confines of the study. But much of it is direct interaction with events, debate, pronouncements, resolutions and appeals to constituencies. Throughout the book an effort is made to set forth the moral ideas and values in systematic and argued form, and to evaluate them within the framework of the history of Christian social teachings and the history and culture of the South.

The historical limits of the period under investigation are the years 1917-1969, inclusive. The year 1917 is used as the beginning of the period which I am designating as "contemporary" because it is the year in which America entered World War I, and marks, perhaps better than any other year, the beginning of a new social consciousness among large masses of Americans. It was the time when such phrases as "the new social order" and "saving the world for democracy" began to fall from the lips of the man in the street.

As to the matter of sources, I have attempted to get as near to the "grass roots" as possible by way of written documents. This accounts for the heavy use of state Baptist papers, Annuals of conventions, and minutes of associations. It just happens that these are the primary sources of Southern Baptist social ethics, although published volumes have also been fruitful.

The literature was approached without preconception as to what the categories of social thought would be. The eight chapters which follow "unfolded" from the sources.

Initial research on the subject of the social thought of Southern Baptists was begun in 1944. This effort culminated in a doctoral dissertation which served as a partial fulfillment of the requirements for the Doctor of Philosophy degree in Yale University.

The overwhelming bulk of the research for this study was done in the library of the Southern Baptist Theological Seminary. I owe hearty thanks to Dr. Leo T. Crismon and his staff for their courtesies and helpfulness to me. Dr. Keith C. Wills of the Southwestern Baptist Theological Seminary and his staff also assisted me in extending my research through the use of their library. To them I am grateful. Finally, I wish to thank the Ford Foundation for the Travel and Study Award which made the completion of research and the final organization and writing possible.

CONTENTS

vii

Chapter I

THE CHURCH

Christian churches have historically sought to validate
their authenticity by tracing their origins to the New Testament and by affirming their undeviating loyalty to New Testament faith and practice.   Southern Baptists are no exception
to this rule.   It may be said that the starting point for any
discussion of the nature of Southern Baptist churches is the
testimony that they are completely in harmony with New
Testament teaching and worshipping communities.   Southern
Baptists are not satisfied with having this affirmation stand
alone.   They go on to the added claim that Baptists are the
only Christian communion that has remained with the New
Testament.   Protestants are said to have emerged from
Catholicism and to have brought elements of Catholicism into
their present structure, life, and thought.   But Baptists
have never been Catholics and are not Protestants, having
maintained their New Testament purity through all the vicissitudes of church history.   Baptists in general, and Southern
Baptists in particular, are therefore subject only to the
Lordship of Christ and are free from every semblance of
"sponsorial"[1] religion.   Every believer is a priest, his
own soul being in direct touch with God through faith.

1.   The Nature of the Church

The church is divine in its origin.   It is divine both
in idea and organization.   "The idea of the church was not
conceived in the brains of men, but in the heart of God.
The organization of the church, the officers of the church,
the ordinances of the church, are divine in their appointment. "[2]

Having conceived the church and appointed its officers
and ordinances, God yet holds it as His own.   God alone is
the owner of the church; men are but the stewards of God
in carrying on its affairs.   "God has never relinquished His
ownership, He has never turned over His claims to another. "

1

This means that Jesus Christ is the true head of the church which is "to be administered under the laws of God and for the glory of God. "[3]

Since the church belongs to God and is rightfully administered under His laws and for His glory, there is only one true and original, ecclesiastical, structural principle. This principle is the Lordship of Christ in all things. Human wisdom and authority cannot properly be substituted for the supremacy of Christ as the head of His churches. The principle of the Lordship of Christ is inherent in the nature of the Church and accords with New Testament example. When human authority is substituted for loyalty to Christ, this can only be due to the weakening of the faith and accommodations to culture.

> How did Christians become separated into different groups or denominations? The explanation is simple and plain. Early in the history of Christendom Greek philosophy penetrated the thinking of Christians. There was a gradual weakening of Christian faith and, at the same time, there was a process of outward adjustment and accommodation to environment. [4]

Not only is the principle of obedience to Christ in all things inherent in the nature of the church and in accordance with New Testament example; this principle is also in harmony with the nature of the Christian religion. Faith in Jesus Christ, says E. Y. Mullins, is the essential of the Christian life, and the church is constituted of men and women who possess such faith. Every believer is a priest and has the right of direct approach to God. The believer is free, responsible, and subject to no ecclesiastical authority. Since the Holy Spirit dwells in every believing heart, the believer has the right even to interpret the Scriptures for himself. The form of church organization is the corporate expression of the spiritual life. "A self governing or democratic church organization, therefore, is the only form which can properly express the meaning of Christianity as a free and spiritual religion. "[5]

When the church is spoken of as a self-governing or democratic organization, Southern Baptists are usually referring to the local church. The overwhelmingly prevalent view among them is that the reality of the church is expressed in the local body of believers. The idea of the

Universal Church is rejected.   Even a denomination does not
constitute a church.   The church is found in the local organization of churches.

> There is no Scripture warrant for a Universal
> Church.   New Testament churches were local and
> distinct bodies,   each an entity in itself.   There
> were churches,   not a church.   In the very nature
> of the case this is the only possible way of having
> congregational or democratic government in the
> churches. [6]

In 1925 the Southern Baptist Convention adopted a
doctrinal statement under the title, "Baptist Faith and Message."   In 1963 the Convention reaffirmed the confessional
statement of 1925 with minor changes.   The doctrine of the
church as a local body of believers in Jesus Christ is set
forth in Section VI of this "official" theological document:

> A New Testament church of the Lord Jesus Christ
> is a local body of baptized believers who are
> associated by covenant in the faith and fellowship
> of the gospel,   observing the two ordinances of
> Christ,   committed to His teachings,   exercising the
> gifts,   rights,   and privileges invested in them by
> His Word and seeking to extend the gospel to the
> ends of the earth.
>
> This church is an autonomous body operating
> through democratic processes under the Lordship
> of Christ.   In such a congregation members are
> equally responsible.   Its Scriptural officers are
> pastors and deacons. [7]

The doctrinal formulation of 1963 adds to this definition of the church a statement that is not included in the 1925
document.   It is that "the New Testament speaks also of the
church as the body of Christ which includes all of the redeemed of all ages."   This affirmation is added without
elaboration but with the appropriate Scriptural citations.   It
may be taken as the basis of the judgment that Southern
Baptists do not deny absolutely the existence of the Universal
Church.   They deny its temporal existence.   This is in-
ferred by E. Y. Mullins when he says that for many people
the New Testament teaching as to Universal Church means
the total assembly of the redeemed in the life to come.
The Universal Church has no existence at present in any
sense; it exists only in heaven. [8]

Mullins himself defines the church as "a local body composed of believers in Jesus Christ who are associated together for the cultivation of the Christian life, the maintenance of the ordinances and discipline for the propagation of the Gospel."[9] This definition does not exclude the idea of the Universal Church, although it appears that it should. Rejecting the notion that the universal church is an outward organization with earthly ecclesiastical functions and powers, Mullins nevertheless declares that "it is most real in that it includes all true believers in Jesus Christ.... The universal church is as real as the Kingdom of God, indeed, it is practically identical with it...."[10] In an address to the Southern Baptists, George W. Truett expresses the same general idea when he says, "Whoever believes in Christ as his personal savior, is our brother in the common salvation."[11] J. B. Gambrell is even more specific in identifying non-Baptists as members of the Universal Church. "All believers in Christ, whether in Baptist Churches, protestant pedo-Baptist communions, Roman Catholic communions, or whether in other communions, or in no communions, are united in an indissoluble bond by their common faith in Christ...."[12]

The prevailing view that the church is a local organization of believers in Christ does not escape direct and explicit challenge. W. O. Carver complains that this way of defining the church is a development of the first half of the twentieth century and tends to place the emphasis on the church as an institution. Prior to the question, "what is the church?" the question should be asked, "why is the church?" A functional definition of the church is needed. First of all, the church should be considered as an instrument in the redemptive purpose of God, and not in the sense of an institution.

> Christ in redeemed men, who constitute His body, is God's hope of achieving His glory in human history. God's glory is to be achieved in the church and in Christ Jesus throughout all the generations of the age of the ages. (Eph. 3:20-21)

> In the light of these major considerations it ought to become clear that any proper definition of the local church should deal with it in terms of its relation to the eternal and agelong purpose and method of God working for the redemption of man-

kind. Such a definition should therefore derive its specifications from the nature and purpose of the Gospel. [13]

In the beginning in Jerusalem, both the Church and a church are discernible. There was a fellowship, a koinonia, a group made one by the common experience of the new life in Christ. This fellowship transcended the limits of a specific church embracing all the saints in love. For New Testament churches, all of the saints constituted the Church. [14]

The idea that the church is essentially a fellowship of the Spirit rather than an organization tends to be correlated with the doctrine of divine purpose.

A church is not simply an organization that men have brought into existence with religious ends and purposes in mind.... A New Testament church exists in history but it is supratemporal in nature. It comes from God. It is God's creation rather than man's organization. [15]

Fellowship, and not organization, is the main thing in a church that is true to the New Testament. "As a divine institution it is not so much an organization as it is a fellowship." Organization is only instrumental to the expression and development of fellowship. [16]

All of the well known symbols of the church of modern ecumenical theology are found in the thought of Theron D. Price. The church is spoken of as the Body of Christ, the people of God, the Elect of God, and the Fellowship of the Holy Spirit. [17] Furthermore, Price, in agreement with W. O. Carver, attacks the abandonment of the historic Baptist position as expressed in the popular view of the church as essentially local. He reminds Southern Baptists that their own confessions of faith attest to the fact that "the true significance of the local church always lay in its being a local embodiment of the Church General." [18]

2.   The Task of the Church

The church is a divine institution. It is administered under the laws of God and for the glory of God. The task of the church is therefore God-given. The church is commissioned by Christ to proclaim the gospel in all the world. Its

primary, basal, and foremost task is to win men from their
sins, to call them unto salvation. Evangelism is the kernel
of this task. "All of the programs of the Kingdom of God
should put evangelism preeminently first and make it the
main, overmastering matter."[19]

The goal of evangelism is both the regenerated individual and the transformed society. But the remaking of society is not a task distinct from the remaking of individuals,
inasmuch as society is transformed only by individuals regenerated through the preaching of the gospel. The service
which the renewed render to society is the fruit of their regeneration and has a transforming effect upon society.

Social service, however, is in no sense "a substitute
for individual personal regeneration and salvation." It is
"the fruit and not the tree...."[21] Proposals which aim at
the renovation of society by means of the elimination of
slums and the creation of better environments offer treatment only to symptoms and fail to reach the deadly disease.
Furthermore, such proposals constitute a method which
"clashes with the spirit and genius of Christianity which be-
gins with the regeneration of the individual units of society."[22]
There is no way of reaching the social order except through
individuals. "The social order is made or marred according
to the nature and motivating impulses of the individual
units."[23] Each Christian must apply Christian principles to
his own life; for Christianity must be applied from within.
The faith can only be applied to the whole of life by the cooperative efforts of individuals. "Christians can never hope
successfully to apply Christian principles to a non-Christian
society."[23]

All of those who would call the church into the arena
of public questions, says P. I. Lipsey, demonstrate a confused notion as to what the church is and what it is for.

> The commission of Christ to His churches was to
> make disciples, baptize them and teach them to ob-
> serve all His Commands. There will be many by-
> products of the gospel which are of great value,
> such as social, economic and government reforms,
> but these are the consequence of preaching a pure
> gospel, and must not be substitutes for it.[24]

The preaching of the gospel and the preaching of the
individualistic gospel are one and the same thing, according

to Leon Macon. In an article in the <u>Christian Century</u>, [25]
Reinhold Niebuhr called upon Billy Graham to preach against
collective as well as individual sins. In response to this
article, Macon displays an amazing ignorance of the prophetic tradition of Christianity and misunderstanding of Niebuhr
by charging Niebuhr with having asked Graham to become a
social reformer, with having criticized Graham for emphasizing the necessity of redemption, and with having minimized
Graham's insistence on conversion and rebirth.

> We trust Mr. Graham will not be swerved from
> his present course by such criticism. God's word
> clearly teaches that the kingdom of God spreads
> like leaven in bread. Conversion and the new life
> come to the individual then he becomes part of a
> process of permeation which acts on society as a
> gradual process and not by programs and plans of
> man. God attacks collective sin through the indi-
> vidual, not through mass reforms. [26]

The idea that the transformation of society awaits the
regeneration of the individual through the proclamation of the
gospel has proved to be a difficult principle to apply amidst
all the vicissitudes of history. The experience of the Southern Baptists adds to the evidence in this connection. Events
occur from time to time which they regard as so crucial and
urgent that they cannot depend on the slow process of preaching to the nation and thus transforming it. They must act
immediately, making use of whatever legitimate social and
political instruments are available for the effecting of social
reform or for the prevention of social decadence. [27] The
fact that this involves deviation from a cherished ecclesiastical principle apparently goes unnoticed by most who hold to
the principle.

The presidential campaign of 1928 placed Southern Baptists in just such a position. To Southern Baptists the election of Al Smith[28] meant the social decadence of America,
for it would allegedly place the control of national politics in
the hands of Tammany and the liquor traffic would run rampant. Preaching could not save the country in this emergency.
The instruments of politics had to be employed. The Baptist papers of the southern states, therefore, increased their
anti-Smith propaganda campaigns, which had begun two or
three years earlier when it was first supposed that Smith
might be the next nominee for the presidency by the Democratic party. But propaganda was not enough. A concerted

effort in the voting booths was called for.   In its report of
1928, the Social Service Commission of the Southern Baptist
Convention unmistakably described and identified Al Smith as
the candidate whom Southern Baptists should oppose, and set
forth the following recommendation:

> Resolved 'that by the adoption of this report we
> enter into a sacred covenant and solemn pledge
> that we will support for the office of president,
> as for any other office, only such men as stand
> for our present order of prohibition, for the faith-
> ful and efficient enforcement of all law, and for
> the maintenance and support of the Constitution of
> the United States in all its parts and with all its
> amendments, ' and that we record our fixed deter-
> mination to oppose actively the nomination or the
> election of any candidate of the opposite type no
> matter by what party put forward nor on what
> party platform they may stand. [29]

The Commission further resolved to request of the
conventions of all political parties meeting in 1928 that they
(1) pledge unequivocally in their platforms and through their
nominee "a program of vigorous and efficient enforcement of
the Eighteenth Amendment and all necessary supporting legislation, " and (2) to nominate candidates who are unqualified
supporters of an effective policy of prohibition enforcement. [30]

The Commissioned also resolved that the president of
the Convention be authorized to appoint a committee of five
to convey this report to the various platform committees.

This action on the part of the Commission and the
Convention did not go unnoticed by all.   R. H. Pitt saw it
as a situational deviation from the Baptist position and labeled it "Regrettable Action. "   He testified that a number of
"our brethren" had written or spoken to him in the same
vein.   Pitt objected to the unmistakable identification of Al
Smith in the resolution.   He asserted that the resolution
ought to have been a declaration of general principles, for
to discuss the relative merits of personal candidates for
presidential nominations is to function as a political body.
Pitt also objected to the appointment of a committee to go
to the party meetings to carry the declaration. [31]   His hesi-
tation and objection were based on two grounds: First, although the temptation to adopt political action is "severe just
at this time, " Baptists cannot afford to interfere in political

contests owing to their great tradition of separation of church
and state. Second, such a course of action is inexpedient,
inasmuch as it undercuts the Baptist witness for a fundamental doctrine when they see similar political action engaged in
by other religious organizations. [32]

Not only do Southern Baptists find it difficult to be
consistent in the application of their theory of the task of the
church in relation to the social order, but occasionally theory
is bent to meet the requirements of practice. Having taken
the line of action which it did with reference to Al Smith in
1928, the Social Service Commission of the Southern Baptist
Convention felt called upon to justify that action in its report
of 1929.

> It has been said before in the reports of your Com-
> mission, but let it be said here again for emphasis
> and because of the special emphasis which will car-
> ry in the light of recent events, Baptist bodies,
> whether churches, associations or conventions, are
> in no sense at all concerned with partisan politics,
> nor, indeed, with politics at all as such, but only
> with the great matters of vital religion, civic right-
> eousness and public morality. The fact that an is-
> sue becomes involved in politics or that an evil
> may become entrenched in government does not in
> any degree lessen the right of the individual Chris-
> tian citizen or group of such citizens to appeal to
> their fellow citizens to join them in denouncing and
> suppressing the wrong and in establishing and up-
> holding the right. [33]

Even R. H. Pitt, who criticized the Social Service
Commission and the Convention for departing from principle
in the case of Al Smith, stated, earlier in the same year,
two grounds on which the church may stand while departing
from the very same principle. In compliance with a request
that he apply the doctrine of separation of church and state
to some modern questions, Pitt pointed out that "two questions
always emerge for thoughtful consideration. " First, if the
issue is clearly and distinctly one of commanding importance,
"then any group of citizens, social, religious, political or
other, has a perfect right to take whatever course their consciences approve. " And secondly, the question of expediency
is almost of equal importance if real service is to be rendered. A group must carefully analyze the situation to ascertain whether it is best for them to press their cause as a

group. [34]

Obviously, if these suggestions are taken by a religious group as a working guide, the group can justify anything under them, from preaching the gospel to forming a political bloc. These suggestions present no objective tests. Who is to determine the importance of the given issue or the expediency of group action but the group itself? Undoubtedly the Social Service Commission of the Southern Baptist Convention considered itself as meeting precisely these requirements in its action on Al Smith.

In 1947, the Supreme Court ruling upholding the transportation of pupils to parochial schools at public expense evoked a departure from the usual content of preaching in some Southern Baptist circles. At a meeting called to discuss the court ruling, members of the Atlanta Baptist Pastors Conference pledged to devote a sermon to the issue. They saw the court ruling as an invasion of the religious freedom of the individual and a violation of the doctrine of separation of church and state. Although the aim was to stress the difference between religious tolerance and religious liberty in the sermons, this emphais on principles could not minimize the fact that a specific judicial-political issue was the sermon topic. In every pulpit, the treatment of this topic had to be a deviation from the traditional understanding of "preaching the pure and simple gospel of Jesus and His love. "[35]

The idea of the prophetic task of the church is not widely accepted among Southern Baptists, but it is very much alive in a minority. Floyd T. Binns complains that the church has been too priestly and too little prophetic. The church should have supported the Christian idealist, Woodrow Wilson, he asserts; and it should work continuously to remove want, fear, race prejudice and other social ills from the world. [36]

The absence of prophetic witness is sometimes due to the misunderstanding and misapplication of the doctrine of separation of church and state. To some Southern Baptists separation of church and state evidently means the freedom of religion from all political responsibility. This is suggested by Z. T. Cody when he says that the doctrine is sometimes misunderstood as being the same thing as the separation of Christ from politics and governmental affairs. Cody agrees that church and state should be separate, but

Christ is the Lord of all of life.   While church and state
are each under rules of their own, each of them is a sphere
of one whole life which exists under the one undivided Christ.
Preachers are both churchmen and citizens, and have a right
to take part in those political questions which affect great
moral interests.   The minister's method in a moral cause is
of course to be carefully adopted. [37]   Cody never says just
how churches and ministers are to function in relation to the
social order, but strongly implies that their task involves
more than evangelistic work.   The religion of Christ, he
says, came not only to teach, heal, forgive, and renew, but
it came as well to cast out demons and to establish God's
authority in Christ over individual men and society.   It is
this work that involves the use of law--the use of the law of
discipline in the church and the use of law in the state. [38]

In an address delivered in connection with an anti-
gambling crusade in the state of Louisiana, L. T. Hastings
vigorously affirms the right and responsibility of preachers
to express themselves in politics where great moral issues
arc at stake, and finds the models for their conduct in "God's
prophets and preachers" whose words and work are recorded
in the Bible.   Hastings cites Moses and Aaron as his first
examples[39] of "political preachers. "   These men, he states,
were commissioned of God to go directly "to Pharoah himself
and demand that he release God's people or suffer the judgments of God. "[40] Obviously reflecting on history and his
own experience of the confused conception of the populace as
to when a preacher is and when he is not in politics, Hastings
adds:

> ... If they--Moses and Aaron--had walked down the
> street with the king, patted him on the back, com-
> mended him for his enslavement of men, women,
> and children, it would have been alright [sic] for
> them to be in politics. [41]

Henlee H. Barnette also turns to the Bible to find the
guidelines of political action, but he adds to these an outline
of the political functions of the contemporary pastor.   In summary, the pastor is obligated "to instruct his people in political principles illumined by biblical truth, and to inspire
them to infuse these principles into the social structure. "
But in this complex and pluralistic society, the exercise of
his political function requires an awareness and pursuit of
certain specific objectives by the pastor.   He must avoid
partisan politics in the pulpit, carefully inform himself con-

cerning political realities, teach his people to consider the
central issues and avoid political sentimentality, teach his
people to consider the political philosophy and competence of
candidates as well as their personal piety and virtue, teach
them to read bills of extraordinary importance and exercise
the ballot, and encourage able youngsters to take up political
vocations. [42]

In its report of 1952, the Committee on Social Service
of the State Convention of the Baptist Denomination of South
Carolina deplored the fact that there are "enemies of Christian social action" within the Christian movement itself. The
reality of hostile forces in an unregenerate society is understandable, but owing to "traditional ways of thinking" within
the church the effective development of a Christian social
order has been paralyzed. The paralyzing attitude of mind
is due to a limited understanding of the nature of the Christian religion. First, it is assumed "by many Christian people that the Christian religion is individual but not social. "
The Christian religion is personal and individual, "but this
does not validate the assumption that... it is not social and
corporate in its expression and influence. "[43] The Kingdom
of God concept of Jesus embraced the ideal of social righteousness, and "he took his stand in the prophetic tradition."[44]
"A second attitude which has hindered Christian social action
is the feeling on the part of so many that the Christian religion is spiritual and contemplative but not active. " This
erroneous notion issues in an unwarranted distinction between
the sacred and the secular, the substitution of religious ritual for simple morality, theological correctness for social
righteousness, and "unlimited emotionalism for unlimited
generosity and concern. "[45]

Joseph Martin Dawson finds that prophetic Christianity
is frequently stymied by a limited notion of salvation. Salvation is first of all a personal deliverance, he states, but
it also involves social obligation. Individual salvation requires a social environment which is conducive to the highest
living. This does not mean that wholesome social conditions
can in themselves save a soul, but they provide the kind of
milieu in which the general orientation of life is in the right
direction. On the other hand, "bad social conditions can
damn and do foredoom people in the mass. "[46]

Coming at the problem from another direction, Dawson affirms that much of the evangelism to which people are
exposed is incapable of inspiring brotherhood and solving so-

cial problems. This incapacity is due to the limited appeal
of evangelism. Some preachers put a larger emphasis upon
justification than upon regeneration. The result is a people
who have faith in justification without the experience of regeneration. Their main business is to get to heaven. They
continue in their insensitivity to any moral obligation to
change unrighteous social conditions because they are the
products of an evangelism which has not drawn upon the
prophetic tradition of Christianity. [47]

In addition to the primary task of evangelism, Southern Baptists consider the functions of the church in society
to be those of an agency of education[48] and social service.
The church is an agency of education not only in the sense
of being a sponsor of formal educational institutions but it
is a community of education itself, in addition to preaching
and worship. "The first church and the subsequent churches
as they arose were each a school of Christianity."[49] Social
service is the fruit of the gospel. It flows naturally from
the Word and worship which constitute its center. [50] The
presence of the fruit is as certainly a witness to the alive-
ness of the tree as the living tree is the source of the fruit.

> Orphanages, hospitals, public sanitation, and law
> enforcement are not Christianity. They are its
> leaves and its fruit. They must, therefore, be
> given plenty of room in the Christian program.
> Take them out of the work of Christ, and nothing
> is left but a bare tree. [51]

3. The Misunderstanding of "Social Christianity"

Much of the opposition to "social Christianity" found
among Southern Baptists is due to the simple fact that it is
not understood. This misunderstanding is expressed in the
very appellations by which this type of Christianity is identified. That which many protestants would designate as "the
prophetic tradition of Biblical faith" or "covenantal religion"
is called "social Christianity" or the "social gospel" by large
numbers of Southern Baptists. These names are very significant in Southern Baptist minds because they express to
them the distortions to which they are endeavoring to point.

The substance of the belief concerning "social Christianity" is that churches which concern themselves with the
transformation of society as well as the regeneration of the

individual eventually lose all emphasis on the latter and become "social agencies" or mere institutions of social reform. [52] In his presidential address to the assembled convention in 1969, W. A. Criswell made a strong plea for
"Christ in faith and work." But he saw the work of the
modern church in general as a pre-occupation with economic
and political considerations, "just one other reforming agency of which there are ten thousand. "[53]

Under the quite appropriate title, "Is the New Social
Emphasis Another Gospel?" John F. Havlik provides a brief
historical account as to why the evangelicals[54] came to react
against social reform and to think of it as inherently secular-
istic and humanistic. In the eighteenth and nineteenth centuries, social reform was a major theme of the evangelical
revivalists themselves. The preaching of the gospel of the
new birth was combined with prophetic criticism of slavery,
child labor, poverty, and other social evils of the day. The
revivalistic tradition of Southern Baptists is rooted in this
heritage.

But two factors "brought about a neutralizing of the
attitude of evangelicals toward social problems." The first
of these is the great reduction of the ministry of mercy as
a direct service of the church. More and more the state
and tax supported agencies assumed the ministry to human
suffering, and church related institutions in this field became only loosely related to the church. "The second factor
that brought about a reaction of evangelicals against social
reform was the fact that the social aspect of the gospel was
emphasized by the liberal wing of the church. "[55] The movement which is properly referred to as the "social gospel"
was informed by a liberal theology. And some of the pro-
ponents of the social gospel were in fact humanists. It is
this humanistic distortion which is identified with all socially
concerned Christianity by Southern Baptists. They simply do
not understand that their protestant brethren in the denominations connected with the National Council of Churches are as
certainly motivated by religious impulse as they are, and
seek to make their social and political decisions under perspectives provided by Biblical faith.

The misunderstanding of "social Christianity" also
takes the form of a lack of awareness of the social and cultural nature of religion. The Christian faith is properly
designated as a religion of revelation. But this does not
mean that it is in no sense a religion of culture. Religion

is man's response to God or that which a man regards as
the ultimate.   This element must be included in any definition.   But since religion is man's response to God it must
in the nature of the case include cultural elements.   In word,
ritual, organization, and life, man is obliged to express himself in terms of the language, categories, thought patterns,
sentiments, and values of time and place.   There is no phase
of the religious experience that can escape this limitation.
But this fact about religion does escape many religious people.   They ascribe an absolute quality to the various aspects
of their religion, forgetting that absoluteness belongs to God
alone.   The fact that God is always first actor where Christian faith is genuine does not mean that man in his role as
second actor becomes a-cultural.   Religion never ceases to
be social and cultural, drawing upon the cultural screen in
all its expressions.   Accordingly, insofar as the church is
not engaged in transforming work, both personal and social,
it is engaged in accommodating work.   Southern churches,
including Southern Baptists, are a prime example of the latter. [56]   Churches engaged in the sanctification of the status
quo are as certainly social in their ministry or "gospel, " if
you will, as the churches which seek to transform the same
society.

It may be said that conversion is the most profound
personal experience in the life of mankind.   But conversion
always takes place in a social milieu and must in part be
understood communally.   The theological conservative who
insists that the transformation of society awaits the conversion of the individual does not understand the impact of cultural influences upon conversion.   He bases his erroneous
claim on a description of the converted person that is socially
and culturally unrealistic.   This description assumes that the
religious symbols and moral values of the new life of faith
completely transcend social and cultural realities.   The converted person is portrayed as being "out of this world, " responsive only to the demands of God directly and unequivocally.   The fact is that the conversion experience involves a
reading into as well as a reading off from the nature and
purpose of God.   That is, the understanding of what God requires of the individual after conversion is drawn from the
religio-cultural community in which he has been reared and
nurtured.   How else can one account for the fact that David,
"a man after God's own heart, " had a deep sense of guilt
about his deeds in connection with Uriah's wife, but felt no
compunction about the fact that he was already a polygamist?
In what other way does one account for the fact that, only a

few generations ago, religiously serious Christian men held
their fellow human beings in chattel slavery in America?
People are always imbedded in a history in every aspect of
their lives. Their understanding of the demands of their
faith is as certainly nurtured in an historical context as are
any other ideas and values.

This means that the transformation of society is re-
ciprocally related to the conversion of individuals. Theological conservatives are correct in stressing the need for newness of life in individual hearts and minds. Authentic personal and social transformation depend on this. But there
must also be an ever richer social and cultural ground in
which conversion takes place. The regeneration of individuals and the transformation of social institutions, values, and
policies must be sought together. For the constitution of the
individual contains a large measure of social substance at
every level of fulfillment.

The idea that the structures of justice and the corporate existence of man belong to God and are subject to his
will is receiving increasing emphasis in a small but growing
circle of the Southern Baptist community. John J. Havlik
makes note of this fact and calls upon Southern Baptists to
preach the "full gospel" and repent of the sin of having
failed to do so. [57] T. B. Maston makes a plea for the
combination of theological conservatism and social liberalism. [58]

In its report of 1969, the Division of Christian Life
and Public Affairs of the Baptist State Convention of North
Carolina addresses itself to "The Nature of the Christian
Life, " with the apparent purpose of correcting some of the
misunderstanding of "social Christianity. " The report states
that "Christianity is not a way of life in a certain area of
our lives, but a certain way of living in every area of our
lives. " The Gospel is to be experienced in two dimensions
of human existence--the personal and the social. "Christian
social action is, therefore, as necessary as personal believing faith.... There is no conflict between the task of evangelism and the requirements of ethical conduct. The first be-
gins the Christian life, even as the second is evidence of its
reality. "[59] The report goes on to say that both evangelism
and social action are needed. The latter is not a substitute
for the former, and the former is not "the end of Christian
witness and obedience. "[60]

John Jeffers reminds Southern Baptists that sin is
characteristic of the social order as well as of the individual
man.   He asserts that a "part of our problem is that we
have too simple a concept of sin. "   The notion of sin is limited to certain specific acts that can be arbitrarily so designated and that assist the accuser in pointing the finger away
from himself.   There is in fact a solidarity of man in evil.
"Sin is both personal and social--individual and corporate, "
and the gospel of redemption must be proclaimed to this
real world of sin. [61]

The claim that we have made that Christianity is always social, even among those who decry "social Christianity, " is attested to by the Christian Life Committee of the
Baptist General Association of Virginia.   We have asserted
that a non-transforming Christianity is an accommodating
Christianity.   Although these two terms must be understood
in a relative rather than an absolute sense, [62] there is a
discernible difference between religious communities that
may be described by the one or the other.   The Christian
Life Committee affirms that "the church is involved in society" and it "has never been and can never be detached
from the social order as long as the world survives. "   The
concern of the committee is to call the church away from
its "un-Christian involvements"--or accommodation.   The
sins of the church are listed as the alienation of denominations and communions among themselves, class cleavage and
racial exclusivism, the narrow and limited social concerns
of the church while ignoring the momentous issues of justice
and mercy, the cultural accommodation of the church on regional and geographical bases including its identification with
sectional and national interests, the shortcomings of the
church in the religious instruction of youth, and its ethically
questionable employment practices. [63]

4.   Anti-Catholicism

Baptists are historically great exponents of religious
liberty.   The doctrine of freedom of conscience is a fundamental tenet and a distinguishing mark of the communion.
The doctrine is believed to be applicable to all groups and
individuals, believers, and unbelievers.   While Southern Baptists do not make an exception of Roman Catholics in the application of this principle, they make it clear that they stand
in direct opposition to Catholics on every important issue of
Christian doctrine.   The theological relation of Baptists and

Catholics is described by George W. Truett in the statement
that "the Baptist message and the Roman Catholic message
are the very antipodes of each other."[64] The prime aim of
the Roman Catholic Church, says J. M. Dawson, is to win
America. "The center of this tremendous effort on their
part is to fix the notion in the people's minds that the Catholic Church is the only true church and that it is the only real
authority in morals."[65] J. B. Gambrell summarizes the religious and theological differences between Baptists and Roman Catholics as follows:

> Immersion is Baptist because of Christ's command.
> Sprinkling and pouring for Baptism are Catholic
> and rests [sic] on the primary assumption of the
> Catholic hierarchy that Scriptural institutions may
> be changed by human authority. Proxy religion is
> Catholic. Individualism in religion is Baptist.
> Baptismal regeneration is Catholic. Regeneration
> by the Spirit, through faith, is Baptist. The sac-
> ramental view of the ordinances is Catholic. Sal-
> vation by grace is Baptist. The independence of
> local churches is Baptist. The over-head control
> of local churches is Catholic. The equality of all
> ministers is Baptist. Orders in the ministry is
> Catholic. The democracy of churches is Baptist.
> Hierarchical control of churches is Catholic and
> so on and on, we might go. [66]

In spite of the depth and strength of the chasm which
lies between Baptists and Catholics in matters religious and
theological, it is fairly evident that Southern Baptist opposition to Catholics does not lie mainly at this point. Southern
Baptists are primarily opposed to Roman Catholics on social
and political grounds, and secondarily on religious and theological grounds. Although they take a missionary attitude toward Catholics, inasmuch as they believe that Catholics are
engaged in false religious teachings, nevertheless these
teachings do not disturb Southern Baptists as much as surface appearances indicate. Like other religious groups in
America, Southern Baptists are accustomed to granting religious liberty to all, and are not greatly excited or fearful
of the existence of contrary religious teaching alongside their
own. But Southern Baptists are genuinely afraid of and excited about the Catholic Church as a political institution and
a political threat in American life.

Admitting the difficulty of viewing without prejudice

the conduct of men of different religious experience, Reuben
E. Alley credits the Catholics with having rendered much
public service in this country and with having accomplished
their growth by good methods, but he complains that they
are doing certain things that constitute "direct attacks upon
the American principles of government."[67] To illustrate this
point, Alley calls attention to the unusual action of Congress
after it received the news of the death of Pope Pius XI in
Rome, the receipt of instructions by the American legation
in Italy to give official recognition to the late Cardinal Mun-
delein when he visited the Vatican, the success of the Catholic lobby in New York in sponsoring a bill in the state legislature providing bus transportation for all school children,
and the interpretation of that law in such a way as to provide
transportation for children attending parochial schools, and
other things.[68] In a later article, Alley points to the pro-
Vatican propaganda in this country conducted by radio, news-
papers, and the newsreel as a part of an effort to establish
control over the social and political life of the nation. He
declares confidently that millions of Americans will resist
this campaign. Then he touches directly upon what he regards as the main point of cleavage between Catholics and
other Americans by saying that closer fellowship among
Christians in the United States would be possible if American
Catholics would repudiate their allegiance to a foreigner and
accept the American Bill of Rights.[69]

The intensity of the fear of the allegiance of Catholics
to a foreigner becomes evident when it is understood that to
some Southern Baptists the Pope is an outright political
schemer. David M. Gardner states that "it is a recognized
fact that Pope Pius XII is among the best trained politicians
and one of the keenest political schemers in all Europe."[70]
An outstanding example of the pope's political conniving was
the collaboration of Marshall Petain with Hitler's forces in
France. This collaborationist plot, asserts Gardner, origi-
nated in the Vatican. It meant political favors to the Roman
Catholic Church because Petain was known to be more devoted to the Roman Catholic hierarchy than to France. After
four years it became obvious that the Pope had backed the
wrong party. France was now free and Petain had departed.
The Pope accordingly "turned a political somersault in an effort to save face in France."[71]

America has not escaped the plotting and scheming
tactics of the Roman Catholic Church. J. M. Dawson states
that the Catholic Welfare Conference "exists for the funda-

mental purpose of establishing control over the entire social
life of the people of this country. "[72] An important technique
in the achievement of this end is the manipulation of news.
Experts are employed to prepare copy for the Catholic
Church with two aims in view: to command the attention of
lay readers and to win acceptance from the secular press.
Annual retreats for newspapermen are conducted by these
experts, "with a view to instructing them to treating news
agreeably to the church. "[73] David M. Gardner charges the
church with the use of pressure tactics "to intimidate civil
authorities to get concessions that will give Roman Catholics
the advantage of other church groups. " Periods of national
and international upheaval are looked upon as especially favorable for the advance of Romanism. [74] A major danger was
seen in President Truman's appointment of an ambassador to
the Vatican: "It puts the government in official business
with the greatest dictatorship in the world. " Such a course
of action contradicts the foreign policy of the nation in its
usual orientation and aligns "us with a hierarchy, the head
of which does not hesitate to claim authority above that of
any and all political leaders. "[75]

The fear of the impact of the Catholic Church upon
the social and political life of America has evoked Southern
Baptist social action to the fullest extent in two presidential
campaigns--those of Al Smith[76] and John F. Kennedy. It
was admitted that some Southern Baptists would not vote for
Al Smith because of religious prejudice, [77] but, in the main,
opposition to Smith was declared to be due to his loyalty to
a political institution dominated by a foreigner. "If the Roman Catholic Church confined itself to religion it would in
the minds of all citizens take its place by the side of other
communions in this country. " But this, says Z. T. Cody,
the church has consistently failed to do. The church is in
politics everywhere, and always with the special interest of
the church in view. Even if the Pope were astute enough
not to try to influence American politics or to minimize his
influence, the election of a Catholic president "would be putting the stamp of approval upon a system that is profoundly
un-American, and would be an opening of the doors to influences that are inimical to our ideals of government. "[78]

"A South Carolina pastor" sets forth in summary fashion twelve reasons why he is opposed to Al Smith. Nine of
these reasons are references to the social and political significance of the Catholic Church.

Because of the responsibility of fraternal relations.
He represents a faith which holds its subjects in
abject physical and spiritual bondage....

The attitude of his particular brand of faith toward
our government and institutions....

Because his first allegiance is to a foreign poten-
tate, and his conduct has already shown this to be
true with him....

Because of the particular brand of faith to which
he belongs. Never in all its history has it been
free from State-Churchism and persecution, if
conditions would admit such.

Because Romanism is an ecclesiastical autocracy.
You must receive your faith and your politics from
Rome....

Because it is a religion-political [sic] institution.
It is a great political machine with religion as a
side issue.

Because its political character makes it seek to
dominate public life--every phase of it. From the
secret thoughts of your heart to every single thing
you read.

Because of its attitude toward our public school system.

Because of its attitude toward religious and civil
liberty. [79]

As had been the case for those who opposed the presidential aspirations of Al Smith, the political nature of the Roman Catholic Church was the theme of Southern Baptists who
opposed John F. Kennedy for the presidency on religious
grounds in 1960. It is the encroachment of the Catholic
Church upon the lives of non-Catholics which must be vigorously resisted, says Edwin L. McDonald. "Roman Catholicism is more than a religion. It is totalitarianism with a
world organization centering in a foreign land and denying the
right of any religion to exist outside its own hierarchy."[80]
McDonald warns those who might be deceived by the "tolerance" of the Catholic hierarchy in America. This show of

tolerance is due only to the minority status of Catholicism in the nation. The long-range objective of Rome is to take America and when this is done, the same ruthless rule will be applied in America which the church applies in every country in which it is dominant. [81]

Joe T. Odle cautions those who may wish to uphold the constitutional guarantee that there shall be no religious test as a qualification for public office. He cites the "Good Citizenship" resolution approved by the Southern Baptist Convention of 1960 which reaffirmed support for this constitutional guarantee. The resolution, however, goes on to say that "when a public official is inescapably bound by the dogma and demands of his church, " and when the position of the church is in conflict with the pattern of American life, "then such conflicts are 'of concern to the voters in every election. ' " Although the "Good Citizenship" resolution neither names a church nor a candidate, Odle asserts that it "has been rightly interpreted as opposition to the election of a Roman Catholic candidate for president of the United States. " From the resolution he draws support for the idea "that the individual Catholic member cannot separate himself from his church. "[82] Leon Macon contends that the opposition to John F. Kennedy is not an attack on a man's religion but a fervent defense of "the principle of separation of church and state as it is firmly fixed in the First Amendment. "[83]

After making a strong, initial declaration that "we will never support any Roman Catholic for President of the United States, " John J. Hurt sets the conditions under which he can support a Catholic candidate. Either the Pope must declare himself for religious freedom everywhere and grant religious freedom to each Roman Catholic, or the candidate must declare his own religious freedom and designate himself a crusader for religious freedom on a universal scale. [84] Hurt is obviously willing to accept verbal declarations. But a set of conditions which involve only verbal declarations is not enough for Ramsey Pollard, President of the Southern Baptist Convention in 1960. In an address to the Mississippi Baptist Evangelistic Conference, Pollard said, "I will never believe what the Pope of Rome says about good will and brotherhood until I see some evidences of it in countries where the Roman Catholic Church is dominant. "[85]

5. Anti-Church Union and Anti-Cooperation

In their own environment Southern Baptists are a
church.   They are large, conservative, influential, puritanical, and sociologically accommodated to the regional culture.
But in their relation to ecclesiastical movements, tendencies,
and ideas outside the southern region and in relation to other
denominations in general, they react as a sect. [86]   They are
aloof, defensive, sure of their orthodoxy (adherence to New
Testament doctrines) and insist on the maintenance of the
New Testament ecclesiastical structural principle (Baptist
polity).   As we have already seen, Southern Baptists fear
and oppose Roman Catholics outright.   While their attitude
and action are not nearly as drastic as this toward the protestant bodies, nevertheless Southern Baptists are far from
being cooperative in relation to these groups.   Through the
years they have consistently refused to join any united and
federated protestant efforts. [87]

This attitude of defensiveness and aloofness is probably a part of a larger pattern of southern defensiveness
which had its origin in the period of abolitionist agitation
and was accentuated by the Civil War and Reconstruction.
The clinging to the old theology is probably a part of a
larger southern pattern of resisting new ideas.   It is also
undoubtedly due to the fact that the old theology lends itself
better than later theologies to giving sanction and foundation
for the past and to the preservation of present patterns and
relations.   Thus motivated, Southern Baptists reject all
church union proposals and all invitations to ecclesiastical
cooperation, interpreting the latter as unionism in disguise.

The principal, expressed cause of anti-unionism[88]
and anti-cooperation among Southern Baptists is the fear of
centralization of control.   This fear seems to be accentuated
by the belief that whatever centralization of control may take
place will surely have its headquarters outside the southern
region.   This is perhaps in part a survival of the Reconstruction psychology.   It may also be a reflection in the area of
religion of the attitude engendered by the control of much of
the South's economic life by northern capital.   Whatever additional reasons may be presented by the opponents of unionism
and cooperation, the centralization of control is generally
given great prominence.   It looms as the major reason of
the opposition even when the World Baptist Alliance[89] or the
union of the American and Southern Baptist Conventions are
topics of consideration.   It is applied to the church council

movement on both the national and international levels.

Expressing his opposition to the Interchurch World Movement (now defunct), J. W. Porter asserted that its real purpose was to coerce the country into church union with headquarters in New York.[90] R. H. Pitt answers appeals for union and cooperation by saying, "we can do best following our accustomed way and the New Testament."[91] He accuses the Interchurch World Movement of leading to a protestant oligarchy, which has no basis in Scripture, and of having violated Christian fraternity in its relation to Southern Baptists "by a policy of invasion and intermeddling after having its appeal answered."[92]

Although a federation even in name, the Federal Council of Churches of Christ in America[93] did not escape the charge of seeking to establish a centralized control over the churches of the nation. W. B. Riley called the Federal Council a corpse of the Interchurch World Movement, and likened it unto the evil spirits which possessed the swine and drove them to their destruction after Jesus had cast the evil spirits out of the two men in the country of the Gergesenes.[94] Speaking in language full of meaning for the late thirties, A. J. Barton called the Federal Council of Churches religious fascism[95] and admonished Southern Baptists to hold their lines against it. He published some recent correspondence between officers of the Federal Council and some officers of the Southern Baptist Convention to show that the persistence of the former is unrelenting and borders on arrogance. He observed ominously that,

> if Southern Baptists are to maintain their independence and freedom and are to be able to maintain their witness and deliver their messages, they will have to resist constantly and resolutely the subtle and insidious efforts of the centralizing agencies and influences to bring them under some sort of overlordship and control.[96]

When the World Council of Churches began its process of formation, an invitation to membership was sent to Southern Baptists just as it was to all other communions who could be thought of as prospective members. The Convention appointed a committee headed by George W. Truett to look into the matter. The special committee drew up a reply to the World Council's invitation which was overwhelmingly approved by the Southern Baptist Convention. The argument

against centralization of control is the highlight of the reply.
The special committee pointed out to the World Council that
the Southern Baptist Convention is a purely voluntary association of churches, devoid of any ecclesiological authority. "It
is in no sense the Southern Baptist Church. " The committee
continued by calling attention to the growing tendency toward
centralization of power in all of the major institutions of
Western civilization, and reported the sensitivity of Southern
Baptists to "the dangers of totalitarian trends which threaten
the autonomy of all free churches. " The reply concludes
with the statement that, "in the light of these considerations,
we feel impelled to decline the invitation to membership in
the World Council of Churches. "[97] A little more than a
decade later, the Committee on Southern Baptists Relations
with other religious bodies, appointed by the Convention,
called attention to some dangerous trends and movements.
Highlighted among these is the ecumenical movement. The
committee saw in the ecumenical movement the tendency toward centralization of power which placed authority "in the
hands of erring men instead of the unerring Scriptures. "
Southern Baptists are advised to have nothing to do with a
protestant ecumenical church which has no scriptural authority. [98]

Closely associated with the claim that the ecumenical
movement is seeking centralization of control is the accusa-
tion that it is seeking to overthrow and undermine the Baptists and to obliterate denominationalism. J. B. Gambrell
charged John R. Mott and the Federal Council of Churches
with seeking to obliterate denominationalism[99] and the Interchurch World Movement with seeking to undermine Southern
Baptists. He predicted a rupture between Southern and Northern Baptists[100] since the latter, having contributed
$10, 000, 000 to put over the union program, have formed an
alliance with people who are seeking to break down Southern
Baptist policies. [101]

B. J. W. Graham put all of the stress on the overthrow of the Baptist denomination and was convinced that
there were several agencies at work on this objective. He
designated the Federal Council of Churches of Christ in
America, the Sunday School Union, the Edinburgh Conference
through its Continuation Committee, the Y. M. C. A. and John
R. Mott as "Co-ordinated Agencies for the Overthrow of the
Baptist Denomination. " He accused them of having taken
advantage of conditions created by World War I to carry out
their program. Specifically the movement established condi-

tions which forced the Home Mission Board of the Southern
Baptist Convention to work with the movement in order to
secure the appointment of Baptist preachers as military chaplains. It was with great difficulty that the Baptists secured
the privilege of appointing camp pastors at all. [102]

Despite all of the denials of their leaders, the ultimate objective of the National and World Council of Churches,
says David M. Gardner, is the death of denominationalism.
He predicts that if that "mammoth monstrosity, " which is
the World Council of Churches, ever gains the authoritative
position in the non-Catholic world which it desires, "it will
be a world church; and what's worse, it will be a worldly
church. "[103]

These charges of seeking sweeping structural changes
in American non-Catholic church life are enough to condemn
the "unionists" in the eyes of Southern Baptists, but the
charge of theological and political unorthodoxy is of no mean
importance. J. W. Porter accused the Interchurch World
Movement of a whole hearted and willing unorthodoxy by saying that the Movement did not even pretend to preach the
whole gospel. [104] "Union" movements are at best spiritually
and doctrinally weak, according to Victor J. Masters. For,
by their very nature, they tend to reach their level at the
point of the least spiritual and doctrinal common denomina-
tor. [105] Even the question of the union of Baptists North and
South gives rise to the charge of "unorthodoxy. "[106]

Criticism of the intellectual climate and activities of
the Federal Council of Churches was also very unsparing
and even vitriolic. W. B. Riley condemned the Federal
Council as modernistic socialistic, semi-political, and anti-
evangelistic. [107] Victor J. Masters charged the Council with
friendship "for radical and socialistic organizations and
propaganda, " and declared that the Council has "interlocking
directorates with a number of radical organizations, particularly the communistic. "[108] The Council was "infiltrated
through and through with communism and socialism, " according to the testimony of Anson Justice, and the schools
related to the constituent communions are "modernistic and
Bible denying. "[109] John A. Brunson cited the activities and
utterances of some of the "recognized leaders" of the Federal Council, namely, Dr. Ivan Lee Holt, Bishop Francis J.
McConnell and Dr. S. Parkes Cadman, to show that the
Council was under the influence of rationalistic theology,
and "is more interested in effecting economic and social

change that make for the temporal betterment of man than it
is in preaching the Old Gospel of salvation by grace. "[110]

Making its report after the formation of the National
Council of Churches, the Committee on Southern Baptists Re-
lations with other Religious Bodies of the Southern Baptist
Convention noted two dangerous tendencies in the ecumenical
movement. The first of these is the centralization of power.
The second is

> the tendency to compromise the truth of the gospel
> of Jesus Christ by recognizing as fellow Christian
> workers those who deny such scriptural truths as:
> the virgin birth, the deity of Christ and the iner-
> rancy of the Holy Scriptures. [111]

Since the ecumenical movement is believed to be constituted of communions which are unorthodox, the preservation of their own orthodoxy becomes one of the motives of
Southern Baptist noncooperation.   One word describes Southern Baptist people.   "It is the word Convictions."   Whenever
Baptists have compromised their beliefs, they have lost.
Interdenominationalism is the medium of compromise.   "There
is an unholy triumvirate of words: Unionize--Compromise--
Suicide."   Unionism of all kinds will eliminate Baptist freedom "and prevent our doing the task which the Lord gave
us. "[112]

Religious isolationism is falsely charged to Southern
Baptists, says Jack L. Gritz.   "Southern Baptists are not
religious isolationists."   They have been cooperative in
many ways and places, such as the American Bible Society,
state temperance associations and the National Temperance
Society, the international uniform Sunday school lesson program and local ministerial alliances.   Southern Baptists have
demonstrated their willingness to cooperate with other religious bodies when such participation does not involve any
compromise of their convictions.   Despite the disagreement
on many beliefs, "we believe there are many saved people
and good Christians in other denominations....   We believe
that where they correctly interpret the New Testament we
are one. "[113]

Oscar E. Sams puts the argument for noncooperation
in the larger context of the need for denominations, not simply the Baptist denomination.   He states that protestantism
has produced a finer civilization than Catholicism.   A factor

in this development has been denominationalism, which has a
purifying effect through the constant examination and criticism
which takes place among those who disagree. The different
denominations, he continues, have particular truths which
would be lost in one great church. If protestantism is united
it will become like Romanism. 114

Charles T. Alexander sees the continuing isolation of
the Southern Baptists from the ecumenical movement as an
outcome of the very nature of a Baptist Church. "We recognize nothing beyond the local 'ecclesia' as having a single
atom of valid New Testament ecclesiastical existence. " Even
the Baptist denomination is not a church. It contains
churches in a fellowship in which autonomy is not at all
compromised. It is not possible for Baptists to unite with
anything outside of their own local organic existence which
might make demands upon their local organic existence. 115

6. Bigotry

That many Southern Baptists believe that "the truth
once and for all delivered to the saints" is now in possession
of the Baptists in general and Southern Baptists in particular
is not to be doubted. An attitude perilously close to bigotry
appears repeatedly in anti-"unionism" literature. 116 Although they declare that they wish to be fair in all things,
the editors of the Word and Way affirm that Baptists have
the true gospel needed alike by Catholic, Jew and Protestant. 117 A. J. Holt speaks in a similar vein when he says
that "the Christian world owes a debt of gratitude to the
Baptists in that we are hard to move from the truth."118
Holt relieves the Baptists of all responsibility for the divi-
sions of Christendom and, in commenting on believers' bap-
tism, says, "we believe God has elected Baptists to be the
conservators of this great ordinance."119 The love and
practice of Christian union, F. M. McConnell writes, are
willed by God. He has declared His will in His word. But
in answering the question, what is Christian union? McCon-
nel describes the beliefs and practices of a church which
are precisely those of Southern Baptist churches.

> Christian union is sincere adherence to Bible truth.
> If repentance is taught, every violator of God's law
> ought to repent.... If baptism is burial in water,
> every converted person ought to be immersed. If
> a New Testament Church was one congregation,

worshipping at one place, and not organically joined
to any other church, every group of people claiming to be a church ought to be that kind of
church. 120

Anson Justice identifies the uniqueness of Southern Baptists
clearly by their sole possession of gospel truth. "If we
don't preach the gospel to this generation, who will?"121
The gem of all statements of the uniqueness and sole pos-
sessorship of total truth on the part of the Baptists is that
of J. B. Gambrell:

> If everything that is Baptist is taken away from
> any one of the protestant pedo-Baptist bodies, what
> remains will be Catholic. If everything that is
> Catholic is taken away what is left will be Bap-
> tist....
>
> The supreme, undelegated authority of Jesus Christ
> is the true and unbending organizing principle of
> every Baptist Church. This principle stands as
> an impossible barrier between Baptist and other
> bodies. Baptists never did symbolize with other
> bodies built on human wisdom contravening divine
> wisdom and the authority of Jesus Christ. They
> never can. What relation have Baptist Churches
> to other ecclesiastical bodies? None. They never
> can have any while their primary principle, obedi-
> ence to the authority of Jesus Christ as given in
> His holy Word, holds the Baptist conscience.
>
> Baptists are not to blame for this separation.
> They remained with the New Testament and others
> went away from it. For long, weary centuries
> they have stood by this principle, even to blood
> and death. Meantime they have been the torch-
> bearers to light the world back to the simplicity
> of the New Testament faith and practice. Baptists
> should today, candidly, lovingly and boldly, accept
> their ecclesiastical isolation and proclaim it for
> the benefit of the present and future generations.
> They are the trustees of the truth and are bound
> to hold it and hold it forth. We do not express
> our lack of love for other Christians when we
> stand by the truth. We can give no higher expres-
> sion of our love for them and the world than to
> hold and proclaim those principles written in the

divine Word by the Spirit to enlighten and bless
the human race. [122]

7. Ecumenicity

The sweeping victories of "anti-unionism" and ecclesiastical isolationism with the accompanying expressions of
bigotry have not been won by a Baptist "Solid South. " They
have been won over a stubborn ecumenical minority. [123]
When Southern Baptists rejected the invitation to membership
of the World Council of Churches, they did so by an overwhelming majority, not unanimously. And when B. J. W.
Graham labeled the Federal Council of Churches of Christ
in America, the Sunday School Union, the Edinburgh Conference through its Continuation Committee, the Y. M. C. A.
and John R. Mott as "Co-ordinated Agencies for the overthrow of the Baptist Denomination" (pp. 22-23), he did not
entirely escape censure. M. Ashby Jones quickly issued a
stern protest, expressing astonishment that such pettiness
represented the viewpoint of a Baptist paper, seriously presented. The preoccupation of the paper with attacks on ecumenical agencies, while the real enemies of Christ and His
Kingdom go about their work unmolested, reminded Jones of
"the days of the Pharisees, when camels were swallowed
with equanimity, while gnats were strained out with punctili-
ous care... " Jones also took the occasion to correct the
notion among Southern Baptists that these movements of
protestant cooperative effort are "unionist. "[124]

Edwin M. Poteat seeks to clarify the nature of the
Interchurch World Movement and disclose to Southern Baptists
the extent of their evangelistic task if they persist in rejecting cooperative protestantism. The Interchurch World Movement, he points out, is not a union movement but a movement of cooperative effort, having its basis on the principle
of cooperation between independent units. [125] Raising the
question "Can Baptists help?" Poteat states that if the answer is "No, " Baptists must assume responsibility for the
world and proceed to meet it:

> We cannot take the position that other Christians
> are disqualified for giving the whole gospel to the
> whole world, and go on at our old pace of attending
> to that job. ... If Baptist orthodoxy is the only sal-
> vation for the world, then in the name of high
> heaven Baptists must get busy on a scale we have
> never dreamed of. ... [126]

The Southern Baptist attitude toward the World Council
of Churches is repudiated by Ernest F. Campbell. He deplores the failure of Southern Baptists to join the World Council of Churches, designating this failure as "a sad blunder."
The Southern Baptists were invited into the Council on the
ground floor which gave them the opportunity to help formulate the organization. Joining this world fellowship would
have entailed giving up nothing "except our selfishness, our
complacency and our unholy ambition and conceit that make
us feel we can save the world by ourselves alone."[127]

The idea that the World Council of Churches and cooperative protestantism in America are agencies driving toward organic union and centralization of control appears as
an obsession in Southern Baptist circles. The repeated
statements of aim by these agencies and the actual facts of
their histories simply do not get through. Southern Baptists
of course look at these organizations from a distance, but
something more serious than distance blurs their vision.

The persistent tendency among Southern Baptists to
confuse the Council of Churches movement with "unionism"
stems in part from the erroneous identification of the positions of certain persons prominent in ecumenical circles
with the official positions of the councils themselves. For
example, B. H. Duncan credits the National Council of
Churches with having taken a saner position on the question
of church union in its biennial meeting of December, 1952,
and of having consequently "forsaken the extreme and radical
positions advocated by many church unionists of the past.[128]
Charles Clayton Morrison and E. Stanley Jones are cited as
examples of vocal advocates of church union. The fact is,
the message of the National Council as it pertains to the
nature of the National Council represents no change whatso-
ever. From the beginnings of the old Federal Council of
Churches in the early part of this century, all councils of
churches have issued the same declarations--that they are
councils of churches and not churches, that they are federa-
tions of autonomous communions and not super-churches, and
that they do not aspire to be super-churches. Furthermore,
two generations of actual history lend ample validity to the
claims of the councils.

On the other hand, there are and have been individuals
who have advocated the organic union of the churches. And
some communions of the same ecclesiastical family have effected unions in recent decades. But these developments

have neither altered the philosophy nor the practices of the
councils of churches.   The fact that the unions of certain
denominations and cooperative protestantism as expressed
through councils of churches are two distinct ecclesiastical
realities has not been grasped by large numbers (undoubtedly
the majority) of Southern Baptists.

The confusion among Southern Baptists concerning cooperative protestantism and the inaccurate statements about
it are perhaps best summarized by Edward Hughes Pruden
in an appeal to his Southern Baptist brethren to be fair.
The most relevant portions of this appeal are as follows:

> We should remember that the National Council of
> Churches is neither committed to organic union
> nor has it been set up for the purpose of promot-
> ing any such idea.... To use the term 'unionism'
> with reference to all those who believe in some
> form of Christian cooperation is most unfair and
> inaccurate.   Let us recognize that the Councils of
> Churches have frequently been denounced because
> of certain statements which a few individuals con-
> nected with these councils are reported to have
> written or said.

> We need to remember that denominations which
> unite with either the National or the World Council
> of Churches must agree to a thorough evangelical
> theological statement which includes acceptance of
> the deity of Christ.

> Whenever it is charged that those who believe in
> closer cooperation with other Christians are lacking
> in courage and are primarily concerned with being
> affable, it should be remembered that many of these
> persons have forfeited a very cherished place in
> the life of their communion in order to follow what
> they believe to be a very profound and inescapable
> conviction.

> Let us be reminded that the terms 'ecumenical, '
> 'united church, ' and 'world church' are frequently
> used very loosely by speakers and writers who
> have reference to nothing more dangerous than
> brotherly cooperation on a purely voluntary basis
> that has no reference whatever to organic union
> or the creation of a super-church. [129]

Notes

1. Every expression of human authority and representation for another.
2. Turner, J. Clyde, "The Church of God," Review and Expositor, XXXVI (July, 1929), 253.
3. Ibid.
4. Gambrell, J. B., "The Relation of Baptists to Other Ecclesiastical Bodies," The Baptist Courier, XLIX (November 14, 1918), 1.
5. Mullins, E. Y., "The Social Life of Religion: The Church and Its Organization," Religious Herald, XCII (July 31, 1919), 4.
6. Brown, Joseph E., "We Believe in Baptist Churches" (Editorial), The Word and the Way, LXXXVII (October 5, 1939), 4.
7. Report of the Committee on Baptist Faith and Message, Annual of the Southern Baptist Convention (Nashville, Sunday School Board of the Southern Baptist Convention, 1963), p. 275.
8. Mullins, E. Y., Baptist Beliefs (Philadelphia, The Judson Press, 1921), p. 64.
9. Ibid.
10. Ibid.
11. Truett, George W., "Baptists and Religious Liberty," Religious Herald, XCIII (July 1, 1920) p. 4.
12. Gambrell, op. cit., p. 1.
13. Carver, W. O., "A Church: The Church," The Review and Expositor, XLVIII, No. 2 (April, 1951) pp. 152-153.
14. Ibid., p. 154.
15. Conner, W. T., "The Nature and Function of the Church," Baptist Standard, 60, No. 14 (April 1, 1948), p. 6.
16. Ibid.
17. Price, Theron D., "The Church and the Churches" The Review and Expositor, LII, No. 4 (October, 1955), pp. 443-450 and "Why I Believe in the Church," Biblical Recorder, 121, No. 40 (October 1, 1955), p. 6.
18. "Why I Believe in the Churches," ibid.
19. Scarborough, Christ's Militant Kingdom (Nashville, Sunday School Board of the Southern Baptist Convention, 1924), p. 126.

20. Report of the Social Service Commission of the Southern
      Baptist Convention, "Basal Principles, " Annual of the
      Southern Baptist Convention (Nashville, Sunday School
      Board of the Southern Baptist Convention, 1933), p.
      104.
21. Gardner, David M., "Modern Crusaders" (Editorial),
      Baptist Standard, LXIII, No. 9 (February 28, 1946),
      p. 3.
22. Ibid.
23. Jones, S. H., "Applying Christianity, " (Editorial) The
      Baptist Courier, 86, No. 6 (February 18, 1954), p.
      3.
24. Lipsey, P. I., "The Church" (Editorial), The Baptist
      Record, XXL (January 30, 1919), p. 4.
25. August 8, 1956.
26. Macon, Leon, "Theologians and Billy Graham" (Editorial),
      The Alabama Baptist, 121, No. 34, (August 23, 1956),
      p. 3.
27. The whole prohibition struggle illustrates this point.
      See Chapter V.
28. Alfred E. Smith is referred to as "Al Smith" because
      this is the way he is designated in Southern Baptist
      sources and was popularly known.
29. Report of the Social Service Commission of the Southern
      Baptist Convention, "The Presidential Campaign" and
      "Recommendations, " Annual of the Southern Baptist
      Convention (Nashville, Sunday School Board of the
      Southern Baptist Convention, 1928), p. 88.
30. Ibid.
31. Pitt, R. H., "Regrettable Action" (Editorial), Religious
      Herald, CI (June 7, 1928), p. 10.
32. Ibid., pp. 10-11.
33. Report of the Social Service Commission of the Southern
      Baptist Convention, "Not Concerned with Partisan
      Politics, " Annual of the Southern Baptist Convention
      (Nashville, Sunday School Board of the Southern Bap-
      tist Convention, 1929), p. 89.
34. Pitt, R. H., "Some Practical Questions" (Editorial)
      Religious Herald, CI (February 9, 1928), p. 10.
35. "News Item, " "Baptist to Preach Sermons on Court Bus
      Ruling, " The Alabama Baptist, 112, No. 16 (April
      17, 1947), p. 4.
36. Binns, Floyd T., "The Church and the Present World
      Crisis, " Religious Herald, CXVI (May 20, 1943), pp.
      4-5.
37. Cody, Z. T., "The Lordship of Christ in Politics"
      (Editorial) The Baptist Courier, LXIV (August 4,

1932), p. 3.

38. Cody, Z. T., "An Unjust Criticism" (Editorial), The
     Baptist Courier, LXII (March 6, 1930), pp. 2-3.
39. Hastings, L. T., "The Preacher in Politics," The
     Baptist Message, 65, No. 4 (January 22, 1948), pp.
     2, 4.
40. Samuel and Elijah are also discussed as examples and
     several major figures of the Bible and church history
     are listed.
41. Ibid., p. 4.
42. Barnette, Henlee H., "The Pastor and Politics," Re-
     ligious Herald, CXXXII, No. 32 (September 10, 1964),
     pp. 7, 20.
43. Report of the Committee on Social Service, "Enemies
     of Christian Social Action," Minutes of the Baptist
     State Convention of South Carolina, November 11-13,
     1952, pp. 124-125.
44. Ibid., p. 125.
45. Ibid., p. 126.
46. Dawson, Joseph Martin, "Brotherly Believers," in
     Preaching the Doctrines of Grace, (Compiled Press,
     1939), p. 107.
47. Ibid., pp. 104-105.
48. See Chapter II for the discussion of education.
49. Carver, W. O., op. cit., p. 155.
50. Price, Theron D., "Why I Believe in the Church,"
     Biblical Recorder, 121, No. 40 (October 1, 1955),
     p. 6.
51. Report of the Committee on Social Service of the Bap-
     tist State Convention of North Carolina, Annual of
     the Baptist State Convention of North Carolina (Ral-
     eigh, Bynum Printing Company), 1926, p. 110.
52. Some of the opposition to protestant ecumenicity stems
     from this misapprehension. See Section 5, Anti-
     Church Union and Anti-Cooperation.
53. Criswell, W. A., "The Two-Edged Sword or Christ
     in Faith and Work," Florida Baptist Witness, 86,
     No. 25 (June 19, 1969), p. 14.
54. It must be noted that there is a conservative segment
     in each of the protestant denominations who are op-
     posed to "the social gospel."
55. Havlik, John F., "Is the New Social Emphasis Another
     Gospel?", Arkansas Baptist, 67, No. 33 (August 22,
     1968), p. 5.
56. See Hill, Samuel S., Jr., Southern Churches in Crisis
     (Boston, Beacon Press, 1966).

36   Social Ethics Among Southern Baptists

57. Havlik, op. cit.
58. Maston, T. B., "Theological Conservatism and Social
Liberalism, Baptist and Reflector, 134, No. 51
(December 19, 1968), p. 3.
59. "The Nature of the Christian Life," Report of the Division of Christian Life and Public Affairs, Annual
of the Baptist State Convention of North Carolina
(November, 1969), p. 162.
60. Ibid., p. 163.
61. Jeffers, John, "The Gospel and the Social Order," The
Alabama Baptist (November 21, 1968), 133, No. 47,
p. 6.
62. Organized Christianity is culturally accommodated
everywhere, and there is undoubtedly some degree
of social transformation impulse everywhere; but
where the prophetic tradition has strength there is
a vital ethical tension in the religious community.
63. "The Church's Un-Christian Involvements," Report of
the Christian Life Committee, Journal of the One
Hundred and Forty Fifth Annual Meeting of the Baptist General Association of Virginia (November,
1968), pp. 68, 69.
64. Truett, op. cit., p. 5.
65. Dawson, J. M. "The Catholics and the Nation,"
Christian Index, 126, No. 45 (November 7, 1946),
p. 9.
66. Gambrell, op. cit., p. 1.
67. Alley, Reuben E., "Baptists and Catholics" (Editorial),
Religious Herald (December 14, 1939), p. 10.
68. Ibid.
69. Alley, Reuben E., "Catholic Propaganda (Editorial),
Religious Herald, CXIII (March 28, 1940), p. 10.
70. Gardner, David M., "The Pope a Political Opportunist,"
Baptist Standard, LVII, No. 4 (January 25, 1945),
p. 3.
71. Ibid.
72. Dawson, "The Catholics and the Nation."
73. Ibid.
74. Gardner, David M., "Keeping Catholicism from Winning
America," Baptist Standard, LVII, No. 12 (March
22, 1945), p. 3.
75. McGinty, H. H., "The Ambassador to the Vatican,"
The Word and the Way, 88, No. 44 (November 1,
1951), p. 6.
76. Southern Baptists also opposed Smith because he was
anti-prohibitionist and a Tammanyite.

77. Cody, Z. T., "Will the South Support Governor Smith?"
     (Editorial) The Baptist Courier, LVIII (November 4,
     1926), p. 2. See also: Funk, R. H., "Why Not
     Governor Smith?" Religious Herald, C (April 28,
     1927), p. 8.
78. Cody, Z. T., "As to a Catholic Candidate" (Editorial),
     The Baptist Courier, LV (May 1, 1924), p. 2.
79. "A South Carolina Pastor, 'Some Reasons Why I Would
     Not Vote for Governor Al Smith,' " The Baptist Couri-
     er, LX (October 18, 1928), p. 6.
80. McDonald, Edwin L., "Should a Catholic Be Elected
     President?" (Editorial), Arkansas Baptist, 59, No.
     28 (July 21, 1960), p. 4.
81. Ibid.
82. Odle, Joe T., "The Good Citizenship Resolution" (Edi-
     torial) The Baptist Record, LXXXIII, No. 23, (June
     9, 1960), p. 4.
83. Macon, Leon, "The Religious Issue is Admitted" (Edi-
     torial), The Alabama Baptist, 125, No. 18 (May 5,
     1960), p. 3.
84. Hurt, John J., "Free Choice for Freedom" (Editorial)
     Christian Index, 139, No. 19 (May 12, 1960), p. 6.
85. News Item, "Opposes Kennedy," Christian Index, 139,
     No. 8 (February 25, 1960), p. 5.
86. The characteristics of the "church" and "sect," indi-
     cated here, are taken in part from Ernst Troeltsch,
     Social Teaching of the Christian Churches (London,
     1931), I, 331 ff.
87. It must be noted that Southern Baptists did cooperate
     with various and sundry organizations in the prohi-
     bition struggle and have been very active in the
     movement to maintain separation of church and state.
88. Here and hereafter we are freely using the word "union-
     ism" because this is the word which Southern Bap-
     tists use to describe the aims of the inter-church
     councils and movements which they oppose. Not
     that these councils and movements actually did and
     do aim at unionism, but that Southern Baptists
     thought and think so.
89. See: Barnes, W. W., "A Baptist World Consciousness,"
     Review and Expositor, XX (July 1923).
90. Porter, J. W., "The Interchurch Movement" (Editorial),
     Western Recorder, 95th year (January 1, 1920), p. 8.
91. Pitt, R. H., "A Statement Concerning the Attitude of
     the Southern Baptists Toward the Interchurch World
     Movement" (Editorial), Religious Herald, XCIII
     (February 26, 1920), p. 7.

92. Ibid.
93. The Federal Council of Churches was one of several
     interdenominational agencies which consolidated to
     form the National Council of Churches in 1950.
94. Riley, W. B., "Federal Council of Churches," Florida
     Baptist Witness, XXXVII (June 5, 1924), p. 6.
95. During the McCarthy period, William A. Merryman
     called the ecumenical movement religious socialism.
     Socialism was sometimes used during this period as
     a synonym for Fascism on the right and Marxism
     on the left. Merryman defines socialism in this
     way. Merryman, William A., "Is Unionism Social-
     ism in Religion?" The Word and the Way," 89, No.
     17 (April 24, 1952), p. 3.
96. Barton, "Can Southern Baptists Hold Their Lines
     Against Religious Fascism?" Baptist and Reflector,
     CV (March 2, 1939), p. 5.
97. "Suggested Reply to the World Council of Churches" by
     Special Committee of the Southern Baptist Conven-
     tion, George W. Truett, Chairman, Religious Herald,
     CXIII (April 18, 1940), p. 10.
98. Report of the Committee on Southern Baptists Relations
     with other Religious Bodies, Annual of the Southern
     Baptist Convention (Nashville, Tenn., 1951), pp.
     459-461.
99. Gambrell, J. B., "Facing a Grave Situation," The Bap-
     tist Courier, XLIX (September 5, 1918), p. 2.
100. Now the American Baptist Convention.
101. Gambrell, J. B., "Can Northern and Southern Baptists
     Hold Together?" Baptist Standard, XXXII (February
     12, 1920), p. 1.
102. Graham, B. J. W., "Co-ordinated Agencies for the
     Overthrow of the Baptist Denomination" (Editorial),
     The Christian Index, XCVIII (July 18, 1918), p. 1.
103. Gardner, David M., "The Aim of Church Unionists"
     (Editorial) Baptist Standard, 66, No. 35 (September
     2, 1954), p. 2.
104. Porter, J. W., "The Interchurch Movement" (Editorial)
     Western Recorder, 95th year, (January 1, 1920);
     p. 8.
105. Masters, Victor J., "Why Southern Baptists are not in
     the Federal Council of Churches" (Editorial), West-
     ern Recorder, CIII (February 28, 1929), p. 16.
106. Masters, Victor J., "Union of Baptists North and
     South" (Editorial), Western Recorder, CXIII (June
     29, 1939), p. 7.

107. Riley, W. B., "Federal Council of Churches," Florida
       Baptist Witness, XXXVII (June 5, 1924), p. 6.
108. Masters, Victor J., "As to Unwise Negro Leadership"
       (Editorial), Western Recorder, CXII (July 7, 1938),
       p. 8.
109. Justice, Anson, "Southern Baptists and the Federal
       Council of Churches," The Baptist Messenger, 39,
       No. 48 (November 30, 1950), pp. 4, 15.
110. Brunson, John A., "Federal Council of Churches and
       Southern Baptists" Western Recorder, CXIII (June
       22, 1939), pp. 4-5.
111. Report of the Committee on Southern Baptists Relations
       with other Religious Bodies, Annual of the Southern
       Baptist Convention (Nashville, Tenn., 1951), p.
       460.
112. Justice, op. cit., p. 4.
113. Gritz, Jack L., "Baptist Isolationism," (Editorial) The
       Baptist Messenger, 43, No. 11 (March 18, 1954),
       p. 2.
114. Sams, Oscar E., "Where is the Ecclesiastical Foch?"
       Religious Herald, XCII (January 16, 1919), p. 4.
115. Alexander, Charles T., "That Ghost of Organic Church
       Union," Baptist Standard, LIX, No. 43 (October 23,
       1947), p. 3.
116. Some writers do not say that Baptist beliefs constitute
       the essence of the Christian faith but they lay down
       "Baptist principles" as the only adequate basis for
       the cooperation or union of the churches.
117. Brown, S. M., and Brown, Joseph E., "Let Us be
       Fair to Ourselves and True to God" (Editorial),
       Word and Way, LXXI (June 14, 1934), p. 4.
118. Holt, A. J., "Denominational Perpetuity," (Editorial),
       Florida Baptist Witness, XXIX (January 11, 1917),
       p. 6.
119. Ibid.
120. McConnell, F. M., "What Christian Union Is," Baptist
       Standard, LVII, No. 9 (March 1, 1945), pp. 1-2.
121. Justice, op. cit., p. 15.
122. Gambrell, J. B., Baptists and Their Business (Nash-
       ville, Sunday School Board of the Southern Baptist
       Convention, 1919), pp. 72 ff.
123. Definitions of the church that accord with the ecumeni-
       cal understanding of the church have already been
       noted. See Carver, Conner, and Price, pp. 8 ff.
124. Jones, M. Ashby, "A Reply to the Editor of the Chris-
       tian Index," The Christian Index, XCVIII (August 1,
       1918), p. 6.

125. Poteat, Edwin M., "The Interchurch World Movement
     and the Baptists," The Baptist Courier (June 26,
     1919), p. 3.
126. Ibid.
127. Campbell, Ernest F., "Southern Baptists and the
     World Council of Churches," Religious Herald,
     CXIII (July 11, 1940), pp. 9, 24.
128. Duncan, B. H., "National Council of Churches Takes
     Saner Position," (Editorial) Arkansas Baptist, 52,
     No. 5. (January 29, 1953), p. 3.
129. Pruden, Ernest Hughes, "Brethren, Let's Be Fair,"
     Biblical Recorder, 117, No. 30 (July 28, 1951),
     pp. 9, 16.

Chapter II

EDUCATION

The social theories of a people can be seen in their philosophy of education. Education is the chief agency in modern times for the transmission of racial, national, and regional ideals from generation to generation. Organized education is the main base for the formation of group attitudes. Since the government at various levels is the chief sponsor of education, the form, content, and aim of education are profoundly influenced by the prevailing hopes, aims, beliefs, and interests of the body politic.

Among Southern Baptists education has more than the usual social significance. It is a doctrine. It is a duty enjoined by Jesus Christ in the great commission:

> It is unusual to refer to education as a doctrine. Yet there is ample warrant in the New Testament for such reference. In the great commission Jesus couples the duty of teaching with the duty of preaching. The teaching and preaching therein enjoined are co-ordinate and equal parts of the great task of Christ's people. The academy, the college, the university, indeed, all forms of organizations for teaching the truth, all institutions for the diffusion of knowledge are the direct and logical outcome of the work of evangelization. The Christian life involves a particular view of the world and of God as its providential Ruler and Christianity in its doctrine of regeneration lays the foundation for education. [1]

1. The Nature of Education

The Southern Baptist ideal of education is essentially that of medieval scholasticism. Like the scholastics, Southern Baptists hold the view that true education is the develop-

ment of all the constituent powers of man's being.   Man "is
body and soul, he has intellect, sensibility and will.   He is
related to the material world, to the human world and to the
unseen spiritual world. "   Education is complete and success-
ful only when it takes into account man's total environment
and when it is as broad as man's personality.   Complete
education sweeps the whole gamut of human life and trains
all elements of personality to their highest capacities. [2]
Since man is a two dimensional being, education must be
both intellectual and spiritual. [3]

    When education meets these requirements it is in
truth the handmaid of religion.   This is its proper function.
It "should be the most powerful arm of the church of Christ
in bringing in the kingdom. "[4]   To the medieval scholastics,
the development of all the faculties in the hierarchical organization of man's soul was a preparation for contemplation--
the soul's highest expression.   Out of their evangelical tradition Southern Baptists do not speak of contemplation but of
fellowship with God.   Education must prepare man for eternal life, a quality of life which refers not merely to the life
to come but to present life lived in fellowship with God
through faith in Christ. [5]

    The unity of the soul with God is only potential in
many men, but it must be made real and vital.   Education
achieves authenticity only when it brings man into unity with
God.   "True education is founded on religion.   This is true
because education is fundamentally an adjustment to environment and man's spiritual environment is God. "[6]   On the
other hand, education devoid of moral and religious control
is a mighty irresponsible power and can never be permanently
constructive.   The culture of men of higher learning is a
curse to the world and a destruction to themselves unless
they love God and their fellow men. [7]

    All education, public as well as private, should be
religious, according to Talmadge C. Johnson.   In addition
to the fact that religion is inherent to the very nature of
education, the realities of formal and informal education in
America demand the yeast of religion.   Both as to quantity
and quality religious education, as conducted by the churches,
is very weak in comparison with secularized public education.   Moreover, certain informal and irreligious agencies,
such as the radio, the motion picture industry, and secular
periodicals, are effectively inculcating their ideals, attitudes,
and practices.   The church alone cannot hope to counteract

and outweigh these. This problem can only be met through
the cooperative efforts of state, educational, and church
leaders in devising a system of public education "which will
perpetuate the best in our national culture and raise the moral standards of all the people. Religion must be the yeast
which leavens the whole."[8]

    While education is the handmaid of the Christian re-
ligion in general, it is a special necessity for Baptists. The
doctrines and practices of Baptist churches place them under
special obligation to foster Christian education. First, "a
regenerate church membership is a cardinal Baptist doctrine." Since the regenerate life is a growing and unfolding
life, in which all the powers of men are alive, education is
required to meet the demands of these powers. Again, Baptists observe the ordinances in a nonsacramental way, requiring intelligence in the participant that their meaning may
be clearly perceived. Thirdly, the local self-government of
Baptist churches and the equality of believers require education. The right of private judgment in the interpretation of
the Scriptures increases the intellectual responsibilities of
the individual believer. And the principle of spiritual leadership instead of episcopal authority governing the ministry requires an educated ministry. Finally, the Baptist method of
working together in the missionary program and all ecclesiastical effort is that of voluntary cooperation. This method
requires intelligence and breadth of view.[9]

    If education is as broad as personality and adjusts
man to his total environment, it follows that the goal of education is the personality developed on all sides and in its total setting. The beginning of such development is the unifi-
cation of the soul itself. Personality is characterized by
many conflicting elements which manifest themselves in in-
congruities and inconsistencies of conduct. At church the
life of a man may be one thing, in business another, and at
home still another. And within the soul there is conflict between aspirations, desires, longing, and ambitions. "The
object of Christian education is to overcome these conflicts
and build a unified personality." It is sin which enters into
the soul as a "strong man" bringing disorder into it. "Christ
is the stronger man who enters in and binds the strong
man."[10]

    The individual, so unified within, will view the world
around himself in broader and richer perspective. True education broadens horizons, develops the power of analysis,

brings inner satisfaction, [11] and adjusts the individual to his natural environment. [12]

Education founded on religion will also have as its goal the complete socialization of the individual. The motive force of this objective is the idea of the Kingdom of God which Christ inspires in the hearts of those whom He possesses. [13] The individual who is actuated by the Kingdom ideal will be internationally minded, one of the great needs of our time since the world is one great neighborhood. "The truly educated citizen must in a very real sense be a world citizen.... Christ was the first great internationalist and every commanding figure since His day has developed the international mind. "[14]

The socialized individual is also consecrated to service, sacrifice, and self denial. He will not seek personal comfort, security, or prestige; rather his life will flow out through channels of usefulness. [15] The end of Christian education may be summarized as freedom, the abundant life, peace of soul, and service to God "by serving humanity to the glory of God. "[16]

2.   Technique and Content

A religiously oriented philosophy of education like that of the Southern Baptists must inevitably serve as a basis of criticism of much that is found in present educational procedure and emphasis. The most general criticism of contemporary education offered by Southern Baptists focuses on the philosophy of life that informs it. Contemporary education is said to be too narrow and this-worldly. It is not as broad as personality and fails to take man's spiritual environment into account. J. Elwood Welsh gives expression to this criticism by saying that contemporary education is sadly lacking from the standpoint of Christian ideals. [17] John W. Shepard complains that modern education "has become ultra-secular and in many cases positively antagonistic to religion. " C. Penrose St. Amant sees contemporary higher education as being too technically narrow even in its secular aspect. The science man is so trained that he knows nothing of the arts; and the arts man is so trained that he knows nothing of science. "The fact of the matter is that the humanities and the sciences need each other and both need the deeper perspective of the Christian faith. "[18] Having fallen increasingly into the hands of the state, modern education is still based on theories drawn from the secular philosophies of the eighteenth and nineteenth centuries. The light of revelation and religion have been largely discarded. [19] The secular and nonreligious character of education is due solely to the fact that the state is the chief educative institution, according to W. J. McGlothlin. [20]

McGlothlin also deplores the narrow intellectualism and fact-centeredness of modern education. The stress has been overwhelmingly on the mere impartation of facts by the teacher and the acquisition of facts by the student. Education has not been sufficiently pupil-centered so that the pupil may acquire independence in the search for facts. "... Even in its intellectual side education is far more useful in the training it gives than in the knowledge it may impart to the mind of the student. "[21] McGlothlin agrees with St. Amant that education has also been too narrowly technical and specialized. The objective of general education is to make a man. Technical and professional education are therefore additions to general education and not substitutes for it. "Men ought to be educated and then trained in the technique of the special vocation which they choose to enter. "[22]

The emphasis on vocational education is often correlated with another objective of modern education which Southern Baptists find unworthy of the Christian man. It is the money-getting goal. John D. Freeman says that the primary motive dominating most schools for two generations has been, "get an education so you can command higher wages and less exacting labor. " Freeman calls for the abolition of this motive in every Christian school. [23]

The tendency toward narrowness in education is also found in denominational schools. W. J. McGlothlin does not overlook this fact. A narrow and rigid intellectualism often characterizes denominational schools but with a different orientation from that of state schools. "As the state school tends to become secular and materialistic, so the denominational school sometimes tends to become ecclesiastical and sectarian.... "[24] Denouncing the same tendency, James E. Hicks makes a plea for freedom of truth, particularly scientific truth, in denominational schools. He condemns the closed shop approach to education and asserts that the new discoveries of modern science must be accepted as the partial revelations of God. "All truth is God's truth and we need not be afraid.... There is no conflict between real science and real religion. All scientific truth is religious truth, and all religious truth is scientific truth. "25

From these criticisms of modern education certain
recommendations for reconstruction follow. W. R. Cullom
continues the stress on truth as the content of education,
placing the emphasis on the wholeness of truth. The whole
truth, he affirms, should be taught about every subject that
is offered. Education must be catholic in the richest sense.26
"The education for today's world must, first of all, seek to
tell the truth, the whole truth, and nothing but the truth. "27

Since all truth is the truth of God, whether it be re-
vealed in history, by science, or in the Bible, 28 every
branch of learning ought to be interpreted as a revelation of
God. 29 C. B. Jackson is distressed because there is no
"Christian graduate school" to prepare people for this kind
of teaching responsibility. He identifies a Christian graduate school as one that is theologically fundamentalist, being
convinced that only a fundamentalist faculty can be depended
upon to interpret every branch of knowledge as a revelation
from God. In the absence of a great Christian graduate
school, the denominational schools of the Southwest "are
forced to turn to the ultra-liberal schools of the north and
east for professors. " The graduates of these schools "have
been compelled to study in an atmosphere which questions
the fundamentals of our faith. " If a great Christian graduate
school were created, the problem of genuine Christian education would be resolved because "such a school should produce writers who would rewrite the text books on every subject. "30

John W. Shepard deplores the fact that modern education ignores the reality of sin. He calls the experience
of spiritual regeneration the corner stone of all true character building, and asserts that education can neither be Christian nor scientific unless it will "take child nature as it is
found in human experience and not as some false or super-
ficial philosophy has interpreted it. "31

Shepard goes on to say that Christianity offers a two-
fold basis for the reconstruction of educational theory--the
principle of spiritual unity and cooperative activity as the
fundamental law of method. The former is absolutely essential to true education. If a person is really educated he is
self-educated. If the latter principle is to be realized there
must first be teacher-activity. His activity consists in se-
lecting those things which will best serve to bring the student

into vital touch with his whole environment and in leading the
student to his best endeavors by holding out the highest ideal.
Thus the teacher leads the student into increasing self-activi-
ty and cooperative activity.

In addition to teacher and student activity there must
be divine activity in education.   Divine power is necessary
to effect the spiritual regeneration of the student through his
personal faith in Christ.   The teacher therefore must constantly invoke divine guidance and help in his work.

In the building of the unified soul, education should
begin early in childhood so that appreciative centers in the
mental system through concrete experiences may be established.   The physical, mental and spiritual in man's nature
should be developed in harmony.   And so should the knowing,
feeling, and willing elements.   The subjects of the curriculum should be so planned that they relate the student to his
total environment--physical, social, and spiritual. [32]

When it is said that subjects should relate the student
to his spiritual environment, this is not a reference merely
to the orientation of courses.   This means also that some of
the content of the curriculum should be in religious subjects.
Southern Baptists believe, as did the scholastics, that education should not only be theistic in basis but that religious
subjects should constitute the crest of the curriculum.   Living in a democratic state, and advocating separation of
church and state, perhaps most Southern Baptists make themselves content with the absence of religious courses from
publicly supported schools, but this does not change their
ideal of theocentric education, nor does it interfere with
making other provisions for religious training wherever
possible. [33]   True and complete education, according to their
view, draws its content from man's total environment, and
aims to develop all his powers.   It therefore includes religious knowledge, and above all seeks to unify the soul with
God.

3.   The Christian School and the Public School

Southern Baptists accept the fact that public schools
are here to stay.   They recognize the invaluable service
which public schools have rendered and are rendering.   In
the popularization of education the public schools have been
an absolute necessity.   Without them the majority of the peo-

ple would have remained destitute of the means of securing an education. Illiteracy cannot be banished without the help of the state. [34]

Normally there is no antagonism or conflict between state schools and Christian schools. Rather, they have much in common and in large measure seek the same ends. They both seek to develop disciplined bodies and minds, and to make better citizens. [35] "In Christian education, we are not competing with state education; we are cooperating with the state in the field of education. . . . "[36] The Education Commission of the Alabama Baptist Convention designates the work of educating the people carried on by the state, denominational, and private institutions as "our common task. "[37]

The recent drive for sex education has met great opposition and hostility in the South, just as it has in other sections of the country. Prominent among the grounds on which the opposition stands is the fantastic myth that the sex education movement is a communist plot to undermine the morals of America. From this extreme point, the range of the opposition includes puritanical tabooism, dissatisfaction with educational materials, techniques, personnel, and other considerations which usually characterize the opponents of sex education.

But a few Southern Baptist spokesmen[38] discern a great need for this form of education, and believe that the public school, at least by the default of other institutions, is the best institution to conduct it. There is general agreement among them that the home is the ideal place for sex education, but parents are generally inadequate for the task and a part of their inadequacy is unwillingness to assume it. The church is recognized as being second in the line of this responsibility. But the churches are too locked in by their own puritanical squeamishness to devise more than a few programs; and even if all churches met this responsibility, large numbers of youth would be untouched.

Admittedly there are problems which a public school program must overcome, but these problems can best be resolved in this institution. Chief among these problems is the selection of effective educational materials and mature teaching personnel. The advocates of sex education assume that the educational program must be ethical as well as scientific in orientation. The selection of the "right" teachers is the means of assuring this objective.

James A. Lester believes that the very nature of sexuality requires the churches to fulfill their responsibility in
the field of sex education. He says, in effect, that sexuality
is a quality of person and therefore must be dealt with in
spiritual terms. He recognizes the presence of puritan con-
cepts of sex in the churches, but affirms that they are un-
biblical and must play no part in a Christian program of sex
education. [39]

Despite the spirit of cooperation and the large measure of community of ends which exist between Christian
schools and public schools, there are certain differences between the two types of schools which make the existence of
the former imperative. One difference is the this-worldly
point of view of public education. "The state school takes
no account of the fact that its pupils have immortal souls--
souls that need to be saved and developed for citizenship
both in this world and in another world to succeed this. "[40]
The Christian school, on the other hand, views the pupil "as
a candidate for citizenship in two worlds. " The second major difference between these two types of schools lies in the
selection of the faculty. The state school cannot make the
faith of a teacher a condition for employment. On the other
hand, a prospective teacher "must be a Christian to hold a
professorship in the right sort of a Christian school. "[41]

In addition to these differences between state schools
and Christian schools, which obviously favor the Christian
schools, there are certain dangerous tendencies in public
education. The first of these is the tendency to monopolize.
"Like every other mighty social force the state school system steadily tends to assume the proportions and prerogatives of a monopoly. "[42] Three attempts at educational monopoly have been tried and each was a disastrous failure.
They were those of the Catholic Church in the Middle Ages,
and of the German and French States in the modern era.
When in control of the school system the state can make the
national will what it will, and tends generally to do so. An
autocracy seeks to make the people think as an autocrat
thinks. Even in a democracy the body politic is not free
from this monopolistic tendency with its accompanying medi-
ocre or low level of achievement. 'In democracies the state
is rarely the embodiment of the highest life of the nation.
We know this in our own country, and it is equally true in
other lands. "[43] Since the monopolistic system will not select
the best, state monopolistic tendencies are always dangerous.

W. J. McGlothlin also sees a serious ideological limitation in public education. The state school, he says, inevitably partakes of the secular nature of the state. When it
teaches religion it does so inadequately. And in dealing with
political theories and ideals, it often lacks freedom. State
institutions of higher learning cannot perform their public
opinion-forming function; rather they tend to cultivate a narrow and belligerent nationalism. [44]

Manifestly the Christian school is needed as a corrective in these areas. It has a definite contribution to
make to the general educational system, and Christian civilization and ideals are dependent largely upon it. [45]

What are some of the special values and characteristics of the Christian school? First, the Christian school
has teachers of vital religious conviction. The faculty of a
Christian college is concerned with the spiritual as well as
the intellectual growth of students. They are men and wom-
en "who are themselves Christians in their beliefs, their
purposes, their lives. "[46] In the second place, an academic
and a worship program are conjoined as forces making for
the growth and maturity of students. [47] The Christian school
is also a community of faith as well as learning. It is a
community in which both faculty and students "are encouraged
to acknowledge Jesus Christ as Lord and to order their lives
by convictions, derived from the main stream of Christian
thought. "[48] The very atmosphere of the campus of a Christian college is Christian. That is, it is an environment in
which there is a prevalence of "such humble virtues as
honesty, helpfulness, kindness, genuineness and understanding. "[49] Christian education inculcates a Christian sense of
values, and gives the Bible a central place in the curriculum. [50]

This does not mean that the curriculum of the Christian school is different from that of the public school. The
strength of Christian education does not lie "so much in difference of content as in its spirit and idealism. "[51] The content of the curricula of state schools and Christian schools
is practically the same outside of a single department.
"The great strength of the Christian school lies in the fact
that the realities openly taught in the department of religion
pervade the spirit and temper, and become the motivation of
the instruction in every department.... "[52] Since man is
constituted for religion, he cannot fully grasp life's possibilities without it. When religion is left out of education "men

become dwarfed and distorted." Christian education alone
therefore completes the task of education.   It meets man's
complete needs, giving him a complete cultural foundation
for his total life. [53]

Among some Southern Baptists, the objective of the
Christian school is clearly sectarian.   One of the strengths
of Christian education, according to J. B. Weatherspoon, is
its contribution to the leadership of the churches and the denomination.   Much of the expansion of the denomination is
due to the schools. [54]   But Weatherspoon does not conceive
the task of Christian education in narrow sectarian terms.
On the contrary, W. E. Denham asserts that the fundamental purpose of the Christian school is the spread and perpetuation of denominational teachings. [55]   While vigorously denying a narrow sectarianism and designating his statement as
one of "fundamental truth," which Catholics and Adventists
alone seem to have the good sense to accept," John D. Freeman calls for an all out denominational emphasis.   He states
that educational institutions that expect generous support from
the churches have the obligation to send students back to the
churches loyal to the faith and better equipped as church
workers.   Freeman attacks those Baptist colleges that would
rather glory in their inter-faith student bodies than boast of
denominational loyalty and make Baptist converts.

> We want every student we can reach, but the de-
> nominational school of the future will exist for the
> sake of the people who support it, and for the pri-
> mary purpose of bringing every possible student
> who attends its classes to become a denominational
> asset. [56]

W. J. McGlothlin ascribes a feature to the Christian
school which produces the effect of a strange note in the
Southern Baptist territory of his day.   He states that the
Christian school is democratic in the broadest and best
sense, transcending racial and national boundaries and class
distinctions.   It is a school that is Catholic in outlook and
sympathies, nonparochial in spirit and outlook, brotherly and
hospitable to truth. [57]   The fact is, not a single school in
the entire South, denominational or public, was democratic
enough to include Negroes in its student body in 1918 when
McGlothlin's words were written.   Nor is there any evidence
that the exclusion of Negroes was challenged at any ecclesiastical centers of decision.   Perhaps McGlothlin means to
describe a school that is "essentially" Christian.

4. Academic Freedom

        If the stated purpose of the Christian school is the
perpetuation of denominational doctrines, and those doctrines
are set forth and understood in rather definite terms, academic freedom is at the outset a very limited notion. But
this is the notion which is prevalent among Southern Baptists.
Academic freedom does not extend to the boundary between
freedom and license; it stops short at the circumference of
an inner circle--the inner circle of denominational belief.

          There is nothing new in the contention of some
          teachers that they should be allowed to teach any-
          thing they may see fit. This coterie seem unmind-
          ful of the fact that they are not employed as ora-
          cles of universal learning, but to teach certain
          doctrines or things. ... If one is engaged to teach
          the Bible in a Baptist school, he is supposed to
          teach it, as believed by Baptists. [58]

        F. W. Boatwright seems to extend the lines of aca-
demic freedom beyond the limits of denominational belief
when he says that professors should be free to present all
aspects of the subjects which they teach. But he quickly
draws in the lines by stating that the teacher's freedom is
bound up with that of the university and all its constituency.
Boatwright adds that the professor must have common sense
and good will as well as character and scholarship. [59]

        H. H. Provence distinguishes between freedom of
thought and freedom of expression, and affirms that everyone has a right to think for himself but freedom of expression can never be absolute. He too, places the boundary
line of academic freedom at the doctrinal limits of the institution served. [60]

        A thoroughgoing institutional and sectarian delimitation
of academic freedom is provided by Allen O. Webb. He even
speaks in the very mundane terms of the paycheck. A professor who is serving in an institution owned, operated, and
supported by and for Baptists must not "exercise his freedom
to undermine the principles and truths he is being paid to
preserve. "[61]

        The problem of restricing the academic freedom of
professors within denominational doctrinal lines is aggravated
within Southern Baptist circles by the fact that there is no of-

ficial creed. In 1925 the Convention did adopt a statement
of faith under the title, "The Baptist Faith and Message."
This statement was reaffirmed with minor modifications in
1963. Although teachers and missionaries must subscribe to
this statement, it is marked by two shortcomings. It is
quite brief; and there is no central ecclesiastical organ
which can give it official interpretation and dogmatic status.
The result is there is disagreement on "Baptist doctrines"
even among Southern Baptists. W. Levon Moore recognizes
this situation, and considers it in setting the limits of academic freedom. Since some members of the denomination
will disagree with him regardless of the position he takes on
most subjects, "the professor is therefore faced with the
question, which Baptist position shall I teach?" Moore finds
the solution of this problem in the professor's use of the
best methods of scholarship but within the context of his denominational position. [62] The question whether these can
really be harmonized is not raised.

Luther Copeland addresses himself to the problem of
the boundaries of academic freedom by introducing the notion
of a theological covenant. "The school and its teachers are
in covenant with their supporting denomination. Usually,
this covenant is witnessed to by a confession of faith to
which the teachers subscribe." The bounds of academic
freedom are set by this covenant. The distinctive elements
in this plan of denominational limitation on academic freedom
are a permissive attitude toward variation and the sense of
the dynamic in the formulation of confessions. Evidently
each denominational seminary is to enter into theological
covenant with the denomination as witnessed to by its own
confession of faith. And although each confession of faith
must be "true to the classical formulations of Christian doctrine, with an evangelical and Baptist interpretation," each
will also be

> flexible enough to permit a healthy diversity of
> theological viewpoint, and to allow a progressive
> interpretation of Christian faith in harmony with
> the best academic principles and with the advance
> of human knowledge in its various fields. [63]

Some Southern Baptists will have none of academic
freedom within any limits. They believe that the very notion is bad in itself. J. D. Mell calls academic freedom
"a polite name for anarchy," "the freedom of the law break-
er, and the destroyer," and "the freedom of the betrayer of

a sacred trust. "[64] Writing five years after the article
quoted above (p. 47), in which he set the teacher's freedom
of expression within the limits of denominational belief, J.
W. Porter takes a completely condemnatory attitude toward
academic freedom. It is a phrase, he says, which is supposed to cover a multitude of scholastic sins. It is used to
justify the theory of evolution and, like that theory, it is
without a semblance of proof. Porter defines academic freedom as unconditional and unlimited license to teach anything
one may believe or desire to teach. [65]

That there are some Southern Baptists who do not
share these attitudes toward academic freedom has already
been implied in the discussion of the "technique and content"
of education. W. J. McGlothlin repudiates the narrow intellectualism of both the state and denominational school. [66] J.
E. Hicks makes a plea for freedom of truth, particularly
scientific truth in denominational schools. [67] And W. R. Cullom states that education must be Catholic in the richest
sense, seeking "to tell the truth, the whole truth, and nothing but the truth. "[68]

In addition to these statements which have implications
for academic freedom, there are others from a minority of
Southern Baptists which explicitly defend academic freedom.
Reuben E. Alley defends the right of a professor to publish
a work which contains theological dissent on the ground that
Baptists reject creeds and disavow fixed and authoritative interpretations of Scripture. He contends that the professor
under discussion adheres to the New Testament as the sole
authority of faith in the development of his thesis. In view
of this fact and the fact that Baptists proclaim both the authority of the New Testament and the competence of individual interpretation, "who, " Alley inquires, "has the competence
to condemn or sit in final judgment upon the interpretations
of a fellow Baptist who adheres to the New Testament?"[69]

George Gordh comes at the matter of academic freedom by defining the concept of tradition as understood by
Baptists. Baptist tradition is "to try to develop those forms
of thought and expression and organization which can be open
to the Word and Spirit. " To state the matter negatively, the
Baptist tradition involves "the determination not to be bound
by any ecclesiastical declarations not to be bound by tradition
itself, but to seek to be governed solely by the New Testament. "[70] Tradition among Baptists is accordingly "an open
book" and the statements which from time to time appear on

"What Baptists Believe" are simply descriptive. Such statements do not refer to what Baptists must believe. Insofar
as such statements are binding, Baptists disavow their own
position of the sole authority of the New Testament. [71] Gainer E. Bryan agrees with the interpretation of tradition as
set forth by Gordh, and testifies that "it is better to err in
the direction of freedom than in the direction of authority, if
Baptists are to remain Baptists. "[72]

A major approach to orthodoxy among Southern Baptists as among creedal protestant churches, is the insistence
on Biblical literalism. S. L. Morgan, Sr. repudiates this
tendency in the name of freedom and enlightenment. The
worst feature of Biblical literalism, Morgan affirms, is that
"it makes God immoral and cruel. Really no one can believe some Bible passages are true--if taken literally. "
Freedom of conscience and enlightenment require that the
Bible be approached as a progressive revelation with the
revelation in Christ as its fulfillment and norm. [73]

From this discussion of academic freedom two things
present themselves to the observer. The first is the attitude of defensiveness which by and large characterizes Southern Baptists. This attitude is frequently manifest in straining the point of the opposition to academic freedom. A cari-
cature is made of the thing being opposed by identifying it in
extreme terms. Academic freedom is defined as absolute
freedom or license, thus the genuine commodity is not ex-
amined. The real issue at stake is not between denominational doctrines, on the one hand, and unlimited freedom to
teach anything, including falsehood, on the other. The issue
is whether the teacher is to be bound within the framework
of limited knowledge and belief, or be free to pursue truth
wherever it leads without reference to predispositions, denominational or institutional interests. In other words, is
truth itself to be the standard, and ever increasing probability the drawing force; or is denominational belief to be
the standard, and denominational thought boundaries the limiting barrier? Has the complete truth been "delivered once
and for all to the saints, " to say nothing of a particular
group of them, or must the human mind ever pursue truth
and the human spirit ever stand in readiness for further
revelation?

The second thing which presents itself to the observer
from this discussion is the fact that the doctrine of freedom
of conscience which involves the right of the individual even

to interpret the Scriptures for himself is a theory among
Southern Baptists and not a working belief. This conclusion
is strengthened by the fact that while Baptist churches generally are not creedal churches, Southern Baptists have
drawn up a creedal statement and require that all teachers,
missionaries and other persons in the employ of the convention sign it. It is further strengthened by the constant appeal to orthodoxy, and the frequent attacks on modernism,
evolution, and the social gospel. When all factors are taken
into account, one cannot escape the conclusion that Southern
Baptists practice a rigid authoritarianism in the field of
thought.

In every major respect, therefore, the educational
ideal of Southern Baptists is that of the medieval scholastics.
Both regard theology or religious knowledge as the core and
spirit of an adequate learning process. And both reserve
for themselves the right to determine rigidly what is orthodox and should be taught.

Notes

1. Mullins, Baptist Beliefs, pp. 74-75.
2. McGlothlin, W. J., "Education and the Future, " The
       Baptist Courier, LI, (June 17, 1920), p. 2.
3. St. Amant, C. Penrose, "Liberal Arts Education in a
       Christian Context, " Baptist Message, 85, No. 47,
       (November 20, 1969), p. 5.
4. Shepard, John W., "Educational Reconstruction on a
       Christian Basis, " Review and Expositor, XXX (July
       1933), p. 236.
5. Cullom, W. R., "The Education That is Needed in To-
       day's World, " Review and Expositor, XXX (January,
       1938), p. 42.
6. Shepard, John W., op. cit., p. 243.
7. McGlothin, W. J., op. cit., p. 2.
8. Johnson, Talmadge C., Look for the Dawn! (Nashville,
       Broadman Press, 1943), p. 139.
9. Mullins, Baptist Beliefs, pp. 75-76
10. Shepard, John W., op. cit., pp. 244-245.
11. Granberry, R. C., "What an Education Should Do for Us, "
       Review and Expositor, XXVI (July, 1949), pp. 319-322.
12. Shepard, John W., op. cit., p. 239.
13. Ibid., pp. 241-242.
14. Welsh, Ellwood, "Some Modern Challenges to the Truly
       Educated, " Review and Expositor, XX (July, 1923),

pp. 286-287.
15. Ibid., pp. 288-289.
16. Jones, S. H., "Christian Education," The Baptist
    Courier, 82, No. 48 (December 7, 1950), p. 3.
17. Welsh, op. cit., p. 282.
18. St. Amant, op. cit.
19. Shepard, op. cit., p. 235.
20. McGlothlin, op. cit., p. 1.
21. Ibid., p. 2.
22. Ibid.
23. Freeman, John D., "The Baptist College of Tomorrow,"
    (Editorial), Western Recorder, 119, No. 23 (June 7,
    1945), p. 5.
24. McGlothlin, op. cit.
25. Hicks, J. E., "The Educational Ideal," Religious Her-
    ald, XCV (March 16, 1922), pp. 12-13.
26. Cullom, op. cit., pp. 39-40.
27. Ibid., p. 39.
28. Carroll, James P., "What is Christian Education?"
    The Baptist Courier, 87, No. 3 (January 27, 1955),
    p. 6.
29. Jackson, C. B., "Christian Graduate School is Needed,"
    Baptist Standard, LVIII, No. 27 (July 4, 1946), p. 1.
30. Ibid.
31. Shepard, op. cit., p. 238.
32. Ibid., p. 237 ff.
33. Ayers, Robert H., "Christian Education in the Post-
    War World," Baptist Courier, 77 (June 7, 1945),
    p. 7.
34. McGlothlin, W. J., "The Christian School and the Fu-
    ture," Religious Herald, XVI (June 13, 1918), p. 4.
35. Baten, A. E., "Christian Education and State Schools,"
    Baptist Standard, XXXIX (January 11, 1917), p. 12.
36. Campbell, R. C., Universal Messages (Nashville,
    Broadman Press, 1935), p. 109.
37. Report of Education Commission of the Alabama Baptist
    Convention, Annual of the Alabama Baptist State Con-
    vention (Atlanta, 1924), p. 95.
38. Daley, C. R., "Sex Education is Needed in Public
    Schools," (Editorial) Western Recorder, 143, No.
    17, (April 24, 1969), pp. 4-5. Hood, Northrup L.,
    "Letter to the Editor," The Maryland Baptist, LII,
    No. 23 (June 12, 1969), p. 2. Maston, T. B.,
    "Sex Education in Public Schools," The Alabama
    Baptist, 134, No. 32 (August 14, 1969), p. 9.
    Puckett, R. G., "The Pros and Cons of Sex Edu-
    cation in the Public Schools" (Editorial), The Mary-

land Baptist, LII, No. 19 (May 15, 1969), p. 2.

39. Lester, James A., "Sex Education, Whose Responsibility?" (Editorial) Baptist and Reflector, 135, No. 38 (September 18, 1969), p. 4.
40. Baten, A. E., op. cit.
41. Ibid.
42. McGlothlin, W. J., "The Christian School and the Future," Religious Herald, XCI (June 13, 1918), p. 4.
43. Ibid., p. 5.
44. Ibid., p. 6.
45. Ibid.
46. Carroll, James P., op. cit., p. 7.
47. Binkley, Olin T., "Qualities of a Christian College," Biblical Recorder, 128, No. 17 (April 28, 1962), p. 4.
48. Ibid.
49. Carroll, James P., op. cit., p. 7.
50. Ayers, Robert H., op. cit.
51. Weatherspoon, J. B., "The Strength of Christian Education," The Christian Index, CXVII (May 13, 1937), p. 4.
52. Ibid.
53. Ibid.
54. Ibid.
55. Denham, W. E., Why Denominational Schools?" The Baptist Courier, XLIX (May 14, 1918), p. 2.
56. Freeman, John D., op. cit., p. 5-6.
57. McGlothlin, W. J., op. cit., p. 6-7.
58. Porter, J. W., "Academic Freedom" (Editorial) Western Recorder, 93rd year, (January 3, 1918), p. 8.
59. Pitt, R. H., "An Admirable Statement" (An editorial report of a statement by F. W. Boatwright), Religious Herald, CIX (May 28, 1936), p. 10.
60. Provence, H. H., "Academic Freedom," The Baptist Recorder, LXV (December 13, 1934), p. 6.
61. Webb, Allen O., "Academic Freedom in Baptist Institutions," The Baptist Record, LXXXIV, No. 46 (November 15, 1962), p. 5.
62. Moore, W. Levon, "What is Academic Freedom?" (The Baptist Record, LXXXIV, No. 21 (May 24, 1962), p. 5.
63. Copeland, Luther, "Academic Freedom in the Seminary," Religious Herald, CXXXVI, No. 7 (February 14, 1963), p. 4.
64. Mell, J. D., "Academic Freedom," Western Recorder CIX (March 21, 1935), p. 5.

65. Porter, J. W., "Academic Freedom," The Baptist
    Recorder XXV (June 21, 1923), p. 5.
66. Supra., p. 42-45.
67. Supra., p. 46.
68. Supra., p. 42.
69. Alley, Reuben E., "Freedom for Seminary Professors,"
    (Editorial), Religious Herald, CXXXIII, No. 19 (May
    2, 1960), p. 10.
70. Gordh, George, Should A Theological Seminary Serve
    a Denomination? Religious Herald, CXXXII, No. 11
    (March 12, 1959), p. 12.
71. Ibid.
72. Bryan, Gainer E., Jr., "Freedom Wins A Round" (Edi-
    torial) The Maryland Baptist, XLV, No. 2 (January
    11, 1962), p. 8.
73. Morgan, S. L., Sr., "Dr. Ralph Elliott, Heretic!"
    Religious Herald, CXXXV, No. 8 (February 22,
    1962), pp. 12-13.

Chapter III

THE STATE

In some aspects of their doctrine of the church, Southern Baptists reflect the emphases of Martin Luther. They assert that the function of the church is the proclamation of the gospel. Luther likewise understood the function of the church as the ministry of the Word; although, in his thought, the Word is not only proclaimed but is set forth as visible in the administration of the Sacraments. Southern Baptists also hold an extremely spiritual conception of the church. Christ is the sole head of the church; it is the body of the Living Christ. It is perpetuated and grows under divine influence, being administered under the laws of God and for the glory of God. This extremely spiritual conception of the church is in direct line with Luther's conception of the church of the Word of God. Luther believed that the Word was completely self-propagating. The church is made and perpetuated through the Word alone, through which Christ acted.

More closely than they follow Luther in their doctrine of the church, Southern Baptists follow Calvin in their doctrine of the state. The direct appeal is to Paul, but it is to Paul by way of John Calvin. Like Calvin, Southern Baptists assume that a relative ethic is the standard in the political realm. The absolute ideals of the Gospel are not applicable to the life of the state. There is therefore no tension between the absolute ideals of the Gospels and the demands of nature and history in Southern Baptist political ethics. There is some recognition that the state is a consequence of, as well as a remedy of sin, [1] but the state does not stand under perpetual judgment because of sin. On the contrary, God works directly through it, and makes it as sacred as is the church. The state has a positive function to perform and, like the church, is divinely commissioned to perform it. In the Southern Baptist doctrine of the state, the God of Grace becomes the God of history who settles down to a temporal task. The good which is realized through the state is not the absolute good of the Gospels, but it is God's good.

1. The Origin of Authority

All authority in law making and law enforcement is a trust from God. Governors, legislators, judges, sheriffs, constables, all civil officers are directly accountable to God in the performance of their official functions. This is true without reference to their religious or nonreligious life. They are accountable whether they be Christians or not, and whether they recognize their accountability or not. They are accountable because all human government is of divine origin and appointment. [2]

In their doctrine of the origin of the authority of the state, Southern Baptists rely mainly on the Scriptures, appealing above all to that famous statement concerning governmental authority uttered by the Apostle Paul: "Let every soul be subject unto the higher powers, for there is no power but from God; the powers that be are ordained of God." (Romans 13:1) Since the powers that be are ordained of God "they are a part of the Divine Order for the government of the world. The state is as much a Divine institution as the church or as the Family."[3] Scriptural ground for political authority is also found in I Peter 2:13-17:

> Submit yourselves to every ordinance of man for the Lord's sake: whether it be to the emporer, as supreme, or unto governors as unto them that sent by him for the punishment of evil-doers, and for the praise of them that do well. For so is the will of God, that with well doing ye may put to silence the ignorance of foolish men: as free, and not using your liberty for a cloak of maliciousness, but as the servants of God. Honor all men. Love the brotherhood. Fear God, Honor the king.

These arguments and exhortations have as their premise, says Charles L. Graham, the words of Christ Himself: "Render unto Caesar the things that are Caesar's, and unto God the things that are God's." (Matthew 22:21). They also have as their premise the act of Christ in submitting to Pilate, and His declaration to Pilate that the power which he exercised was given from above. [4]

Although they represent a minority of voices, some Southern Baptists also find the origin of the state in the social nature of man. [5] R. A. Venable supports the doctrine of the Divine ordination of the government, but he also elaborates a doctrine of Natural Law as the foundation of the state. Men are born into civil authority just as they are born into the family, Venable contends. This civil authority is the inevitable outcome of the social nature of man. God in creation impressed upon the constitution of human beings certain laws which they must follow to attain the end of their being. "The individual cannot attain the end of his being in isolation. He finds his complement in others; association with others leads to self discovery, and development. " Upon this social necessity the state and statutory laws are elaborated. Thus Venable sees the state as a product of Divine Reason as expressed in the Law of Nature. Like Thomas Aquinas, he asserts that human laws are discovered, not made. They are elaborations and formulations of the Law of Nature. [6]

Although the authority of the state is involved and even affirmed in his doctrine of the origin of the state, Venable is convinced that origin and authority must be distinguished to make room for direct investiture. Appealing to the words of Paul concerning the ordination of the public powers, Venable says that the authority of the state is derived from God; it is an investiture from Him, and its mandates are imperial, being limited only by the public welfare. Perhaps this distinction between the origin and authority of the state is made because Venable felt that the doctrine of the state as a product of Divine Reason did not make the appointment of authority sufficiently direct to accord with the words of Paul. [7]

A peculiar feature of the Southern Baptist doctrine of political authority is their placing of the Apostle Paul and John Locke in juxtaposition to each other, apparently without the slightest notion of their incongruity. This statement that Paul and John Locke are incongruous does not mean that they are totally incongruous. It means that they differ widely on the matter of political authority. For Locke sovereignty has its source in the people and remains in the people. The rulers are delegated authorities, who must rule rationally and justly. If they do not they abuse the authority that has been delegated to them, and may expect the people to take it back from them, even by the extreme measure of revolt if necessary. This the people have a right to do.

On the other hand, for Paul, the state is a divine agent of justice and punishment. The existing authorities are constituted by God. God is the source of their authority. The only proper response of the people is obedience. Like Locke, Paul does enunciate a doctrine of natural law, but he does not apply it to political authority. Political authority is by direct investiture.

This peculiarity of conjoining Paul and Locke in Southern Baptist thought well illustrates the fact that no thinker can take a standpoint outside his own historical period. Southern Baptists, just as most American Christians, are heirs of the Pauline political ethic, but they also live after John Locke and the democratic revolution, and in a country whose creed is thoroughly democratic. They, therefore, cannot escape the influence of the democratic idea of the origin and position of political authority, and the influence of that political philosopher who made a heavy impact upon the development of American political thought. Accordingly, both Paul and Locke are affirmed, whether a clear relationship between them is seen or not.

Charles L. Graham, who proclaims the doctrine that the "powers that be are ordained of God, " and calls for allegiance and obedience to them, also says the "laws of the State ought always to represent the crystallized sentiment of the majority of the people. " In spite of his conviction as to the righteousness of the prohibition law, he states that he believes it would be a mistake "to attempt to write prohibition into the laws of the land against the majority sentiment of the people, even if it were possible to do so."[8] Watkins M. Abbitt echoes this sentiment in asserting that a good government is a government of laws and not men, and expresses the collective will. [9] The Social Service Commission of the Southern Baptist Convention also reflects John Locke in convicting the Federal Congress and the Legislatures of some of the states of "embezzlement of power. "

> Legislative bodies, both the Federal Congress and the Legislatures of some of the several states, have utterly ignored and flouted the principles of democracy in dealing with this question the liquor traffic.... Some of our State Legislatures, judging by their acts, would set themselves up as fully posessed with all the powers of a dictatorship with perfect right to ride roughshod over the will of the people. [10]

Clearly these statements represent the view that sovereignty rests in the people, and that the state is a product of a kind of social compact. This view assumes that the legislators and executives are appointed by the people, and have the responsibility to carry out their will since sovereignty remains in the people. It is inconsistent with the view that magistrates are directly and solely responsible to God, and have their power as a direct investiture from Him. No attempt is being made here to say that representative democracy cannot be derived from the doctrine of Divine sovereignty. The intent is to point out that the ideas of the Divine origin of government and the sovereignty of the people cannot be held in conjunction without further ado. There must be a theological understanding of the relationship of the two sovereignties--that of God and that of the people.

Good government is government of laws and not men. [11] Since law enforcing as well as law making is a sacred trust, the enforcement of laws is as urgent a duty of magistrates as is legislating. The dignity and sanctity of the law is expressed in both enactment and enforcement. It is upon this religious ground that the Social Service Commission of the Southern Baptist Convention makes its plea for law enforcement and a campaign of education in its report of 1921.

> What is needed, and what we must have, is a campaign of education. The dignity of the law and the necessity for the equal and impartial enforcement of all law, must constantly be impressed upon the hearts and minds of the people. We suggest and recommend that our pastors preach frequently upon some phase of civic duty and law enforcement, and that your Commission on Social Service be authorized to suggest, as early as expedient during the coming convention year, a period for such a campaign.

The report goes on to suggest the formation of citizen leagues or law enforcement organizations in every city "of considerable size" and in every county. Pastors and people of Southern Baptist churches are urged to take the leadership in the formation of such organizations when this is necessary. Special reference is made to the out-lawing of the liquor traffic and drinking habit. [12]

In the light of a strong tradition of extra-legality in

America, and particularly in the South, Southern Baptists
have an important practical reason for stressing law enforcement.   But during the prohibition period, their pleas for law
enforcement showed a marked weakness.   The weakness of
the pleas lay in their exaggerated concern for the enforcement of one law--the Eighteenth Amendment.   Evidently sens-
ing this undue concern with the enforcement of one law and
at the same time addressing himself to a particular issue,
J. J. Taylor urges the enforcement of all laws and declares
all to be equally sacred.

Taylor's immediate concern is with Senator Carter
Glass' apologia "for what many regard as Southern violation
or evasion of the Fifteenth Amendment. "[13]   In his critique,
Taylor sets this apologia against the background of the Senator's ardent urging of the observance of the Eighteenth Amendment.   He points to the fact that Senator Glass claims the
authorship of the items in the Virginia Constitution prescrib-
ing qualifications for registering to vote and suggests that
the Senator

> will remove every doubt and settle the issue for-
> ever in the mind of every honorable man, if he
> will say the said items were not intended to extend
> the suffrage to certain persons and at the same
> time withhold it from others on account of race,
> color or previous condition of servitude. [14]

But having made this disclaimer, the Senator must then explain why the ratio of voters to the population is larger in
West Virginia than in Virginia.   "To the disinterested observer the easy explanation seems to be that in Virginia
some citizens are debarred from registration on account of
race, color or previous condition of servitude while in West
Virginia all alike are permitted to register. "[15]

Taylor further directs attention to the nature and
consequences of the violation of law.   He asserts that all
violators of law dislike the law they violate, and that the
violation of one law because it is distasteful naturally leads
to the violation of other distasteful laws.   But the violation
of the law or the making of apology for the violation of law
by the higher talent people, like Senator Glass, is especially
pernicious because of their wide influence.   "The violation
of law by whatever means and for whatever cause, is a haz-
ardous adventure. "[16]

2.   The Function and End of the State

Southern Baptists are Calvinists in their understanding of the function of the state. The government exists as a restraint upon the evil doer, but the state also has a positive function to perform. The end of this positive effort Calvin called "the glory of God." Southern Baptists call it "human welfare."

The public welfare is the only limit on the state's authority. The state has a right to impose any restraints or promote any programs, outside the sphere of religion, that may be conducive to public welfare. It is not confined to mere police or even utilitarian functions; it is concerned with the public welfare in all aspects. With the public good as the governing principle of action, the state can take private property, conscript for military service, quarantine against contagious and deadly diseases, regulate business, levy taxes, punish offenders by imprisonment or death, establish institutions of public education and institutions of benevolence. "In a word, it can project and carry through any undertaking which will promote the comfort, happiness and prosperity of the people at large."[17]   T. B. Maston summarizes the functions of the state as the maintenance of order and peace, the provision of justice, the protection of liberty, and the promotion of the security of the people, including economic security.[18]   Foy Valentine finds himself in agreement with a broad consensus that the function of government is "to maintain law and order, suppress crime, preserve peace, serve justice, protect the inalienable rights of the people, advance liberty, and promote the general welfare."[19]

The question as to whether the law can be an agency of morals and an effective instrument of social change has been much debated among protestants. Southern Baptists have participated in this debate and, like other protestants, have produced protagonists on both sides of the argument.

After a profession of his opposition to discrimination in employment because of race, creed or color, Joseph E. Brown proceeds to attack Fair Employment Practices Legislation on two grounds. First, since it is impossible for a government agency to ascertain precisely the motives that entered into an employer's decision making, "the delegation of such power to government smacks of the inquisition, the pillory and the stake." Secondly, human motives can only

be changed from within by the transforming power of Christ;
they cannot be changed by law. [20] Brown is manifestly unaware of the operation and purpose of anti-discriminatory
laws.   The administrators of such laws make no attempt to
ascertain motives; rather, they discern a pattern of behavior.
Secondly, no laws seek to change motives; they aim to regulate behavior.

Reuben E. Alley reflects the laissez faire sociology,
initiated by William Graham Sumner of Yale in the early
part of this century, in contending in effect that the mores
cannot be changed by stateways.   "Social progress cannot be
accelerated by legislation or decree.   Efforts to force moral
patterns beyond the norm of a social group provoke responses
which are reactionary."   Alley goes on to apply this view to
the Supreme Court decision on the desegregation of the public schools, illustrating the reactionary responses in sentiment and action to this decision. [21]

On the other side of the debate, E. S. James expresses agreement with a writer in the journal, the Christian
Crusader, who states that although it is true that morality
cannot be legislated, it is also true that legislation can create an atmosphere in which it is easier to be moral.   The
writer might have gone a step further, says James, to point
out that "while legislation does not make a man moral it
may prevent his being immoral."

> The primary purpose of legislation has never been
> to produce a situation but to prevent one.   Laws
> have never made a good man, but laws may prevent
> his being bad until God has a chance to lead him to
> the good.   Experience proves that unrestrained man
> often becomes so bad that it is impossible for
> right and righteousness to hold any appeal for him.
> Legislation does not even help to make a Christian,
> but it may help him to be a decent citizen. [22]

The Christian Civic Foundation of Arkansas, Inc. attacks the "You Can't Legislate Morals" notion in defense of
the temperance movement.   The Foundation contends in its
report that the practice of the law does tend to make good
men and good citizens.   This is true because the law is an
integral part of the moral and ethical ideals of the people.
Secondly, in the long run, the majesty of the law, with its
full weight on one side of an issue, does affect the moral
character of the people.   Finally, "the purpose of legislation

is not to change the moral character of individuals, but to
restrain individuals and groups from the commission of immoral and anti-social acts." Restraint upon the overt forms
of evil behavior provides the people with a much better
chance at the good life. [23]

Despite much debating of the issue that people cannot
be made moral by law, American people probably embody
their ideals in law more than any other Western nation.
Support of and more frequently opposition to legislation of
moral import relate to particular issues. When an issue
which is urgent and important to him is at stake, the same
person who previously opposed legislation under the principle
that laws do not moralize may support the impending legislation. It is more frequently than not a matter of issues
rather than principle. People are quick to support a law
"agin it," if an issue is important to them, whether they
think they believe "you can't make people moral by law" or
not.

Daniel R. Grant rightly designates the "you can't
legislate morals" doctrine as "one of the oldest myths in
the rhetoric of opposition speeches in the field of race relations." The conduct of the members of the two camps
generated by civil rights legislation provides clear evidence
that people apply this doctrine to selected issues and not as
a working principle.

> Some of those who have argued most strongly
> against civil rights legislation because it will not
> change the hearts of men, have been leading
> spokesmen for legislation to prohibit sale of al-
> coholic beverages, gambling, narcotics, and por-
> nographic literature.
>
> In all fairness, it should be pointed out that 'liber-
> als' opposing legislation against liquor, gambling,
> or obscene material because you can't legislate
> morals' are usually in the forefront of those fight-
> ing for civil rights legislation. [24]

When the Depression came and the New Deal was in-
augurated, Southern Baptists had no difficulty supporting the
New Deal despite the moral overtones of some of the new
legislation. They could support the New Deal because they
believed it served the end of the state--the public welfare.
Speaking to the "economic situation" in 1932, the Social

Service Commission of the Georgia Baptist Convention calls
for governmental regulation and coercion.

> Social and governmental regulating should be more
> and more brought into exercise. Good laws are a
> great aid to a righteous and just civilization. It
> is a weak sentimentalism which would ignore the
> necessity for coercive action. There are evils in
> society that moral suasion or even a gospel appeal
> would not reach in a thousand years. [25]

By the time the Convention met in 1933, the New Deal
program was under way. In its report of that year the Social Service Commission was unstinting in its praise of
President Franklin D. Roosevelt for his national recovery
program. "Never in so short a time has so much been done
in the interest of social justice as has been done by the present national administration in the short time it has been in
office. "[26] The Committee on Temperance and Social Service
of the Missouri Baptist General Association called the ideals
underlying the national Recovery Act basically Christian, thus
heaping their highest praise upon it. [27]

Although the promotion of human welfare involves matters of moral import, it is also the function of the state to
aim specifically at moral ends. John Calvin conceived the
moral ends of the state within the framework of a theocracy
in which it was the function of the state to assist the church
in the promotion of Christian righteousness. Southern Baptists take their stand on the principle of separation of church
and state, but regard the state as having a share in the promotion of righteousness within its own jurisdiction, namely,
civic righteousness. Law is thus conceived as an instrument
of education. Legislation helps to build up a public moral
conscience, a healthy moral atmosphere and moral psychology
favorable to the growth and enforcement of morals. [28] It is
with confidence in the educative value of law that much Southern Baptist zeal is expended behind certain types of legislation, particularly prohibition legislation.

Southern Baptists subscribe to the plan of legislation
even in the field of ideas, if the ideas are judged to be in-
jurious to public morals. Even where religious interpretation is involved, some Southern Baptists sacrifice the doctrine
of the separation of church and state in the interest of the
legislation, if the general welfare is threatened. John D.
Freeman says "the church must recognize the rights of the

state to oversee its conduct in matters affecting the general
welfare. " He includes the ethic of war among these areas
in which the state may properly oversee the conduct of the
church. The state "has the right to demand that its citizens,
regardless of religion, help defend it against aggression from
enemy forces. " To permit a band of pacifists to grow up in
the state means the destruction of the state. [29]

A specific case which involved legislation on religion
was the passing of a law prohibiting the teaching of evolution
and requiring the reading of the Bible in public schools by
the state of Tennessee in 1925. R. H. Pitt deplored the
fact that the law was passed, stating that it contravened the
doctrine of separation of church and state, and would lend
credence to the view that when Baptists are in the majority
they are as willing to tyrannize as anybody else. [30]   Z. T.
Cody also expressed his opposition to anti-evolution laws on
the ground that they contravene the doctrine of separation of
church and state: "A legislative act on this question inevitably means that our courts must decide on the interpretation
of the Bible and must put the power of the state back of that
interpretation. "[31]

George R. Pettigrew rejects Cody's conclusion concerning the interpretation of the Bible by the state, asserting
that

> the best of our common and statutory law, the very
> back-bone of our jurisprudence, is based directly
> or indirectly upon Christian or Biblical principles
> .... In enforcing these State laws, however, there
> is no recourse to scripture [sic] interpretation, but
> they are interpreted according to their own terms. [32]

Pettigrew further states that the teaching of evolution
is conducive to immorality. An anti-evolution law therefore
can be passed in the interest of good morals. Just as Sabbath laws are enacted and enforced on economic grounds,
anti-evolution laws may be enacted and enforced on the theory that they militate against good morals. [33]

In the end, Pettigrew vitiates his argument that anti-
evolution laws do not involve the issue of separation of
church and state. Having dismissed the issue of the state's
involvement in Biblical interpretation to his own satisfaction,
he brings the doctrine of separation of church and state back
as a problem by making an appeal to infidelity. He says

that evolution promotes infidelity and infidelity promotes immorality.   If this be the case, an anti-evolution law would
serve primarily to protect faith and secondarily to protect
morals.   Thus, in the final analysis, the law does contravene the doctrine of separation of church and state.

3.   The Death Penalty

There appears to be no prevailing Southern Baptist attitude toward capital punishment.   Both the views, that capital punishment is right and that capital punishment is wrong,
appear with strong Biblical support. [34]

According to E. G. Quattlebaum, God commanded that
governments should punish murderers by death.   He forbade
for His own reasons the execution of Cain, the first murderer, but since iniquity increased God brought the Deluge, after
which He announced a complete change in governmental affairs. [35]   "Surely your blood, the blood of your lives will I
require, at the hands of every beast will I require it; and
at the hand of man, even at the hand of every man's brother,
will I require the life of man.   Whoso sheddeth man's blood
by man shall his blood be shed; for in the image of God
made he man. "   (Genesis 9:5-6) Under the law of Moses,
God reaffirmed the governmental duty of punishing murderers
with death, and Paul affirms it when he says that the magistrate "beareth not the sword in vain. "   Quattlebaum concludes
that "it is a libel on Christianity to claim that the current
anti-capital punishment cry is Christian.   It is not Christian,
but rebellion against God. [36]

False conclusions concerning capital punishment, says
G. C. Musick, are due to "sentimental and humanitarian
reasons, those who attempt to reach conclusions based on
the Word of God who know not God, those who fail rightly to
divide the Word of truth, and ignorance of dispensational
truth. "[37]   A correct understanding of God's relation to capital punishment as well as the Word of God itself is dependent upon the grasp of dispensational truth.   In the beginning
God placed man under conscience with the responsibility to
govern himself.   But when man failed under conscience, God
added to man the burden of human government, the obligation
to govern other men.   This change in governmental affairs
took place in 2350 B. C.   For one hundred years under Noah
human government was tested.   The testing time ended in
2250 B. C. , but the responsibility continues and will continue

"until all government passes into the hands of the Lord Jesus, when he comes to reign and rule."[38]

Having accounted for the origin of government, Musick proceeds to explain the source and meaning of the right of the government to take life:

> Along with the governing burden God also gave man the right to take life for life. This is the basic principle of all government, and whenever it is set aside for sentimental or humanitarian reasons will always result in confusion.... The word law would be meaningless without a penalty, and no law is stronger than its penalty. The law is inexorable and so inflexible that God Himself conforms to it without deviation. He never pardons but always punishes....
>
> The institution of capital punishment reveals to us that God holds human life as sacred and, therefore, it is to be regarded by man.[39]

Opposition to capital punishment based on the sixth commandment, Musick asserts, is due to erroneous understanding. God is not prohibiting killing in the commandment; He is prohibiting murder. Israel, to whom the law was given, engaged in much killing through international war. This was evidently God's method of dealing with the nations in judgment. Furthermore, God incorporated capital punishment in the law and legal system of the Hebrews. Killing, which is permitted, must not be confused with murder, which is prohibited.[40]

Musick concludes that capital punishment has not been done away with in the dispensation of grace. In language reminiscent of Martin Luther, Musick declares that Christians whose distinctive sphere is that of grace must also respect and obey the laws of the land in the sphere of justice.[41]

In addition to Biblical sanction, F. M. McConnell finds a practical reason for favoring capital punishment. He testifies that we need capital punishment because it is about the only thing that will deter cruel bloodthirsty murderers. McConnell also states, with Biblical support, that it is the criminal who puts himself to death, not the jury, judge, or witnesses.[42] The practical value of capital punishment is also supported by Jack L. Gritz, who can think of no more

effective means of punishment. Gritz believes that murder,
rape, high treason, and perhaps other crimes ought to be
punishable by the death penalty. He rejects as weak the
argument that the innocent are sometimes put to death, and
asserts that the logic of this argument would turn the legal
and judicial system into a shambles. "We do not see punishment as being corrective only. We believe in punishment
for punishment's sake. "[43]

With the announcement that he sees "no wisdom in a
hasty move to do away with capital punishment, " John E.
Roberts makes society an absolute arbiter. The principal
issue, as he sees it, is the determination of the purpose of
the penal system. "If we imprison a man only to 'punish'
him with no effort made toward rehabilitation then it is as
fitting to deprive him of all of his life for a major crime
as to take a part of his life for a less serious offense. "
Roberts raises no questions concerning norms which should
inform society's definition of purpose. [44]

Finley W. Tinnin speaks in terms similar to those of
F. M. McConnell's claim, on Biblical grounds, that it is the
criminal who puts himself to death. Tinnin makes the same
claim on social grounds. Capital punishment is right because the murderer has forfeited his right to live. No one
has a right to live who places in jeopardy the right of others
to live also. [45]

A modified consent to capital punishment is provided
by Z. T. Cody. The purpose of punishment, he states, is
to express society's recoil from crime, which is a reflection of God's recoil. Since society is weak in righteousness,
however, it may be better to do away with capital punishment and substitute life imprisonment as the extreme penalty.
Undoubtedly we would then see society's extreme abhorrence
of an outrageous crime more often expressed. But if society
were righteous it would be better to have the death penalty
because society's capacity for recoil would be equal to the
degree of the penalty. [46]

It is evident from the foregoing that those who say
capital punishment is right rely heavily on the Old Testament. It is equally noticeable that those who say capital
punishment is wrong rely just as heavily on the New Testament. M. C. Collins states himself specifically on the authority of the two testaments relative to each other:

The mistake many people make is trying to accept
all scripture as equally valuable and equally authoritative.   To the most casual student of the New
Testament it must be fully apparent that Jesus intended his teachings to supersede certain sections
of the Old Testament.   This in no way detracts
from our faith in the Bible as the inspired word
of God.   It simply means that we accept Christ as
the LAST word of God, and that where his teachings
are intended to supersede the Old Testament, we
cease to be bound by that particular portion of the
Old Testament. [47]

On the basis of this observation, Collins proceeds to
indicate why capital punishment is not Christian, supporting
his thesis by an appeal to the teaching and spirit of Jesus.
He says that capital punishment is an expression of the rejection of the application of the teachings of Jesus to social
relationships; it is brutal; it is "not Christian because it is
unfair and unjust"; it is not Christian because it is merci-
less, destructive of life, loveless, and manifests a lack of
faith in man. [48]

The idea that some sections of the Old Testament are
superseded by the New Testament is supported by L. L.
Gwaltney.   Gwaltney admits that capital punishment was ex-
acted for murder in Old Testament times; but adds that
many other crimes also carried the death penalty.   If the
Old Testament exactions of the capital penalty remain permanently in Christian civilization, they ought to apply to all
those infractions of the law to which they then applied.
Furthermore, if the categorical commandment, "Thou shalt
not kill, " is wrong for the individual, it is wrong for the
state.   A thing which is morally wrong in one instance cannot be morally right in another.

Gwaltney cites the case of Cain and Abel to show that
God Himself did not use capital punishment when He alone
was in control of things.   He pronounced a curse on Cain,
and proceeded to put a mark on him to prevent others from
killing him.

Speaking constructively, Gwaltney asserts that the Old
Testament law of capital punishment does not permanently
abide in civilization under sanction of the New Testament
scriptures; Jesus' dealing with the woman taken in adultery
is a clear illustration of the nullification of the teachings of

Moses with reference to capital punishment. Neither capital
punishment nor war can be sanctioned on the basis of the
Sermon on the Mount. [49] Leon Macon applauds the abolition
of the death penalty in England, saying that capital punishment cannot be reconciled with Christian conscience. "If we
were living under the Old Testament law then we would have
foundations for such procedure but we live in an age of grace
where mercy is a common factor. "[50] The Christian Life
Commission of the Georgia Baptist Convention also calls upon
Baptists to adhere to the New Testament: "In the New Testament the emphasis is on the rooting out of the attitude that
produced murder. Jesus died to save men from all sin, regardless of its heinous nature. His is a gospel of transfor-
mations, even for the murderer. "[51]

Opposing capital punishment on the practical ground
that it is not superior as a deterrent to other forms of punishment which have been substituted for it, R. H. Pitt presents statistical support and testimony for his position. He
first shows that, during the period from 1912 to 1919, Penn-
sylvania and Connecticut combined executed a higher percentage of persons sentenced to death than did Massachusetts
and New Jersey, yet the combined homicide rate of the latter
two states was lower. Secondly, by comparing states in
which capital punishment has been abolished with states of
corresponding quality of population which still require the
death penalty, he shows that the homicide rate of the former
is lower than the latter. To the contention that the abolition
of capital punishment would be followed by an increase in
the number of lynchings, he replies that "the facts and figures show that lynchings are practically confined to the
states in which capital punishment already obtains and is
most frequently used. "[52] Additional points of consideration
suggested by Pitt are the growth of adverse sentiment, making it difficult to secure convictions when the death penalty
follows, and the cutting off of the possibility of reformation
for the offender by the death penalty. [53]

Pitt also cites the testimony of governors of states
in which capital punishment has been abolished and the testimony of Warden Lewis E. Laws to show that capital punishment is not superior to other forms of punishment. The
governors express entire satisfaction with present conditions,
and Warden Laws says that "the murderer rarely considers
that penalty. "[54]

In issuing a clarion call for a rehabilitation oriented

penal system, James H. Smylie puts the stress on the hu-
manization of society. He agrees with those who suggest that
the death penalty "degrades the community and is the 'law's
darkest crime.'" As a form of punishment, it is retributive,
partial, [55] capricious, "cruel and unusual."[56] Smylie pleads
for a life affirming penal system, which treats "even the
most despicable culprit as a human being," and strives to
achieve his rehabilitation. [57]

4. Relation of Church and State

Southern Baptists have made a more vigorous effort
to remain with the New Testament in matters pertaining to
ecclesiastical organization and administration than in any
other phase of Christian life and thought. Some of their
conclusions concerning New Testament practice are of course
debatable. Principally, they may be accused of overlooking
the reality of the Presbyterian and Episcopal forms of church
organization in the New Testament in the interest of establishing the sole warrant for the congregational form. But the
fact remains that they believe that the Baptist polity is the
sole legitimate descendant of the New Testament church.
Similarly they believe that New Testament thought and the
practice of the New Testament church validate their ideas
concerning the relationship of church and state. The summary of this view is that the state has no ecclesiastical functions and the church has no civic functions. [58] And the appropriate institutional expression of this division of function
is separation of church and state.

The idea that separation of church and state has a
Biblical basis does not mean that the Bible explicitly teaches
the doctrine. "The Biblical basis for the separation of
church and state is not found in proof texts but in principles
which are central throughout the Scriptures."[59] Those passages of Scripture which teach man's creation in the image
of God, his infinite worth and freedom, the sinfulness of his
nature, the divine ordination of both church and state and the
distinctiveness of their contributions, set forth the doctrine
of separation of church and state by implication. [60] "The
very nature of religious experience also argues for the
principle of separation of church and state." As a personal
and spiritual experience, religious commitment is inherently
voluntary, being prompted by the Holy Spirit alone. [61] In the
thought of R. H. Pitt, the idea of the nature of the Christian
religion and the nature of the state are conjoined to establish

the foundation for the doctrine of separation of church and state. The doctrine rests on two fundamental facts: 1) that religion is a matter of choice and in it compulsion is a contradiction, and 2) that the state is a matter of force since all government finally rests on physical force. [62]

The emphasis on the Biblical foundations of the doctrine of separation of church and state has not caused Southtern Baptists to neglect a full statement of the principle in terms that pertain specifically to the thought patterns and social and political conditions of the present. In 1925 the Southern Baptist Convention adopted a statement on the Baptist Faith and Message which included the following article on religious liberty:[63]

> God alone is the Lord of conscience and he has left it free from the doctrines and commandments of men which are contrary to his Word or not contained in it. Church and state should be separate. The state owes to every church protection and full freedom, in the pursuit of its spiritual ends. In providing for such freedom, no ecclesiastical group or denomination should be favored by the state more than others. Civil government being ordained of God, it is the duty of Christians to render loyal obedience thereto in all things not contrary to the revealed will of God. The church should not resort to the civil power to carry its work. The gospel of Christ contemplates spiritual means alone for the pursuit of its ends. The state has no right to impose taxes for the support of any form of religion. A free church in a free state is the Christian ideal, and this implies the right of free and unhindered access to God on the part of all men, and the right to form and propagate opinions in the sphere of religion without interference by the civil power. [64]

Two issues have especially tested the Baptist idea of separation of church and state in America. They are the questions of Bible reading in the public schools and the appropriation of funds to sectarian schools. For a long time, Southern Baptists stood solidly against the latter. In 1920 the Convention sought to lay the issue permanently at rest, unanimously endorsing a resolution calling for an amendment to the Constitution of the United States to prohibit the appropriation of public funds to sectarian institutions. [65] But the

matter of Bible reading in the public schools has divided
Southern Baptists from the beginning.

As an opponent of Bible reading in public schools,
George W. McDaniel takes his stand on the principle that
the state, whose foundation is force, has absolutely no religious function, religion being a matter of personal decision.
Addressing himself directly to a bill in the Virginia legislature, designed to make Bible reading compulsory in the
public schools of that state, McDaniel presents the following
objections to the bill:

"It violates the Golden Rule. "[66] The people of Virginia have no more right to require the reading of the Bible
in the public schools than the people of Utah, predominately
Mormon, have to require the reading of the book of Mormon.

"It violates the equality which ought to be the basis
of every law. "[67] Those who do not wish to read the Bible
should have the same freedom in their choice as those who
do desire to read it.

"It violates the same principle of equality by granting
peculiar exemptions to some. "[68] Parents or guardians who
desire to have their children excused from hearing the Bible
read may do so.

In addition to these violations, the law denies freedom
of conscience to some teachers, wrongs some of the children
both among the excused and the unexcused from the class-
room, mars the religious harmony of the community, places
the reading of the Bible indiscriminately in the hands of the
believers and unbelievers, and "transfers to, or divides
with, the state a responsibility which properly belongs to
the homes and churches. "[69]

The objections of McDaniel to Bible reading in the
public schools evoked a reply from Abe C. Jones, who took
the occasion to answer R. H. Pitt also.   Jones contends that
the Baptist fathers, having suffered persecution at the hands
of governments because of their religious beliefs, developed
an undue fear of the state in its relation to the church.   But,
as a matter of fact, "the State has demonstrated its capacity
for rendering aid to the propagation of religion in a variety
of ways.... "[70] In America the government has favored religion as respects taxation, through giving railroads the privilege of granting passes or reduced fares to ministers and re-

ligious workers, and through blue laws and laws against pro-
fanity. Furthermore, the Christian religion is part of both
the common and statute law of America.

Jones denies the validity of McDaniel's assertion that
the Christian religion does not need the assistance of the
state. "God works through governments as well as individuals." The Virginia legislature is a case in point. This
body is a group of earnest Christians trying to promote a
better knowledge of the Bible among the people. [71]

Speaking to certain specific objections which McDaniel
raised, Jones makes the following observations:

1. It is not true that the state always exercises
force. It frequently presents a free choice as in such matters as offering loans to farmers, in road building, and in
providing counties with health officers.

2. The Golden Rule is not to be applied in a strict
and literal sense. If so, we "would annul very much of the
noblest and most beneficent work in our world. Through our
prohibition laws, we have taken from some millions of people what we would not wish to have taken from ourselves, if
we were in their place."[72]

3. The objection that "it [the bill requiring the reading of the Bible in public schools] places the reading of the
Bible in the hands of those who may not believe in the Bible"
is inadequate, for "we should not forego some great good because of some possible attending evil."[73]

4. The objection that it may wrong the children by
developing a distaste in them for things religious is unsound.
Compared with the few who may develop a distaste there
would be many times their number who would be thankful. [74]

It may be seen in these statements that Jones does
not proclaim the separation of church and state in the thoroughgoing Baptist sense. He admits that the state may and
often does render valuable aid in the propagation of religion.
While Jones is under no illusions concerning his position,
some Southern Baptists are. Many who think that they are
adherents to a thoroughgoing doctrine of separation of church
and state, in practice lend their support to anti-evolution
laws on religious grounds and laws requiring the reading of
the Bible in public schools. Occasionally there are also

statements, perhaps inadvertent, which bear testimony to the
significance of the state in the spread of Christian ideas and
ideals.   J. F. Love, writing on "The Outlook for Palestine,"
announces that the terrible rule of the Turk is broken and
the British are here. The new British hegemony will mean
religious freedom for all and an influx of English literature,
expressing Christian ideals, motives, and achievements. [75]
Charles E. Maddry points to the enlarging significance of the
Monroe Doctrine as enhancing the strategic missionary opportunity of Southern Baptists in Latin America, thus admitting,
perhaps inadvertently, that the missionary follows the flag. [76]
These statements certainly do not accord with those of Southern Baptist writers who say that the Christian religion is not
dependent on any particular form of government.

        Those Southern Baptists who proclaim complete sepa-
ration of church and state are not lacking in a reply to Jones'
affirmation that the state often renders aid in the propagation
of religion.   Those things which he describes as evidencies
of state aid in the propagation of religion, the protagonists
for complete separation of church and state refer to as evidences of the relatedness of church and state:

> The fact that church and state are separated does
> not mean that they are in no way related or that
> they do not act and react on each other....
>
> As concerning religion, the sole function of the
> state is to guarantee to all the right to worship as
> their consciences may direct and to guarantee to
> them quiet and peace in the free observance of all
> their religious beliefs and forms so long as such
> beliefs and forms shall not interfere with the rights
> of others or with the public peace and morals.
> The state is not concerned with beliefs but with
> acts, not primarily with character except as char-
> acter expresses itself in deeds....
>
> The church...is concerned with beliefs, with faith
> and with the making of character and influencing
> and determining conduct and actions which are the
> expression of character....   The church supports
> education, fosters morals, creates ideals and sets
> up standards of conduct, supports law and order
> and in ways without number contributes to the
> peace, prosperity and permanency of the state and
> of social order as a whole.   The church thus in-

fluences the state and ought to influence the state.[77]

The Supreme Court decision on prayer in the early
1960's extended the discussion of religion in the public
schools so that it included "devotions." Despite the fact
that the Court's decision supports the Baptist position on
separation of church and state, many Southern Baptists were
among those Americans who criticized the decision as a violation of the right to pray. E. S. James seeks to correct
this misinterpretation, warning Southern Baptists that of all
people Baptists should be the happiest with the decision. "It
[the Court] has simply ruled that prescribed and controlled
religion shall not be forced upon students by the power of
government."[78] James F. Cole makes the same plea to
Southern Baptists, citing the failure of the mass media both
in reporting the full text of the Court's decision and in properly interpreting it, thus creating confusion among the people.[79] John E. Roberts appeals to the people of South Carolina to understand the decision correctly--as a ban on officially prescribed prayer. The decision does not prohibit
prayer in the public schools that is not officially prescribed,
nor does the ruling on Bible reading prohibit Bible reading
that is not required.[80]

The debate concerning governmental aid to religion
moves between two poles, which for some are held in tension and for others are irreconcilable. The two poles are
historical realism and religious liberty. Officially Southern
Baptists have opposed the use of public funds for sectarian
institutions for decades, but breaches in "the wall of separation" have also been occurring for decades as practical
expediences. A generation ago, W. W. Gaines pointed out
that separation of church and state in America is by no
means absolute, in essence confirming the position taken by
Abe C. Jones many years earlier. The facts to which Jones
had appealed were the existence of army and navy chaplains
paid by the government, the existence of chapels for religious
service on state college and university campuses, the compulsory laws requiring the reading of the Bible in public
schools, and state laws against blasphemy.[81] Gaines calls
attention to the fact that the Constitution of the United States
nowhere specifically uses the phrase "separation of Church
and State." The essence of the Constitution is freedom of
religious belief. Laws therefore which do not interfere with
or control religious belief are entirely constitutional.[82]

In the post-World War II period and especially in the

last decade, the tension between historical realities and religious liberty has been severely aggravated for Southern Baptists, owing to changes in the historical realities. The Federal Government has greatly expanded its services in education and social welfare. Since Southern Baptists must help
pay for these services in the form of taxes, and since they
must share the burden of increasing inflation with their fellow
Americans, their own institutions which rely solely on voluntary giving are sorely troubled. Abner V. McCall addresses
himself to this problem in historical perspective, and states
that "I have come to the conclusion that in this social welfare state in which we live in 1965 in America there are no
simple, easy answers to the various church-state issues."[83]
The burden of McCall's appeal is the proposition that other
values must be weighed in the scale to determine the degree
of rigor with which the principle of separation of church and
state can be applied in the specific situation. He provides
historical evidence to show that Baptists have often done this.
Religious liberty is the cherished value and goal of Baptists;
separation of church and state is a "general political principle" or mode of instrumentalizing religious liberty. Mc-
Call admits that in all of the cases cited there is some violation of separation of church and state, but denies that there
is any evidence of a loss or reduction of religious liberty.
He contends that the failure to cooperate with governments
in those cases would have resulted in a loss of other values
than separation of church and state, namely, the closing of
schools, the reduction of their quality, the inability to admit
many prospective students, the turning away of the poor and
sick from hospitals, etc. [84]

In contrast to McCall, William M. Pinson, Jr. is
convinced that separation of church and state is relevant in
contemporary America. [85] Pinson recognizes separation as
a policy rather than an end, but believes that history, contemporary developments, and a reasonable interpretation of
current trends indicate a strong preference for separation
over tax support for church related institutions.

1. The separatist position is preferred over the co-
operatist position because this latter "tends to harm
churches." "Tax support given to churches tends to sap
their spiritual strength," generate anti-church sentiment,
and probably results in "loss of control by churches of their
institutions."

2. Tax support to church institutions is harmful to

the state. In this connection Pinson's statements take the
form of unproved possibilities.

> Tax support to church-related institutions <u>threatens</u>
> to weaken public institutions.

> Another possibility <u>would be</u> that all institutions,
> including the church-related ones, would become,
> for all practical purposes, public institutions.

> The state <u>may lose</u> a potential voice of conscience.

> Tax support to church institutions <u>could be</u> a long
> step down the road toward totalitarianism.

> Competition among religious groups for public
> funds <u>could create</u> internal strife and contribute
> to national disunity. [86]

3.   Tax support for churches results in injustices for
citizens in the forms of unequal distribution of benefits, sectarian self-interested administration of welfare programs,
and the coercion of taxpayers in the support of programs in
which they do not believe.

4.   Tax support of churches is theologically inconsistent because a free and uncoerced response is of the essence
of Christian faith. [87]

Garrett and Ward agree with Pinson that voluntary
and nonpublic support of church-related institutions is a via-
ble alternative to a system which involves supplementary tax
support but they are prepared to make the final sacrifice.
They reluctantly agree that some institutions may die,

> but if Baptists fail to support them, let them go
> down in unflinching loyalty to the biblical and his-
> toric principle of separation of church and state--
> not in compromise of our witness to truth.

Garrett and Ward choose this as the preferred alternative
because they are convinced that the religious permeation of
the entire curriculum is impossible with public support and
thus "the very purpose of the religiously oriented school is
thereby threatened. "[88]

Owing to the pressures of the situation and their own

religious concerns, the Southern Baptist debate concerning
Federal aid to education inevitably moved to the college presidents themselves. In dialogue with his colleagues in college
administration, G. Earl Guinn of Louisiana College agrees
that religious liberty is the chief concern, not separation of
church and state which is "a political device." Guinn recognizes the importance of the service concept and agrees that
Southern Baptist involvement has been inconsistent. But he
insists that the acceptance or rejection of tax aid must be
justified. If justification for the acceptance of public support
can be found at all, it is found "in the nature of religious
freedom, the nature of our Baptist colleges, the nature of
the aid accepted, and whether the aid will fortify or compromise religious liberty. "[89]

Federal aid to education cannot be justified on the
nature of religious freedom because it is a denial of religious
freedom. Federal aid is only possible as a part of a system of compulsory support of religion, and compulsory support of religion is as certainly a violation of religious freedom as is suppression in the exercise of religion. [90]

Federal aid to education cannot be justified on the
nature of the Baptist college because "church colleges are
religious in nature and serve religious purposes." They are
indivisible in their functions and religious throughout, presenting all subject matter "from a Christian perspective by
a teacher whose orientation is Christian. "[91]

In considering the various positions concerning the
forms of Federal aid, Guinn does not make a clear choice
of his own, but he goes on to assert that tax support will
compromise religious liberty because church colleges will
inevitably become more secular. [92]

Employing a "positive interpretation" of the principle
of separation of church and state, a group of Guinn's colleagues seek to answer some of the questions which he
raises. Interpreted positively, separation of church and
state involves "cooperation that seeks to preserve both independence and interdependence. " The presidents contend
that no funds must ever be accepted which will bring undesirable controls, but some governmental influences and
controls are a fact of life of all institutions in the field of
general education. The actual facts of life make the basic
question one of cooperation rather than simply the acceptance
of federal grants. [93] It is not possible to avoid some outside

control of colleges. "All of the arguments against governmental controls apply equally well to controls by accrediting
agencies. "94

As to the questions of undesirable trends in government and the alteration of the colleges, the presidents believe that the best answer to the former "is faith in Christian education and our American concept of government";
and, although the latter is a vital issue, noncooperation is
more crucial than cooperation.

> If our Baptist colleges withdraw from cooperation
> with our government and community, the nature of
> our colleges will certainly be altered. They will
> become inconsequential and uninfluential in the to-
> tal field of education. 95

The question of compulsory support of religion, the
presidents contend, is not now before Southern Baptists.
The issue has been decided. Federal law authorizes direct
federal aid for the construction of certain academic buildings
on the campuses of church related colleges. The only decision available to Southern Baptist colleges "is whether they
are going to refuse to accept the return of some of the tax
money paid into the public treasury by their own constitu-
ents. "

Finally, the presidents respond to Guinn's question
concerning what is right or what is wrong. They agree with
him that the principle of religious liberty is of great importance. "But we believe that redemptive service in obedience
to the missionary impulse is just as urgent and vital, if not
more so. "96

It is evident that the notion of complete separation of
church and state is a fiction. It does not harmonize with
the realities of social existence. Two entirely distinct communities cannot comprise one social order. The idea is not
only out of harmony with the facts, but with the doctrine of
the Divine ordination of government. Calvinism does not
lend itself to the idea of the complete separation of church
and state. The government is ordained to punish the evil
doer, but it is also a positive agency of righteousness under
the law of God. When Calvinism is applied, as Southern
Baptists do, to the contemporary democratic state, whose
end is every phase of human welfare, it is inevitable that
church and state will work together at some points.

5. Duty of the Citizen

        The authority of the government is divine in origin.
The citizen accordingly owes obedience to the state as an
act of obedience to the will of God as expressed in the laws
of the state. [97] And since the Christian is aware of the Divine source of governmental authority, his obedience should
never be a mere expression of outward conformity to the
law or an expedient to get by. [98]

        The citizen also owes obedience to the state because
the purpose of the state is to promote the good and suppress
the evil doer. Those who do good can only have praise for
the governmental authorities while those who do evil are
fearful and invite judgment. Allegiance to the state is a
reflection of the inner life. "The conscience of the believer
is involved in his attitude toward the State. His duty is
moral and vitally related to the religious requirements of
his nature. "[99] The foundation of good citizenship is found
in justice, kindness, and reverence, which are generated in
human life by authentic religion. [100]

        The duty of the religiously sensitive is not exhausted
in their obedience to the state. Recognizing as they do that
the government is ordained to promote the good and suppress
evil, members of the religious community must support the
government and participate in political action to the end of
establishing the good and preventing evil.

        In theory, participation in political action is the re-
sponsibility of the individual. But in practice, Southern Baptists have exercised their responsibilities as citizens through
corporate action as well as individually. Political action by
Southern Baptists is concentrated at the present time in three
principal areas: "opposition to legalized liquor, gambling,
prostitution, and related vices. " In addition to these, Southern Baptists have been active in the past in other areas,
namely, as opponents of Sunday business activities and violations of separation of church and state. [101] Donald R.
Grant advises Southern Baptists that the time has now come
to enter into new fields. In so doing they must "accentuate
the positive" in political action more than they have in the
past. In an urban mid-twentieth century world, "we need
to reclaim Christ's concern for alleviating human suffering--
sickness, hunger, and sorrow. "[102]

        Speaking in a vein very similar to the above, the So-

cial Service Commission of the Baptist Convention of South
Carolina calls for an active interest in the burning civic issues of the day. Outstanding among these are the voting responsibility of the individual and the rights of the underprivileged, including their economic rights. [103]

In addition to obedience to and support of the state as
the chief agency in the promotion of the good and the suppression of evil, the citizen must cheerfully bear the expen-
ses which the state incurs in carrying on its work. He must
pay the taxes which the state has a right to levy. [104] In
short, the citizen must meet all the obligations which the
state imposes upon him within its own jurisdiction. Christians, however, are citizens of two realms--the temporal
and the spiritual. Each carries its own obligations. [105]

The state accordingly must never invade the sacred
precinct of religious conviction. The citizen must be free
to exercise his personal convictions in discharging his duty
to God in worship and service. Authority in the realm of
personal conscience belongs to God alone. If the state does
usurp such authority, it is the duty of the Christian citizen
to follow the law of conscience and suffer the penalty imposed
by the civil authorities. He must passively disobey. [106]

There appears to be little of the spirit of democratic
revolution in the Southern Baptist political ethic. The stress
is overwhelmingly on the side of divine ordination and the
direct responsibility of the governing powers to God. There
is very little of John Locke and the rights of the people when
the duties of citizenship are being defined. P. I. Lipsey em-
phasizes the honor due the office of governing when he says
that no official

> has any claim upon an office which he does not
> honestly and efficiently fill. But as long as he
> stands in the place of authority he must be honored
> according to the teaching of God's word. Jesus
> condemned the scribes and rulers of His day, but
> to the people He said they sat in Moses' seat and
> were to be obeyed insofar as they taught the way
> to live in obedience to the commands of God. [107]

Z. T. Cody echoes the thought of Thomas Hobbes
when he says that it is better to have a bad government than
anarchy, thus suggesting that the attempt to change an abusive
government issues inevitably in no government. Cody adds

that usually it is only the evil doer who needs to fear the
government anyway. [108]

Charles L. Graham takes up the inverse side of the
question, pointing up the harmony that exists between the
good citizen and the government. Instead of entering into
conflict with the state, the Christian is the most loyal of
all citizens. The Scriptures do not indicate an inherent antagonism between duties to government and duties to God. [109]

Graham further declares that obligation to the authority of the state is not diminished in any degree by the imper-
fection of governments. In support of this view, he cites
the fact that when Paul wrote that "the powers that be are
ordained of God," he was speaking about the Roman government in the early part of Nero's reign. The social and political environment was as alien and incongruous to the spirit
of Christianity as could be.

> The principle is therefore clear cut that the civil
> government... whatever its form and... however im-
> perfect it may be, however oppressive or unjust in
> some or many instances, is a divinely ordained
> institution, which has a claim on the respect and
> allegiance of all its citizens, and to which all who
> live within its territory must submit as law-abiding
> subjects. [110]

This is a clear statement of unconditional obedience
on the part of the subject. It would appear that the case is
closed with this statement. But Graham adds:

> While the Scriptures teach that the existing order
> of political and civil society is ordained of God,
> and thus makes loyalty the religious duty of sub-
> jects, the Apostle Paul turns the light on the other
> side of this relationship, and declares it the will of
> God that rulers under the penalty of Divine dis-
> pleasure shall be just.... [111]

With this idea of the duty of rulers as a basis, Graham proceeds to contradict his statements concerning unconditional obedience by affirming the right of revolution. The
arbitrary usurpation of power, tyranny, the violation of liber-
ties and consciences of citizens, and the ignoring of their
protestations are acts on the part of the rulers which call
forth the right and perhaps the solemn duty of resistance by
force. [112]

Graham makes no effort to harmonize these two views. But the added statement that "Christian people will exercise patience and long suffering to the last degree before they will suffer themselves to suspend compliance with a plain dictate of the Almighty" seems to suggest that revolution is a purely practical measure for which there is no theological or philosophical justification. The absence of a theory of revolution conjoined with the presence of revolution as a practical measure is undoubtedly due to the fact that Graham depends entirely upon a Calvinistic interpretation of Paul for theory in defining the duty of citizens, while in practice he is under the influence of the democratic ideas of his own day. As has been seen, the ideas of John Locke sometimes appear alongside those of Paul and Calvin in Southern Baptist political ethic, but the ethic is prevailingly Calvinistic and Pauline. Consequently, it does not hang together consistently at all points.

In the thought of A. T. Robertson, however, the theoretical problem is resolved. It is resolved by a consistent application of Lockean theory.

> There is a limit to obedience. When civil government, meant to be the organ for order and freedom, becomes the agent for tyranny and oppression, the right of protest exists. Government is of God per se, but it may be exercised in the spirit of the devil. The people have had to wrest from their rulers the right to govern themselves. This is a God given right, not the divine right of kings. The Bill of Rights rests upon the very nature of man and society. Every liberty enjoyed by Anglo-Saxon freedom has been won at a great price. Resistance to government can only be justified when it is a serious effort to establish another government that will bestow the liberty that has been taken from the people. A brave spirit must say like Luther: 'I can do no other. So help me God.' It was this spirit that made Peter and John defy the Sanhedrin; 'for we cannot but speak the things which we saw and heard.' (Acts 4:20).... [113]

The contemporary scene--with its increase in protests, demonstrations, riots and disruptions--has evoked a more concentrated stress on "law and order" among Southern Baptists than ever before.

At one end of the spectrum, Herschel H. Hobbs calls civil disobedience sinful. He makes no allowance for variations in spirit, form, and purpose. Civil disobedience is a crime and a war against one's government, just as are deeds of violence. Such rebellion brings judgment from the forces of the law and from God, "whether one be a beatnik, a hippie, or wears the collar of the clergy."114 Quoting the words of Paul as his text, "for rulers are not a terror to good works, but to the evil" (Rom. 13:3a), Hobbs comes close to making a total denial of the reality of police brutality. 115 But since he is not certain that righteousness and power are unequivocably combined in the government, Hobbs does not escape a contradiction. He concedes that Christians should defy laws that interfere with their relation to God, and even accepts revolution as an alternative "when every means of redress has failed."116

With the Columbia University riots, the Poor Peoples Sit-In at Resurrection City, and the rhetoric of Stokeley Carmichael and Rap Brown as illustrations of disorder, Hudson Baggett calls for "some limitations upon liberty in this country before it is too late."117 He suggests a legal positivist solution of the problem of freedom and order inasmuch as he defines freedom in purely contextual terms and provides no norms for the contexts and institutions. 118

John J. Hurt recognizes the fact that some policemen "are too quick with the billy club and possibly too quick with the gun" in every city of any size; but he virtually exonerated the Chicago police in connection with the Democratic Convention protests, even before the evidence was in. He asserts that one of the great needs of the country is a campaign in support of the police, and unashamedly expresses indifference toward the protesters.

> Frankly, we are not concerned about the demonstrators who got banged about a bit. Some of them may behave like angels, but it is difficult, if not impossible to identify them in the company they keep. 119

The flaunting of the law by the very people who sit in the seats of law enforcement has not gone unnoticed among Southern Baptists. Richard Brannon decries the action of a governor who defies a federal law by standing in a school house door, the action of another who prevents the legitimate desegregation of one school child by calling out the National

Guard under the guise of peace, and the rhetorical response
of the police commissioner of a great Southern city that the
application of a desegregation law in his city will cause
blood to run in the streets. [120] And Erwin L. McDonald
condemns the violation of the Arkansas liquor law at the ball
of the very people who made the law--the Arkansas legislature. [121]

    At the opposite end of the spectrum from Herschel
M. Hobbs stands T. B. Maston, who insists that law and
order must be maintained with justice[122] and affirms the
right of nonviolent civil disobedience from the perspective
of the Bible. Maston makes it clear that "any disobedience
by Christians should be done regretfully," and participation
should be of such a nature that constituted authority is up-
held in the very act of disobedience. [123] This is a statement of the classic Christian doctrine of passive disobedience.

Notes

1. Valentine, Foy, Citizenship for Christians (Nashville,
   The Broadman Press, 1965), pp. 25-27. Russell,
   Chester F., "Jesus and the State," Baptist and
   Reflector, 132, No. 23 (June 9, 1966), p. 16.
2. Lipsey, P. I., "Civil Officers Responsible to God"
   (Editorial) The Baptist Record, XXXIV (April 14,
   1932), p. 4.
3. Graham, Charles L., "Obedience to Law," Western
   Recorder, CII (August 16, 1928), p. 6.
4. Ibid.
5. Valentine, Foy, op. cit., pp. 25-26. Venable, R. A.,
   "Civil Government" (Sunday School Lesson), The
   Baptist Record, XXVII (February 19, 1925), p. 10.
6. Ibid.
7. Ibid.
8. Graham, op. cit., p. 7.
9. Abbitt, Watkins M., "Christ as the Answer to the Question of Good Government," Religious Herald,
   CXXIII, No. 15 (April 13, 1950), p. 4.
10. Report of the Social Service Commission of the Southern
    Baptist Convention, "Embezzlement of Power," An-
    nual of the Southern Baptist Convention (Nashville,
    Sunday School Board of the Southern Baptist Conven-
    tion, 1941), p. 133.
11. Abbitt, op. cit., p. 4.
12. Report of the Social Service Commission of the South-

ern Baptist Convention, "Campaign of Education, "
Annual of the Southern Baptist Convention (Nashville,
Sunday School Board of the Southern Baptist Convention, 1921), p. 81.
13. Taylor, J. J., "Senator Glass' Apology, " Religious
Herald, CI (March 29, 1928), p. 8.
14. Ibid.
15. Ibid.
16. Ibid.
17. Venable, R. A., op. cit., p. 10.
18. Maston, T. B., "The Role of the State, " Western Recorder, 125, No. 10 (March 8, 1951), p. 7.
19. Valentine, Foy, op. cit., p. 28.
20. Brown, Joseph E., "Fair Employment Practices Legislation" (Editorial) The Word and the Way, 83, No. 5
(August 2, 1945), p. 2.
21. Alley, Reuben E., "Social Progress Slow under Pressure" (Editorial), Religious Herald, CXXVII, No. 40
(October 13, 1955), p. 10.
22. James, E. S., "Legislation and Morality, " Baptist
Standard, 70, No. 51 (December 17, 1958), p. 2.
23. Report of the Christian Civic Foundation of Arkansas,
Inc., Annual of the Arkansas Baptist State Convention, One Hundred Tenth Annual Session, November
4-6, 1963, pp. 78-79.
24. Grant, Daniel R., "Can Morals Be Legislated?" The
Christian Index, 147, No. 41 (October 10, 1968),
p. 7.
25. Report of the Social Service Commission of the Georgia
Baptist Convention, "Economic Situation, " Annual of
the Georgia Baptist Convention (Atlanta, 1932), p.
31. See also Report of the Committee on Social
Service and Civic Righteousness of the North Carolina Baptist Convention, North Carolina Baptist Annual (1934), p. 45.
26. Report of the Social Service Commission of the "Georgia
Baptist Convention, "The Economic Situation, " Annual of the Georgia Baptist Convention (Atlanta, 1933)
pp. 43-44.
27. Report of the Committee on Temperance and Social
Service of the Missouri Baptist General Association,
"Implications of the NRA Program, " Annual of the
Missouri Baptist General Association (Kansas City,
1933), pp. 149-150.
28. Taylor, O. W., "You Can't Legislate Morals into People" (Editorial), Baptist and Reflector, CV (March
23, 1939), p. 2.

29. Freeman, John D., "The Church and the State,"
    Western Recorder, (Editorial), 119, No. 32 (August
    9, 1945), p. 5.
30. Pitt, R. H., "Religion and the State" (Editorial) Re-
    ligious Herald, XCIII (April 2, 1925), p. 11.
31. Cody, Z. T., "The Anti-Evolution Laws (Editorial) The
    Baptist Courier, LVIII (February 17, 1927), p. 2.
32. Pettigrew, George R., "Anti Evolution Legislation,"
    The Baptist Courier, LVIII (March 10, 1927), p. 6.
33. Ibid.
34. In 1969 a Baptist Viewpoll was conducted. A 92 per
    cent response was achieved involving 600 Baptist
    Viewpoll panel members. In this poll, pastors re-
    corded a 65. 2 percent approval of the death penalty.
    This percentage is higher than that of Sunday School
    teachers, much higher than that of the general pub-
    lic, and comparable to the 60 percent approval of
    male Americans in a Gallup poll of the same year.
    "Church Leaders Take 'Hardline' Position on Death
    Penalty" Baptist and Reflector (July 17, 1969), 135,
    No. 29, p. 5.
35. Quattlebaum, E. G., "Concerning Capital Punishment,"
    The Baptist Courier, LXXI (July 13, 1939), p. 5.
36. Ibid.
37. Musick, G. C., "Should Capital Punishment Be Abol-
    ished?" Religious Herald, CVIII (June 27, 1935),
    p. 6.
38. Ibid.
39. Ibid.
40. Ibid.
41. Ibid.
42. McConnell, F. M., "Capital Punishment" (Editorial)
    Baptist Standard, LI (February 23, 1939), p. 3.
43. Gritz, Jack L., "Should Capital Punishment End?"
    (Editorial) The Baptist Messenger, 52, No. 19 (May
    9, 1963), p. 2.
44. "Should We Abolish Capital Punishment? (Editorial),
    The Baptist Courier, 98, No. 26 (July 7, 1966),
    p. 3.
45. Tinnin, Finley W., "Capital Punishment, Murder,
    Maudlin Sentiment," (Editorial) The Baptist Message,
    XLV (January 26, 1928), p. 6.
46. Cody, Z. T., "The Death Sentence" (Editorial), The
    Baptist Courier, LV (September 18, 1924), p. 2.
47. Collins, M. C., "Is Capital Punishment Christian?"
    The Baptist Courier, LXXI (April 27, 1939), p. 7.
48. Ibid.

49. Gwaltney, L. L., "Capital Punishment and the Scrip-
     tures" (Editorial), The Alabama Baptist, LVIII
     (September 30, 1926), p. 3.
50. Macon, Leon, "Britain Abolishes the Death Penalty"
     (Editorial), The Alabama Baptist, 121, No. 13
     (March 29, 1956), p. 3.
51. Report of the Christian Life Commission, "Capital
     Punishment," Minutes of the One Hundred and Forty-
     Second Anniversary of the Baptist Convention of the
     State of Georgia, November 11-13, 1963, p. 124.
52. Pitt, R. H., "Ought the State to Kill?" (Editorial),
     Religious Herald, XCVIII (September 10, 1925), p. 3.
53. Ibid.
54. Ibid., p. 23.
55. See also Maston, T. B., "Capital Punishment," Baptist
     and Reflector, 134, No. 40 (October 3, 1968), p. 5.
56. Smylie, James H., "Rehabilitation vs Capital Punish-
     ment," Religious Herald, CXXXXII, No. 19 (May 8,
     1969), p. 6.
57. Ibid., p. 7.
58. Mullins, E. Y., "The Social Role of Religion: Church
     and State," Religious Herald, XCII (August 7, 1919),
     p. 4.
59. Texas Christian Life Commission, "Biblical Basis for
     Free Church in Free State," The Baptist Message,
     79, No. 8 (February 22, 1962), p. 4.
60. Ibid.
61. Allen, Jimmy R., "Our Troubled Baptist Conscience in
     Separation of Church and State," Christianity and
     Political Action, Messages from the Christian Life
     Conferences on Christianity and Political Action,
     Glorietta and Ridgecrest, August 11-17 and August
     25-31, 1960, p. 49.
62. Pitt, R. H., "A Little Philosophy" (Editorial) Religious
     Herald, (September 26, 1918), p. 10.
63. This article was reaffirmed in 1963 when the larger
     statement on Baptist Faith and Message was also
     reaffirmed.
64. Quoted from Mays, Blanche, "The Proper Relationship
     of Church and State as Viewed and Held by Baptists,"
     The Christian Index, CIX (August 29, 1929), pp. 30-
     31.
65. Report of the Social Service Commission, "To Prohibit
     The Appropriation of Funds to Sectarian Institutions,"
     Annual of the Southern Baptist Convention (Nashville,
     Sunday School Board of the Southern Baptist Conven-
     tion, 1922), p. 99.

66. McDaniel, George W., "The Bible and the Public
    Schools," Religious Herald, XCVII (March 20, 1924),
    p. 4.
67. Ibid.
68. Ibid.
69. Ibid.
70. Jones, Abe C., "The Bible in Public Schools," Re-
    ligious Herald, XCVII (September 11, 1924), p. 6.
71. Ibid.
72. Ibid.
73. Ibid., p. 7.
74. Ibid.
75. Love, J. F., "The Outlook for Palestine," Religious
    Herald, XCIII (February 5, 1920), pp. 5-6.
76. Maddry, Charles E., "Mobilizing for World Conquest,"
    Religious Herald, CXIII (February 20, 1941), p. 9.
77. Report of the Social Service Commission on the Southern
    Baptist Convention, "Related though Separated," An-
    nual of The Southern Baptist Convention (Nashville,
    Sunday School Board of the Southern Baptist Conven-
    tion, 1929), p. 90.
78. James, E. S., "Prayer in the Public School (Editorial)
    Baptist Standard, 74, No. 27 (July 4, 1962).
79. Cole, James F., "The Supreme Court Decision" (Edi-
    torial) The Baptist Message, 79, No. 26 (July 12,
    1962), p. 2.
80. Roberts, John E., "Worship Has a Place in Public
    Schools" (Editorial) The Baptist Courier, 98, No. 11
    (March 24, 1966). p. 3.
81. Jones, op. cit.
82. Gaines, W. W., "Our Doctrine of Separation of Church
    and State," The Christian Index, CXIX (July 20,
    1939), pp. 7, 29, 31.
83. McCall, Abner V., "Some Views on Church and State,"
    Baptist Standard, 77, No. 46 (November 17, 1965),
    p. 6.
84. Ibid., pp. 6-10.
85. Pinson, William M., Jr., "The Relevance of Separation
    of Church and State," Baptist Message, 85, No. 16
    (April 10, 1969).
86. Ibid., p. 8.
87. Ibid., pp. 12-13.
88. Garrett, James Leo and Ward, Wayne E., "Baptists at
    the Crossroads," Arkansas Baptist, 64, No. 1 (Janu-
    ary 7, 1965), p. 10.
89. Guinn, G. Earl, "Can Baptist Colleges Afford to Accept
    Federal Aid?" Baptist and Reflector, 131, No. 31

(August 5, 1965), p. 10.
90. Ibid.
91. Ibid., pp. 10, 11.
92. Ibid., pp. 11.
93. McCall, Abner; Blackwell, Gordon W.; Harris, Rufus C.; Edmunds, J. Ollie; Tribble, Harold W.; "Can Baptist Colleges Afford Isolation instead of Cooperation?" Baptist Standard, 77, No. 40 (October 6, 1965), p. 6.
94. Ibid., p. 7.
95. Ibid.
96. Ibid.
97. Venable, R. A., op. cit., p. 11.
98. Paschal, George W., "The Christian and His Government" (Editorial), Biblical Recorder, CIV (June 29, 1938), p. 6.
99. Venable, R. A., op. cit., p. 11.
100. Abbitt, op. cit., p. 5.
101. Grant, Donald R., "Baptists and Political Action Today," Christianity and Political Action, Messages from the Christian Life Conferences on Christianity and Political Action, Glorietta and Ridgecrest, August 11-17 and August 25-31, 1960, p. 36.
102. Ibid., p. 38.
103. "The Responsibilities of Christian Citizenship," Report of the Social Service Commission, Annual of the State Convention of the Baptist Denomination in South Carolina, One Hundred and Twenty - Nineteenth Session, November 15-17, 1949, pp. 126-127.
104. Venable, R. A., op. cit.
105. Owen, Richard M., "The Child of God and His Citizenship," Baptist and Reflector, 119, No. 27 (July 2, 1953), p. 2.
106. Venable, R. A., op. cit.
107. Lipsey, P. I., "Civil Officers Responsible to God," (Editorial), The Baptist Record, XXXIV (April 14, 1932), p. 4.
108. Cody, Z. T., "Christianity and the Nation," (Editorial), The Baptist Courier, LVII (September 8, 1927), p. 2.
109. Graham, op. cit., p. 6.
110. Ibid., p. 7.
111. Ibid.
112. Ibid.

113.   Robertson, A. T., The New Citizenship (New York,
       Fleming H. Revell Company, 1919), pp. 51-52.
114.   Hobbs, Herschel H., "The Sin of Civil Disobedience, "
       Baptist and Reflector, 133, No. 36 (September 7,
       1967), p. 5.
115.   "Police Brutality?" Baptist and Reflector, 133, No.
       37 (September 14, 1967), p. 5.
116.   "God and the Government, " Baptist and Reflector, 133,
       No. 35 (August 31, 1967), p. 5.
117.   Baggett, Hudson, "In the Name of Freedom, " The
       Alabama Baptist (Editorial), 133, No. 27 (July 4,
       1968), p. 2.
118.   "What Is Freedom?" (Editorial), The Alabama Baptist,
       133, No. 27 (July 4, 1968), p. 2.
119.   Hurt, John J., "Specter of Anarchy" (Editorial) Bap-
       tist Standard, 80, No. 37 (September 11, 1968),
       p. 6.
120.   Brannon, Richard, "America's Crucial Problem: Law
       and Order, " The Baptist Courier, 100, No. 29
       (July 18, 1968), p. 7.
121.   McDonald, Erwin L., "Poor Leadership for Law Ob-
       servance" (Editorial), Arkansas Baptist, 68, No.
       8, (February 20, 1969), p. 3.
122.   Maston, T. B., "Law, Order, and Justice," Baptist
       Message, 85 No. 2 (January 9, 1969), p. 3. See
       also McDonald, Erwin L., "Our Obligation to In-
       sure 'Justice for All, '" (Editorial), Arkansas Bap-
       tist, 68, No. 13 (March 27, 1969), p. 3.
123.   Maston, T. B., "The Bible and Civil Disobedience, "
       Baptist and Reflector, 135, No. 44 (October 30,
       1969), p. 3.

Chapter IV

WAR AND PEACE

One of the purposes of the state is the punishment and restraint of the evil doer. Within its own borders and within the family of nations, the state performs this function. Ordained by God, the magistrate does not bear the sword in vain.

When the state punishes and restrains the evil doer within the community of nations it engages in war. Nations, like individuals, are addicted to criminal behavior and need to be restrained and punished. War therefore belongs to history. The question whether wars are absolutely inevitable is not specifically raised and answered by Southern Baptist spokesmen, but it is strongly implied that wars are inevitable. They are the instruments of God to punish the evil doer, and even to chastise His own and make them return to Him.

A strong Biblicism governs the Southern Baptist attitude toward war. But the stress of justification is not primarily on the New Testament, as they claim it is for all things; rather, it rests largely on the Old Testament. For the general theory of the origin and function of the state, Southern Baptists look to the New Testament. But to give validity to the position that the state is the instrument of restraint, punishment or chastisement in God's hands, they direct attention to the Old Testament.

1. The Ethics of War

The prevailing war ethic among Southern Baptists is a reproduction of the ethic of "person" and "office," elaborated by St. Augustine and Martin Luther. The term "person" and "office" are not employed, but the essential idea is expressed in a clearly separate private and public morality. The Christian individual must harbor no private resentment and must make no effort to redress wrong. He

must be motivated by love and good will, prompted by the
Holy Spirit. But the Christian is also a temporal and civil
person, and is subject to temporal rights and laws. On this
plane his duties are imposed upon him by his citizenship.
In the civil realm the evil doer must be punished, property
secured, the weak defended, and justice vindicated. All of
these are prerogatives of the state.

> Again, it should be said that the standard of ethics
> for the individual is in the very nature of the case,
> different from that of the state or the nation for
> the reason that their prerogatives are different.
> The individual, as such, has no right to punish
> his fellow man, but the state has. The individual
> has no right to set up standards of right for the
> community, or, in other words, to make laws for
> the community, but the commonwealth has.... 1

The government is the divinely "appointed means of
preserving order, protecting the innocent and punishing the
guilty.... Human government is founded on force and can
be preserved in no other way."2 It is the duty of the state
to resist evil and to protect its citizens from injury, whether
it be perpetrated by agents that are within or without.

Since it is the duty of the state to resist evil, it follows that it is the duty of the citizen to serve the state in
the exercise of this function. Service to the state in war is
not a mere privilege; it is a duty. The principle of obedience
requires it. It is binding and obligatory on the individual as
a function of "office."

> According to the Scriptures, a nation is not only
> permitted to go to war against another nation that
> attacks it. Under such circumstances, the attacked
> nation is held responsible for its own defence, un-
> der penalty of a curse. 'Curse ye Meroz, said
> the angel of the Lord, curse ye bitterly the inhabi-
> tants thereof; because they came not to the help of
> the Lord, to the help of the Lord against the mighty'
> (Judges 5:23). Again: 'Cursed be he that keepeth
> back his sword from blood.' (Jer. 44:10).

> Now how does all this apply to a soldier who kills
> another man in battle? It applies in this way:
> The soldier is not acting from his own initiative,
> and as an individual. He is the servant of and

under authority from his government, which, as we
have seen, derives its authority from God. Therefore the soldier, who is a representative of and in
service for his government, which is an instrument of God is NOT a murderer. He is a messenger and servant of his country and his God.
His position is stated in a nutshell in Rom. 13:4.
'For he is the minister of God to thee for good.
But if thou do that which is evil, be afraid; for
he beareth not the sword in vain: for HE IS THE
MINISTER OF GOD, A REVENGER TO EXECUTE
WRATH UPON HIM THAT DOETH EVIL. '3

In addition to noting the defense of property, life and
honor, self defense, and the defense of weaker peoples as
justifiable grounds for Christian participation in war, D. H.
Wilson also stresses the minister of God role of the soldier.

We are engaged with God in the punishment of evil
doers. We strike as God's strong right arm to
punish criminal nations.... We are now engaged
in the high and holy business of executing divine
wrath against impenitent sinners. 4

For the very reason that the soldier is executing the
divine wrath, he must not be vindictive. He must execute
the wrath of God in the spirit of God. A Christian nation
and Christian soldiers must prosecute their war in the
Christlike attitude. God is ever ready to forgive the penitent sinner, and punishes with a desire to reclaim. This is
what God demands of Christians when He uses them as His
right arm. "So we shall punish Germany, not because we
hate the German people, but with a desire to help them, to
show them the better way, and to safeguard the world
against their crimes.... 5

If a citizen-soldier is a messenger and servant of his
country and his God, what is the difference between the citizen-soldier who is a Christian and one who is not? If the
Christian soldier really is an executor of the divine wrath,
he must be both wrathful and merciful, for the wrath of God
is the "strange work" of His love. In other words, he must
perform the extreme function of killing in loyalty to the Jesus' ideal of love and mercy, even though he is at the same
time serving as an avenger. In commenting on what he calls
the proof text of the pacifist--"But I say unto you, resist not
evil; but whosoever smiteth thee on the right cheek turn to

him the other also. "--J. M. Burnett resolves for himself the
tension between mercy and wrath in terms of the ethic of
"person" and "office. " He declares that a Christian soldier
can meet the demands of Jesus if he goes to war with the
legitimate motive of a loyal citizen without hate and revenge.
Loyalty to Jesus involves the maintenance of the proper attitude and spirit; it is not a matter of the outer deed. The
protection of the citizen from injury to person and property
is the first duty of the government, and its appropriate instrument is physical force. Neither the state nor the individual soldier violates the spirit of Jesus' command when
the legitimate and essential function of the state is being
carried out. 6

In addition to the fact that love is inherent to newness
of life in Christ, it is a positive force whose fruits are discernible in history. Love is a positive spiritual force for
good. And this is what Jesus wants, "to stop the forces
producing evil and to put to work the positive forces producing good. " Secondly, love is itself a fighting motive, and
is superior as a fighting motive to hate and revenge. Christians must, therefore, go forth with a positive, creative good
will and a determination to make a better world. They must
oppose the forces of evil, not out of revenge, but because
these forces obstruct the good. And in opposing evil men,
Christians must be a positive spiritual force even for their
good. 7

It would appear from what has been said that sheer
self-defense could never be a Christian motive for war.
Sheer self-defense is to be distinguished from the vindication
of justice because it may be attached to a system of domination or a prior aggression. Without qualification, however,
the Social Service Commission of the Alabama Baptist Convention adopts self-defense as a sufficient motive for war.

> War is horrible and yet the right of self-defense
> remains.... War is un-Christian and yet Jesus
> recognized the right of self-defense when he said
> 'How shall one enter a strong man's house and de-
> spoil his goods until he has first bound the strong
> man?' We are pacifists until our liberties, our
> homes, and our nation are put on the execution
> block and then we would resist.... 8

Writing under the title, "The Place of the Church in
an 'All-Out' War, " S. Lewis Morgan, Jr. justifies World

War II only on the ground that it is the lesser of two evils
and repudiates the ethic of "person" and "office." The task
of the church in such a crisis as World War II is to keep
before the world the truth that war is not in God's design
for living, that it is the result of sin, and that it is wrong.
But Christians must oppose the forces of unrighteousness as
the lesser of two evils in order to save as much as possible
of the achievements of Christian civilization upon the basis
of which a more Christlike way of life may be established in
the future.

Morgan rejects the notion of putting a uniform on Jesus, a gun in his hand, and following him into battle. He
also denies the right of the church to ascribe divine sanction
to war. Rather it is the task of the church to purge war of
the emotion of hate, to teach that both friend and foe are the
children of God and the objects of his love, and to pray for
all mankind. [9]

The ethic of "person" and "office" is repudiated because it falsely locates the good and calls for transformation
only in the inner life.

> The Christian gospel is too often relegated, even
> by the church, to an isolationist position: namely,
> the gospel is essential for the eternal well-being
> of man's inward parts, but it had best not become
> entangled in efforts to achieve his external well-
> being. The church must be brought to realize that
> the gospel is the power of God unto salvation wher-
> ever it is believed; that men can be spared this
> result of their sins, if the power of God has made
> them victor over their sins; that war will be re-
> duced to a minimum--if not completely eliminated--
> in a world where men follow, even if imperfectly,
> the will of God as revealed in Jesus Christ. [10]

The idea that Christian decision concerning war can
be reached best under the theory of the just war is supported
by M. L. Fergeson. A war is just when it is defensive and
when the lesser evil is accumulated on the side of the state
to whom the just cause is ascribed. [11] Jimmy R. Allen also
favors the just war position, seeing in it the least ambiguous
relationship between idealism and realism. [12]

Espousing an absolute pacifist position, John Calvin
Slemp makes a complete and clear break with the ethic of

"person" and "office." He denies that a thing can be wrong for an individual and right for a company, corporation or nation of which he is a part. A man is not a Christian who acts like a Christian in personal affairs and often like a pagan in social, economic or international affairs. Such action emanates from a failure to take Christ seriously. Failure to learn the meaning of Jesus' words and to take him seriously account for the fact that we are at war today. [13]

W. Clyde Atkins believes that sacrificial love is not only a spiritual ideal; it is the only effective political strategy in a military situation. Sacrificial love alone can transform a foe into a friend. The Christians of the first three centuries were committed to the sacrificial idea. "They believed in peace. They were willing to die rather than to go to battle and kill someone else. They manifested the spirit of Christ." The militarization of Christianity was a result of the official recognition granted by Constantine. [14] Atkins stresses the fact that he is not pleading for passive resistance to armed force, but for love. Love is the first law of Christianity, and the greatest power and force known to man. It is the only way Christians can conquer. It is the very essence of life, not something extraneous to life that may or may not be brought to bear upon it. [15]

Atkins sharply criticizes the Southern Baptists in their attitude toward peace, in the light of their claim to have remained with the New Testament. Baptists are right in going back to the New Testament for theology, doctrines, and teachings concerning church polity and the ordinances, "but we have left it to the Society of Friends or Quakers to apply the teachings of the New Testament concerning Christianity and peace. "[16]

2. God and War

The relation of God to war is understood in a variety of ways among Southern Baptists. At times God appears as the active agent of war; at other times He is spoken of as permitting and using war, with the question of the initiating agency of the war left unclear. While these two views may be said to be prevailing interpretations, war is also thought of as God's judgment in the sense that it is a consequence of man's sin. And, in at least one case, God's relation to war is set forth in immanental terms, God being immanent in the human spirit.

In a discussion of World War I, M. H. Wolfe sees
God as its active agent. All recorded history shows that the
Almighty uses men to perform heroic deeds. "Under the
ruling hand of the Almighty God, the time came when this
monster evil must be destroyed." The task of "destroying
the god of German militarism" was assigned by God to
America and her allies; "and to the performance of this
righteous service we must dedicate every drop of blood that
flows through our veins."[17]

Many voices may be heard testifying either to God's
agency in the origin of wars or to His agency during and at
the end of wars. Victor J. Masters, following M. P. Hunt,
states that God not only permits but uses war to chastise
His rebellious people. He cites as cases in point Second
Chronicles 24, where God used the Syrian army to conquer
a great host of the soldiers of Judah, and Habakkuh 1:6,
where God says: "I raised up the Chaldeans, that bitter and
hasty nation, which shall march through the breadth of the
land to possess the dwelling places that are not theirs."[18]
In support of the notion of the divine use of war, H. W. Battle asserts that God used Woodrow Wilson to humble the
Kaiser and checkmate the devil. "God is in and around and
back of life."[19] Declaring that it is not by might or power
but by the spirit of God that men come through great crises,
Thomas V. McCaul describes the intensity of the prayer life
among the Allies in 1918, when defeat seemed inevitable. In
England, America, and France, multitudes of men from the
streets sought sanctuaries in which they could pray. In Ar-
cadia, Florida, McCaul's own soul was stirred to the depths
by the sight of a "poor Negro" praying in the streets.

> And I said, Oh God, look at him, that poor negro!
> [sic] He is earnestly invoking Thy blessing upon
> our boys over there. He is praying for the young
> men who have left this town for the front. Per-
> haps he is praying for the son of his employer;
> perhaps he is praying for his own black boy who
> has gone. Oh, Lord, give us the victory, for we
> are fighting for justice, right and humanity.

> God gave us the victory....[20]

The idea of the divine agency in war is softened by
J. B. Gambrell, becoming divine permission. God does not
lift men and nations out of the bog of sin in such a way as
to abrogate their power of self determination. "God redeems

humanity from evil through the efforts of humanity. " War
has a place in the divine scheme of dealing with sin. "All
wars occur under the permissive decrees of God, " and serve
two purposes:

> They are the surgery of civilization. Evils which
> become obdurate and beyond the reach of moral
> remedies are often eradicated by war....
>
> War is also God's rod of correction. Nations, not
> wrong on great national issues, are sometimes
> prideful, pleasure-loving, selfish, God-forgetting
> and God-defying.... [21]

The relation of God to man through war is further
softened by Gilbert Guffin, who sees war as God's judgment
upon man only in the sense that it is the consequence of
man's sin. God does not experience an impish glee from
the sight of dying men. He does not desire that men should
come to the consequences of their sins. Men do so because
it cannot be otherwise in a moral universe. God permits
the judgment of war upon men because He is forced to allow
it in a moral universe which He has ordered according to
His moral nature and plan. And secondly, He allows the
judgment of war from the desire to correct men. [22]

Addressing himself to the problem of the relation of
God to World War I, E. Y. Mullins finds the solution in the
doctrine of divine immanence. God is immanent and omnipo-
tent in His world, but omnipotence does not mean the same
thing in the physical and moral realms. In the physical
realm, God can "do as He pleases" with created things. In
the moral realm, He achieves His ends through free persons, and therefore imposes restraint upon Himself. Divine
restraint is not a reflection of finitude in the moral realm
but a self-limitation for moral ends in a kingdom of free
persons.

God must restrain His power in the moral realm, for
otherwise there would be no moral achievement. The good
must be chosen freely by man, he must be internally moved
toward it, not externally compelled. The more independent
he is in the pursuit of the good, the more Godlike man becomes. That is, the indwelling God becomes effectual for
moral ends in him in the degree to which his choices and
moral attainments become his own. [23]

What bearing do these ideas have on God's relation to
World War I? Presupposing that democracy in its ultimate
form will be the manifestation of the sons of God, Mullins
views God's relation to World War I in terms of His immanence in the human spirit striving toward the democratic
good. 24

A novel turn is given to the idea of God's relation to
war by John A. Brunson, who identifies Jesus with Jehovah
of the Old Testament. "Jehovah of the Old Testament was
Jesus the Christ in his preincarnate state. Jesus the Christ
when he was on earth was Jehovah incarnate. The risen and
glorified Jesus as he is in heaven now is Jehovah--Jesus in
his post-in-carnate state. "25 There are three states or
spheres of manifestation but only one person.

Jehovah-Jesus never changes. All that Jehovah did
or sanctioned in Old Testament times, therefore, accords
with the mind and character of Jesus now. This includes
the conferring of civil powers on man and the approval of
war. Jehovah-Jesus has never approved all wars or all
things done in war, "but since the flood war has been and
is a divinely chosen means of punishing evil doers and of
destroying evil. ... 26

The words of Jesus in the Sermon on the Mount--"Resist not evil" and "Love your enemies"--do not alter these
facts. In this teaching, Jesus was referring to the personal
relations between man and man. He Himself said that He
came not to destroy, but to fulfill the law. The doctrine of
nonresistance did not do away with the magisterial office,
civil obligations and responsibilities, or convey the idea that
armies and navies are not needed in this age of grace. "So
my conclusion is that Jesus today does approve of righteous
wars and uses them to hold evil in check. "27

3.   World War I a Crusade

World War I was regarded as a great crusade, just
and holy, by American Christians in general. Southern Baptists shared this view. The war was just in that its aim
was to redress wrong done; and it was holy in that it was
being fought for God, Christian principles, and the establishment of a new order. It was at bottom a war between
Christianity and Anti-Christ. 28

In an address to soldiers in a South Carolina camp, Chaplain G. C. Schwartz greets them as the New Crusaders. Describing in poetic detail the "age of glory" created by the Old Crusaders as it passes before him "in a panorama of valor and might, " Schwartz announces that "the new Crusaders are here. " He then proceeds to set before the soldiers the objectives of the New Crusade. It seeks, he says, to avenge the outraged national honor of America, to rescue an outraged and exploited humanity who have been subjected to unbridled cruelty and barbarism, and to protect American principles of democracy and freedom. "And so...from sainted hill, from smiling valley, from fruited plain, we come one people, united and indivisible, engaged in a holy crusade for God, humanity, and for Motherland. "[29]

Setting forth the objectives of the war in terms of the establishment of a new order, W. L. Hargis perceives that order as a very high level of spiritual achievement;

> We are fighting for a principle that is dearer than life. We are fighting to establish in every land the things that Jesus brought to the world and for which he laid down his life; namely, democracy of thought, word, act and human conscience. [30]

In a quotation from an address by president William DeWitt Hyde of Bowdoin College, Hight C. Moore also states that the objective of the war is the extension of democracy to European nations, and asserts that no nation ever engaged in a holier war. [31]

Some Southern Baptists are not content to speak of the establishment of a new democratic order, but must let the world know that these are Baptist principles. The Committee on World Crisis of the Southern Baptist Convention declared in 1918 that "the great objective of the war on the part of our country is nothing less than the firm establishment of our own Baptist organizing principles in the political life of the world. "[32] In a reply to those persons who criticize certain pastors for preaching "too much war, " the editors of The Baptist Courier contend that the war is not a mere state or political question. It is being fought for Baptist principles. "If Baptist principles ought to be brought into our pulpits, then this war must be brought there. "[33]

World War I was not only holy; it was also just. A "monster from the pit has burst the crust of the world and emerges from the tilled fields, the image of forgotten gods of the Canaanites, Moloch and Baal and Ashtaroth. "[34] Justice must be vindicated because atrocities have been perpetrated upon citizens, ships sunk, babies murdered, and citizens drowned. It is in this just cause that America bears arms--in a war to destroy autocracy, prepare the way for and establish democracy. [35]

In this war, both holy and just, the soldier at the front is likened to Christ in the sacrifice on the cross. Ascribing a clear conscience to American Christians concerning the righteousness of the war, John E. White says that they are also convinced "that our boys who have gone to the altars of sacrifice are flinging their bodies unselfishly on a cross not wholly unlike the great cross of the great Christ of God. "[36] In a "prayer for Soldier Sons, " it is stated boldly that the soldiers follow in the footsteps of the Master:

> In their sacrifice, offering their lives that others may live, they were following in the footsteps of the Son of God Himself who died to make men free from the power of evil. We trust them, O God, to Thy infinite love, and to Thy ever-watchful eye. Hold them as in the hollow of Thy hand, for they are doing Thy work and fulfilling the teachings of Him who spoke as never man spake, when He taught that greater love hath no man than that he is willing to lay down his life for others. [37]

The crusading spirit in the Southern Baptist attitude toward World War I is further evident in the prevailing ideas concerning the relation of the church and the Christian religion to the war. As an institution without temporal power, the church was not expected to provide divine sanction and fighting energy through the power of the Christian religion. In this war, asserts E. Y. Mullins, there need not be any conflict between absolute loyalty to Christ on the one hand and to country on the other. Americanism and Christianity may both be saved intact and entire. Thinking about the war may be unified and correlated without sacrificing anything required by either loyalty. The imperative duty of Christian leaders today is "to correlate and unify the law and the gospel in a way which will give a new vision to the Christian soldier and put new energy into his fighting and a sense of the righteousness of his cause. "[38]

The Christian people of America, says, J. B. Gam-

brell, ought to express themselves as favoring the freest
possible preaching in the camps, limiting it only by the necessities of military order and discipline. The need for
free preaching is imperative because "nothing will do so
much as to make a great army as to put a sense of God and
of righteousness in the souls of men."[39] The freest possible
preaching is also necessary because no force is equal to the
Christian religion in its power to produce good soldiers.
"The best soldier is a man with a clear vision, with a firm
grip on eternal verities, committed by all of the sanctions
of Christianity to the full discharge of his duty."[40] Gambrell
illustrates his thesis by reference to General R. E. Lee's
army of Northern Virginia. No army, he asserts, has been
more religious than Lee's army since the day of Cromwell's
invincible prayers. And, by the consent of history, Lee's
army was one of the most efficient the world has ever
seen.[41]

4. World War II a Just War

        Between the two world wars a peace crusade swept
the American churches. Although they passed some resolutions on peace, Southern Baptists did not participate in the
peace movement as such. Consequently, when World War II
came, Southern Baptists did not have a pacifist tradition to
cast off. But, without the help of pacifist teachings, by the
time of Pearl Harbor they had freed themselves of the crusade idea about as thoroughly as had other American churches.
Along with American churches in general, Southern Baptists
regarded World War II as a just war[42]--speaking more precisely and using the phrase of Roland Bainton, a "relatively
just war."[43]

        Describing the war as just in object, A. L. Goodrich
admonished Baptists to approach it with just intention and to
engage in just conduct. The objective of the war is to save
American political and economic freedom, and her territorial
possessions. Baptists must approach the war as "Christian
fighters," hating only the evil designs and deeds of the enemy, but loving their souls and engaging in no shameful practices no matter how unfair the enemy may be.[44]

        Viewing the enemy as analogous to gangsters whose
aggressive action must be dealt with by force, Ryland Knight
states that the objective of the war is the freedom of all. It
is a war to defend the weak, whose infirmities the strong

must bear. [45]

 Knight reiterates the idea of the justice of the war in
a discussion of "Christian Youth in a Warring World, " but
also expresses an attitude that reflects pacifist teachings.
He asserts that the youth of today have been trained in the
true and the beautiful and now stand bewildered. War must
be stripped of its glamour. It is the antithesis of what
Christ stood for. The choice for Christians today is not a
simple one. It is not between war and peace, but between
war and "passing on the other side, " as did the Pharisee. [46]

 The Social Service Commission of the Southern Baptist
Convention is certain that the nation will prosecute the war to
a military victory, but manifestly sees the nation in a forced
situation as a vindicator of justice--"the threat to free democratic life, the revulsion of social conscience against the
ruthless violence of renascent tyranny, all urge upon us that
necessity of determined battle. "[47]

 It may be seen from what is said above that World
War II was approached reluctantly, and perhaps even negatively. It was something forced upon the people against their
wills, and from which they could only hope to restore peace
and vindicate justice by stopping the perpetrators of evil.
The war itself could not establish a new order or even prepare the way. At best it could only stop those forces which
would destroy the framework of a better order. The establishment of a new order belongs to the spiritual forces, which
alone are able to perform this function. Informed by this
outlook, when Southern Baptists call upon the church to gird
herself in World War II, it is for quite a different purpose
than that in World War I:

> The church must gird herself for the task of hold-
> ing fast to the ideals of our puritan fathers. The
> church cannot escape its obligations to mankind,
> but must intensify her activities for spiritual guid-
> ance. The church now as never before must make
> America and the world conscious of the gospel
> truths of God's plan, man's welfare on earth.
>
> . . . .
>
> Armies and navies win battles, but gunfire cannot
> build a Christian social order. The building of a
> permanent peace with love for all peoples is dic-

tated by the moral fibre of the victor. Upon the
church in these days rests the responsibility of
evangelizing America and preparing her for the
role of a spiritual lighthouse for the rest of the
world. [48]

5. Gains from War

If God permits and uses wars, it is to be assumed
that wars produce real gains. The idea that wars do produce
real gains finds much support among Southern Baptists.
God's agency in and the fruitfulness of the wars of the Old
Testament are by and large taken literally. And since God
has not ceased to use and permit wars, they still serve
God's purposes.

Examining World War I from the point of view of its
fruits, A. J. Holt cites twelve blessings of that war:

1. Twenty nations are allied in the battle for freedom of the whole world.
2. America's vast wealth is being used to secure
for all humanity the freedom which she enjoys.
3. Hundreds of thousands of young Americans whose
lives were purposeless now have a great and noble contention
in which they endeavor.
4. Hundreds of thousands of young Americans who
were subject to no authority have now learned to obey.
5. America had become wasteful but has now learned
to conserve her food supply.
6. Hundreds of thousands of people have learned to
eat wholesome food at which they formerly sneered for no
other reason than the fact that it did not suit their pampered
palates.
7. Patriotism has increased and all Americans love
each other better.
8. Sectionalism has been wiped out.
9. Un-Americans are being weeded out.
10. Religious activity has been quickened. Many
soldiers will hear the gospel who had heretofore given it
no attention.
11. The Bible is being circulated and read much more
widely.
12. The war is being fought over lofty ideals. This
is a blessing since these ideals are held constantly before
the people.

Holt admits that these blessings may not compensate
for the destruction of life and property, but he believes that
they will prove of incalculable benefit to America and all
mankind. 49 Unfortunately, these alleged blessings are a reflection of the naivete of Holt rather than the realities of the
situation. Holt's naivete is manifest in the ascription of an
unqualified idealism to America and the Allies, his confidence in the lasting and generalized quality of what appear
as war-time "virtues, " his apparent belief in the permanence
of military alliances, and the confusion of a negative coalition
of peoples with positive unity.

Similar gains for America are suggested by J. Calvin
Moss. The war helped America find itself--its vast might.
New leaders for every type of service, missionaries of truth,
and servants of mankind arose because of the war. The war
caused Americans to subordinate excessive individualism for
the common good and called forth stewardship in the administration of personal values and talents. It destroyed the pro-
vincial outlook of multitudes through "overseas" service and
stimulated giving. It has brought America to world power
and responsibility. And America has proven to be an unself-
ish servant of mankind. 50

Other gains from World War I in which the whole
world will share are suggested by George W. McDaniel. The
gains are the end of oppression, the expulsion of the Mos-
lems from Palestine, the overthrow of militarism, the dis-
solution of the church and state, and a just, universal and
lasting peace. 51

Good was also wrought out of World War II. God
never fails to bring good out of evil. Pain and tragedy make
for the gains of human life. "The Japanese have been used
to call out the deepest and most elemental qualities in the
Chinese, and to weld them into a union never known before."
And in all the lands that have been overrun by the Nazis,
and even among thousands of Germans, "we have such a
vindication of the human spirit and an assertion of man
against the machine as the world has never before witnessed
on such a scale. "52

A great service was rendered to the Christian religion
by World War I. It destroyed the power of the military
class in Japan and thereby removed "the greatest threat to
the spread of the gospel in the Orient. " The war also discredited the humanistic philosophy and the naturalistic theory

of evolution. "Germany has been the hotbed for the culture of these anti-Christian philosophies." "Is it too much to hope," H. H. Provence rhetorically inquires, "that the sufferings which the Germans must endure before the war ends will open their eyes to their need of God?"[53]

The view that war issues in gains is not unanimous among Southern Baptists. Raising the question, "Does War Settle Anything?", already posed and answered in the affirmative by Arthur J. Barton, John Calvin Slemp responds in the negative. Referring to the American civil war, he suggests that arbitration would have been a far better method, and hints that the issues were not really settled by the war, but in spite of it. Slemp adds strength to his contention by reference to World War I which was supposed to make the world safe for democracy. But, he says, "the truth is that the World War created more issues than it settled." The democracies are in greater danger now [1940] than in 1918.[54]

6.   Pacifism and Conscientious Objection

Pacifism and conscientious objection are rare forms of commitment among Southern Baptists. The conscientious objector is an oddity, and when he does appear, he is vigorously attacked. As has already been observed, the peace crusade of American Christianity between the two world wars did not find fertile soil among Southern Baptists.

Deeming pacifism essentially unchristian, Victor L. Masters attacked the anti-war propaganda between the World Wars as a product of international communism.[55] A few years later, during the early stages of World War II, he stated that modern Christendom makes the serious error of tending toward a high idealism in the name of the faith of Christ, and thus fails to take into account the basic sinfulness of man. In the Old Testament, wars are clearly sanctioned by God as means of gaining righteous ends and of disciplining the Israelites. While the New Testament has no direct teaching on war, it does declare the authority of the state. Pacificts cannot sustain their position by appeals to the teachings of Jesus inasmuch as the Old Testament, which sanctions war, was authoritative for Jesus. The words of Jesus about turning the other cheek obviously refer to individuals, and, furthermore, he did not intend for this saying to be taken literally. When he was struck while on trial before the Sanhedrin, Jesus did not turn the other cheek, thus

inviting further abuse; rather, He rebuked the offender. "Nor
did Paul take these words literally when he was struck in the
face in a court trial. "[56]

According to F. M. McConnell the position of the
conscientious objector is wrong and criminal under certain
conditions and circumstances.   A nation has a right to defend its property and liberty.   And anyone who refuses to
oppose an invasion which would rob the people of these possessions is guilty of criminal behavior. [57]

The editors of The Baptist Courier are convinced that
conscientious objectors belong in the same category with
slackers and traitors since "their works and words contribute
to the same end. "   The difference between them lies only in
their degrees of culpability.   If a conscientious objector is a
Baptist, he is in strange company.   And although he doubt-
less has a right to his position under the doctrine of freedom
of conscience, "while thus shielded he ought to thank God that
there are men who are willingly giving their lives on the bat-
tlefields of France for the preservation of that very doctrine
beneath which he has taken shelter. "[58]

By making several generalizations, which "flow naturally" from the position of the conscientious objectors, H. L.
Winburn seeks to show the shallowness and confusion of their
ideas and practices.   He infers that they incorrectly interpret
the Scriptures by pointing out that their objections are based
on "the interpretation of the same Scriptures that Pershing
and Haig and most of the great fighting men of the English-
speaking world loved and reverenced. "[59]   The conscientious
objectors, Winburn continues, do not distinguish between war
of aggression and war of defense.   They profess a greater
love and understanding of Christ than other people.   But Jesus "seized the nearest weapon and did violence to the money
changers who prostituted his Father's house of prayer. "[60]
Conscientious objectors are willing for others to fight for
their freedom and possessions, engaging in noncombatant
service in the meantime, thus encouraging the hardier brethren who fight for them.   Many of them bought war bonds and
stamps during the war to provide munitions.   All of them are
willing to use the police in defense of their homes.   The general principle is inescapable that, if it is right to have a
state, it is right to defend it.   If it is right for the state to
use force in restraining the lawless it is right for every citizen to support the use of necessary force.   If the objection
to the use of force by the state in its defense will stand in

ethics and religion, government is an absurdity. And "if
these objections really lie in the realm of conscience at all,
the conscientious objector either must hold the 'holier-than-
thou' attitude toward his less conscientious neighbors who
preserve his home for him or he must surrender all moral
right to the benefits of citizenship. "[61]

The conscientious objector is not left entirely defense-
less among Southern Baptists. In 1946 the Committee on Social Service and Civic Righteousness of the North Carolina
Baptist Convention deplored the continuing confinement of
conscientious objectors in detention camps, and called upon
"the president of the United States and the military authorities to grant amnesty at the earliest possible moment to all
who are so confined. "[62]

In an appeal for the public defense of the conscientious
objector, T. B. Maston calls attention to the connection between conscientious objection and the Baptist doctrine of freedom of conscience.

> It may be that they are wrong, but if we are con-
> sistent, as Baptists we will come to their defense.
> We believe that the individual should be supremely
> loyal to the will of God in his life. We stand for
> freedom of conscience for those of other religious
> faiths and for no faith at all. Surely we ought to
> do as much for those within our own ranks. [63]

Maston continues by noting the fact that the Southern Baptist
Convention publicly defended conscientious objectors in its
1940 assembly by approving the report of the Social Service
Commission in which the right of conscientious objectors was
recognized. Upon this authority, he especially urges state
conventions, associations, churches and pastors to do likewise in order to give their public defense the character of
completeness. [64]

A bill before the House of Representatives in Montana,
making conscientious objection a crime and denying the right
of property ownership to conscientious objectors, evoked a
response from Leon Macon in the name of freedom of conscience. Not a pacifist himself, Macon expresses appreciation for the high aims of authentic conscientious objection,
namely, the end of all warfare. If a conscientious objector
refuses the provision of noncombatant service, Macon believes he should be punished by temporary confinement, but

there is no justification for "making it criminal to stand by one's conscience" and for prohibiting property ownership. 65

7. The Peace Settlements

(1) World War I

The effort to establish the conditions of peace at the end of World War I gave rise to two topics of discussion among Southern Baptists.   First, what is the proper attitude toward the enemy?   And second, what should be the nature of the peace machinery?

The editors of The Baptist Courier became the center of a discussion of the former topic when they declared that hate and war have done their work, if they were ever needed. What the world needs now, as never before, is the gospel of reconciliation. 66

Attacking their position as absolutely erroneous, Richard H. Edmonds says:

> Hate and war are not necessarily Christianity, and yet they may be Christian.   This war was certainly a holy war of Christianity on the part of the Allies and of the United States, as holy a war as Almighty God ever permitted in the world's history, and God sent forth his chosen people to war.   Hatred in the sense of righteous wrath against black criminals is righteous in the sight of God we are sure.
>
> This is not the time for the 'gospel of reconciliation. '   It does not require any courage to preach reconciliation and no courage is needed to stand for that.   All that is required is a sickly sentimental misinterpretation of the teachings of Christ. 67

Edmonds goes on to say that when Christ was on the cross he forgave the penitent sinner and promised his entrance to paradise, but did not utter a word to the unrepentant sinner.   Failure to impose a stern punishment upon the German nation will make Americans unworthy to do the work of the Almighty, and will bring the collapse of civilization because of the moral degradation and rottenness produced by this dereliction of duty.   "Failure to punish is not according to the teachings of Christ.   Nowhere from Genesis to Reve-

lation, we believe, is there one single word which, rightly
interpreted, can call for a 'gospel of reconciliation' with an
unrepentant nation of criminals."[68]

The idea of stern punishment for Germany is echoed
by R. H. Pitt. Stern and righteous retribution is due the
German people for their "shameless organized, deliberate
persistent and unprecedented lawlessness and violence."
However, punishment must be administered without the spirit
of vengefulness.[69]

On the other hand, John E. White lends support to
the "gospel of reconciliation," and condemns the position of
Richard H. Edmonds, affirming that God did forgive us while
we were yet sinners. Appropriate New Testament passages
are employed to substantiate the argument: "Father, forgive
them; they know not what they do...." "God was in Christ,
reconciling the world unto himself, not imputing their tres-
passes unto them, and hath committed unto us the word of
reconciliation...." "God commended his love towards us in
that while we were sinners Christ died for us."[70] White
says further that Edmonds "must explain that God so hated
the world 'in the sense of a righteous wrath against black
criminals,' that he sent his only begotten son?"[71]

Henry Watterson approaches the problem by distinguishing between the German masses and their leaders, suggesting
mercy for the former. He states that brave men never gloat
over a fallen foe, and compares the Teuton masses with the
mob in Jerusalem, declaring that the former knew as little
about what they were doing as the latter. The Teuton Masses were "bamboozled" by their leaders.[72]

In 1921 the controversy concerning the treatment of
Germany was revived by the German reparation bill. Z. T.
Cody takes his stand on the side of forgiveness for Germany,
but this time he distinguishes between the attitude of forgiveness and full forgiveness. It is true, says Cody, that full
forgiveness can never come except to the penitent, but
Christianity inculcates the attitude of forgiveness towards all.
Christian forgiveness involves both the principle of forgiveness and that of justice. Forgiveness considers primarily
the criminal; justice considers primarily the victim. The
attitude of forgiveness makes the principle of justice effectual in forgiveness. "It seeks the conditions of peace and
brotherhood. It strives to reestablish God's order and fellowship, not forgetting justice and not waiting till the crimi-

nal has made himself good. "[73]

Against this background of interpretation, Cody affirms
the need for the attitude of forgiveness toward Germany on
the part of Christian nations. If the nations deal with Germany out of an attitude of forgiveness, they will require that
Germany pay heavy penalties, thus giving evidence of repentance. But this attitude will cause them to seek the peace of
the earth in Christian ways. [74]

R. H. Edmonds immediately issues a reply to Z. T.
Cody, reiterating the fact that Jesus offered no forgiveness
to the unrepentant criminal, and saying that unless the German people repent of their crimes in sackcloth and ashes
and pay for their deeds to the extent of their powers, "civilization will place a premium on war for looting purposes
and thus help to destroy itself. "[75] Cody contends, in response, that Edmonds overlooked his distinction between full
forgiveness and the attitude of forgiveness. While Christ
did not receive the unrepentant sinner, He did have an attitude of forgiveness toward him, and He did not denounce
him. The right spirit toward Germany does not mean that
she will be spared the heavy burdens of reparation, but it
means that the paths of conciliation will be sought and those
things will be done which will lead to world fellowship. [76]

The attitude of Southern Baptists toward the peace
machinery was generally favorable. The new condition of
interdependence and mutuality of responsibility was fully
recognized. In view of America's new responsibility for
the welfare of the world, the editors of The Baptist Courier
advocate America's entry into the League of Nations and the
abolition of her pre-war attitude toward Europe. [77] R. H.
Pitt expresses total sympathy with the effort to create an
enduring alliance for the administration of international justice, and charges that "the opponents of the League have
failed utterly to offer any constructive program as a substitute for it. "[78] E. C. Routh supports the League on the
grounds of the interdependence of nations, stating that they
must plan their future policies together. [79] Urging America
to regain her position of moral leadership and service occupied at the close of the war, the Social Service Commission
of the Southern Baptist Convention asserts that this can be
done by associating herself with the world court. [80]

While the opponents of international machinery for the
administration of justice are less numerous than the advo-

cates, the former are nevertheless just as vocal as the latter. As a staunch opponent of international organization, R.
H. Edmonds advances the following arguments: (a) the proposed League of Nations is similar to the proposed League
of Denominations which is a weakening rather than a strengthening union.   (b) the League of Nations proposes to force all
races, nations and creeds into a united organization for the
purpose of ruling the world.   "Who can believe that man can
thus accomplish what the Almighty has never achieved?"
(c) Rich and powerful America will be brought down to an
equal voting power with such petty countries as Liberia,
Haiti, Hedjaz or South Africa.   America would not long
stand for this.   (d) America will lose her individuality, independence of action and sovereignty.   (e) the League as
now proposed would create wars instead of preventing them.
It would give monarchical, heathen and backward countries
a deciding voice in determining what American shall do or
not do. 81

    These statements from Edmonds evoked the following
reply from Maryus Jones: (a) There is no similarity between the proposed League of Churches and the League of
Nations by virtue of the nature of the church and the state.
(b) The League of Nations does not propose to force various
peoples and creeds into a united organization; the League is
a voluntary organization to prevent the strong from oppres-
sing the weak.   (c) America will not be brought down to an
equal voting power with Liberia, Haiti, Hedjaz or South
Africa.   The "covenant provides that the vote of the council
or of the assembly shall be unanimous. "82

    Writing in the Manufacturers' Record, of which he is
a publicist and R. H. Edmonds is editor, Eugene Thwing condemns the League of Nations on moral grounds. 83   (a) "The
League of Nations is a device of Man's contrivance, which
was built without recognition of God's governing hand in the
affairs of men, it was constructed without any public ac-
knowledgment of Him, and without any public appeal for His
guidance. "   (b) The League is in direct disobedience to God's
command: "Be ye not unequally yoked together with unbelievers.... "   The United States, a Christian nation, having
only one vote among thirty-two nations, many of which are
pagan, is "unequally yoked together with unbelievers. "84
Only evil can come out of this.   (c) The League is an instrument of evil.   Its first acts have been acts of injustice.
(d) "The League of Nations is foredoomed to utter failure because of its disobedience to God and its own inherent weak-

ness. "85

All plans of its type have failed. The present League
is weak in that it is made up of jealous and hostile groups;
it is without God as its leader and righteousness as its governing principle, secret intrigues and realignments are already going on, the basis of its power lies in the strong nations, and it is inconsistent and insincere in its aims. 86

These claims are immediately challenged by W. R. L.
Smith. First, he asserts that Thwing does not know that the
League was built without recognition of God. The statement
is based on an unwarranted assumption. "Woodrow Wilson
and Lloyd George are men of prayer." Second, the claim
that the League "is in direct disobedience to the commands
of God" is established on "incompetent quotation of texts, as
in the old battle against missions." Third, the proposition
that "the League is an instrument of evil is untrue since the
preceding indictments are untrue. Fourth, the prediction
that the "League is foredoomed to failure" is based on bold
and unproved charges of moral evil in the measure itself,
and on "a new volley of impertinent texts of Scripture. "87

(2) World War II

Even before World War II came to a close the Social
Service Commission of the Southern Baptist Convention called
upon the nation to do away with isolationism and develop a
sense of community, which is the only basis for a permanent
peace. This means, the Commission asserted, the substitution of a recognized interdependence for absolute sovereignty
and self-sufficiency, cooperation among all nations instead of
competition between groups of nations, and an international
police force rather than separate national armies strong
enough to withstand all possible enemies. 88

Southern Baptists disavowed any desire to be officially
represented at the peace table, but, in the annual meeting of
the Convention in May, 1944, adopted a Christian moral platform for international relations, designated as "our Baptist
interpretation of the teachings and spirit of Christ in relation
to the present world situation. "89 The platform includes the
idea that the Law of Love condemns the policy of national isolation; an affirmation of the universal right of nations to self
government "and the obligation of the strong to protect the
weak"; the necessity of an international organization with power sufficient to guarantee national security; a condemnation of

racial hatreds as undermining and destroying the human respect and goodwill upon which an enduring peace must rest;
a rejection of tariff barriers which protect the stronger nations and injure the weaker; and a plea for religious liberty.

When the San Francisco Charter was adopted by Fifty
United Nations in conference, the Southern Baptist Committee
on World Peace urged prompt United States Senate ratification. The Committee expressed the conviction that on the
whole the Charter commends itself to the Christian conscience
"and warrants our firmest support." Certain provisions of
the Charter were lifted up for special praise, namely, those
relating to human rights and freedoms, and to religious liberty. The Committee also called upon every Baptist in the
Southland, who shared the Committee's convictions, to com-
municate immediately with his senator urging ratification. [90]

The punitive and even vindictive attitude toward the
Germans which characterized American Christians in general
and Southern Baptists in particular after World War I was
not evident in any general way after World War II. Joseph
E. Brown, however, does express a modified punitive view,
while rejecting the spirit of hatred and revenge. Brown is
convinced that the German people have demonstrated that
they are a lawless nation. They must accordingly "be held
in custody until the spiritual forces of right and justice so
permeate their thinking and their lives that they shall aban-
don their ways of crime." In the meantime their leaders
"need to be tried and punished as a deterrent to future lawlessness."

But, in addition to this, Brown recommends the reform of the defeated. Just as released criminals need to
return to an environment of righteousness to assist them in
being law-abiding, so does a guilty nation. [91]

The historical background of World War II, its philosophical environment and the technological resources with
which it was waged produced post-war issues unknown to
World War I.

The first of these was the new threat of atomic death.
After a review of the vast destructive power of the atom
bomb and an expression of certainty that the scientists of all
countries will soon know its secrets, Joseph E. Brown calls
for the propagation of the gospel of good will on an unprecedented scale. "Good will is the only antidote for national

and racial misunderstanding. "92

        In an obvious effort to justify America's use of the
atomic bomb against the Japanese, David M. Gardner displays an astounding naivete concerning the power struggles
of nations. The whole world, he suggests, should be un-
ceasingly thankful "that the secret of atomic power was discovered by peace loving America. That means it will be
used as a force of destruction only until the foes of freedom
are crushed. "93 Thus Gardner suggests that his nation is
immune to the universal tendency to define "national interests"
in less than ideal terms.

        A more realistic position is taken by W. O. Carver
in relation to the issue of the restoration of Western dominance in the world. As World War II approached its end,
Carver feared it would merge into a new war due to "power
politics for sectional superiority. " The peaceful end of Western domination of the Orient and the prospect of friendly cooperation were in sight.

            But the course which Great Britain and the United
            States seem to be plotting with a view to giving a
            new era of extended white (Ango-Saxon) domination
            heads inevitably to speedy revolt of all Asiatics--
            and African--peoples. Unless some radical change
            is quickly made in British-American policy this
            war will not end.

Carver concludes that if America assists in restoring the
old colonial empires, "we shall be attempting the impossible
and the immoral and unethical. "94

        The third post-war issue peculiar to World War II
was an awful sense of national insecurity. The new weapons
of mass destruction, disillusionment owing to the failure of
the hopes of World War I, the long period of totalitarianism,
and the continuing threat of Communism all conspired to
create a security mood based on military preparedness. The
immediate result was the demand in some quarters for universal military training. Southern Baptists firmly opposed
this tendency.

        In 1945, the Convention adopted the report of the So-
cial Service Commission in which "peace time military training" was opposed on practical and moral grounds. The Commission stated that such a program was not necessary be-

cause of the large pool of trained men left by the war; the
exact nature of the program could not now be determined in
view of the emerging United Nations organization; it would
be a vast annual expense out of proportion to the demands
of national defense; it would prolong "the period of education
of all American youth and break off permanently the education of many thousands" with negative economic and professional results in the life of the nation; it would involve a
huge armaments stockpile which must constantly be renewed;
and it would change the American attitude toward war and in-
tensify nationalism. [95]

In 1946, the Committee on Social Service and Civic
Righteousness of the Baptist State Convention of North Carolina reflected in its report the ideas adopted by the Southern
Baptist Convention during the previous year, and suggested
that the Baptists of North Carolina ponder a list of considerations against conscription pointed out by the National Council Against Conscription. [96]

In 1955, the Southern Baptist Convention adopted a set
of "Recommendations" addressed to the political leaders of
the nation. Among these was the statement

> That, while we recognize the necessity of prepara-
> tion for national defense, we deplore any effort of
> the military to establish a continuing policy of uni-
> versal requirement of military service, believing
> that the selective service law is sufficient and that
> the fruits of universal military training would fur-
> ther weaken the principle of freedom and increase
> the danger of our becoming a military civilization
> tempted to world domination. [97]

Once the United Nations organization was achieved, the
Southern Baptists, who had supported international organization as a proposal, now supported it as a fact.   The Baptist
Convention of North Carolina in its 1946 assembly expressed
confidence that the United Nations had "accomplished much
toward the establishment of a permanent peace. "[98]   The
Alabama Baptist Convention[99] and the editor of the Religious
Herald[100] praised the United Nations for its contributions to
peace through the Korean victory.   Through the years the
Southern Baptist Convention has adopted the report of the Social Service Commission, urging prayerful support of and
continuing participation of the United States in the United
Nations as the best instrument for peace.

8. Vietnam

The Vietnam War has undoubtedly produced more moral anguish among Christians than any other in which America has engaged. Some Southern Baptists have shared this anguish. Based on the authorities of congressmen and generals, including the late President Eisenhower, that war is sometimes pursued from questionable motives and even selfish interests, Frank Stagg raises some telling questions about Vietnam:

> Except for those who are deriving money and political power from us, do we have any friends in Vietnam? Is the extensive 'pacification' program itself an admission that we must persuade the people to let us 'liberate' them? After eight years of war, we are still capturing the same villages--for we are fighting South as well as North Vietnamese! Why?[101]

Stagg rejects the claim that Vietnam is essential to American security in view of the facts that America is vulnerable only to land invasion and missiles, and Vietnam is ten thousand miles away. He concludes that the war is politically and morally unwise and should be stopped. [102] Jack V. Harwell editorially reproduced the substance of Stagg's statement and announced his own editorial support of Stagg's conclusions. [103]

Owing to the wide differences of opinion among Christians concerning American involvement in Vietnam, the Christian Life Commission of the Southern Baptist Convention eschews a definitive position, but calls upon the constituency to enter into open discussion of the issues. "Such open discussion and public debate are necessary if we are to achieve a sense of moral certainty about the course of our action."[104] The report continues by raising certain crucial questions which should stir the conscience of the nation, and calls upon the churches "not to be blinded by distorted appeals to false patriotism so that they lose sight of the personal tragedy, the great sorrow, and the fantastic costs attached to the present conflict. A spirit of solemn repentance is in order. "[105]

The Southern Baptist approach to war and peace after World War II shows a marked increase in the influence of democratic ideas and the teachings of Jesus. Whether the

topic of discussion be the ethics of war, the relation of God
to war, the two world wars, the attitude toward the defeated
enemy, Vietnam, or the problem of international machinery
for the administration of justice, an increased appeal to
democratic ideas and the teachings of Jesus is observable.
In the matter of its theological and philosophical ground, the
Southern Baptist ethic of war and peace is decreasingly dis-
tinguishable from that of other major protestant groups of
America. [106]

Notes

1. Brown, S. M. and Maiden, R. K., "The Christian At-
    titude Toward War" (Editorial), The Word and the
    Way, LIII (April 26, 1917), p. 2.
2. Lipsey, P. I., "Danger of Pacifism" (Editorial) The
    Baptist Record, XXVI (July 31, 1924), p. 5.
3. Sloan, W. A., "Is Man a Murderer Who Kills Another
    in Battle?" Western Recorder, CXVI (September 13,
    1942).
4. Wilson, D. H., "The Christian and the War," Alabama
    Baptist, XLIX (October 23, 1918), p. 6.
5. Ibid.
6. Burnett, J. M., "Non-Resistance" (Editorial) The Bap-
    tist Courier, LXXII (August 29, 1940), p. 3.
7. Burnett, J. M., "No Hate, No Revenge" (Editorial),
    The Baptist Courier, LXXIV (February 5, 1942),
    p. 3.
8. Report of the Social Service Commission of the Alabama
    Baptist Convention, "War," Annual of the Alabama
    Baptist Convention (1939), p. 101.
9. Morgan, S. Lewis, Jr., "The Place of the Church in
    an 'All-Out' War," Biblical Recorder, CVIII (Febru-
    ary 25, 1942), pp. 9-10.
10. Ibid., p. 10.
11. Fergeson, M. L., "Is There Such a Thing as a Just
    War?" The Baptist Student, 41, No. 5 (February,
    1962), pp. 8-10.
12. Allen, Jimmy R., "The Bible Speaks on War and
    Peace" in Peace! Peace! Foy Valentine, editor
    (Waco, Texas: Word Books, 1967), p. 45.
13. Slemp, John Calvin, "Why Do We Fight?" (Editorial)
    The Biblical Recorder, CVI (March 20, 1940), pp.
    4-5.
14. Atkins, W. Clyde, "When Friend Meets Foe," Review
    and Expositor, XXXV, (January, 1938), pp. 27 ff.

15. Ibid., pp. 30-31.
16. Ibid., p. 28.
17. Wolfe, M. H., "When the War Will End," The Religious Herald, XCI (April 11, 1918), p. 7.
18. Masters, Victor J., "War Has a Place in the Plans of God" (Editorial), Western Recorder, CXIV (June 27, 1940), p. 7.
19. Battle, H. W., "Dr. Battle's Address," The Religious Herald, XCI (November 21, 1918), p. 6.
20. McCaul, Thomas V., "Putting the Emphasis Where the Emphasis Belongs," Religious Herald, CI (February 9, 1928), p. 8.
21. Gambrell, J. B., "God and War," Baptist Standard, XXX (April 18, 1918), p. 11.
22. Guffin, Gilbert, "What is God Doing in this War?" The Christian Index, CXXIII (May 27, 1943), p. 4.
23. Mullins, E. Y., "God and the War," Review and Expositor, XXI (October, 1924), pp. 454ff.
24. Ibid., pp. 457-458.
25. Brunson, John A., "Does Jesus Ever Approve of War?" The Baptist Courier, XLVIII (August 16, 1917), p. 1.
26. Ibid.
27. Ibid., p. 2.
28. Advertisement by Home Mission Board of the Southern Baptist Convention, "Matching Religion and Patriotism," Religious Herald, XCI (March 28, 1918), p. 2.
29. Schwartz, G. C. Chaplain, "America and the Crusade Splendid," The Word and the Way, LV (October 17, 1918), p. 5.
30. Hargis, W. I., "Why Are We Fighting?" The Baptist Record, XIX (November 8, 1917), p. 7.
31. Moore, Hight C., "The Cause for Which We Fight" (Editorial) Biblical Recorder, LXXXIII (July 25, 1917), p. 2.
32. Report of Committee on World Crisis of the Southern Baptist Convention, Religious Herald, XCI (May 23, 1918), p. 11.
33. Cody, Z. T. and Keys, J. C., "Too Much War" (Editorial), The Baptist Courier, XLIX (July 11, 1918), p. 4.
34. Hahn, B. D., "The Soldier of the Republic," The Baptist Courier, XLIX (September 12, 1918), p. 3.
35. Ibid.
36. White, John E., "Conscience and Country," The Religious Herald, XCI (February 28, 1918), p. 5.
37. "Prayer for Soldiers," Religious Herald, XCI (February 21, 1918). p. 23.

38. Mullins, E. Y., "Shall We Be Brutalized by the Beast?" Religious Herald, XCI (July 18, 1918), pp. 5-6.
39. Gambrell, J. B., "Christianity in the Making of an Army," The Baptist Courier, XLIX (September 26, 1918), p. 2.
40. Ibid.
41. Ibid.
42. A just war is one whose object is just (its purpose is to vindicate justice and restore peace), which has a reasonable chance of obtaining its objective, which is conducted under the authority of government, which has a just intention (love toward the enemy), and which is characterized by just conduct.
43. Bainton, Roland H., "The Churches and War: Historic Attitudes Toward Christian Participation," Social Action (January, 1945), p. 59.
44. Goodrich, A. L., "Baptist Behavior in a World at War," The Baptist Record, LXIV (January 22, 1942), p. 4.
45. Knight, Ryland, "Southern Baptists and World Peace," Religious Herald, CXVII (August 10, 1944), pp. 4-5.
46. Knight, Ryland, "Christian Youth in a Warring World," Review and Expositor, XXXIX (April, 1942), pp. 161 ff.
47. Report of the Social Service Commission of the Southern Baptist Convention, "War," Annual of the Southern Baptist Convention (Nashville, Sunday School Board of the Southern Baptist Convention, 1943), p. 104.
48. Report of the Social Service Commission of the Southern Baptist Convention, "Responsibility of Church," Annual of the Southern Baptist Convention (Nashville, Sunday School Board of the Southern Baptist Convention, 1942), pp. 91-92.
49. Holt, A. J., "The Blessings of the War," Florida Baptist Witness, XXX (November 8, 1917), p. 6.
50. Moss, J. Calvin, "What the Great World War Did for Baptists and Others; the Fourteen Points of Blessing," Religious Herald, XCII (October 16, 1919), pp. 4-5.
51. McDaniel, George W., "Gains from War," Religious Herald, XCI (August 29, 1918), p. 5.
52. Porter, Henry Alfred, "What on Earth Is God Doing?" Religious Herald, CXIV (December 18, 1941), pp. 4-5.
53. Provence, H. H., "God's Hand in History," The Baptist Courier, LXXV (September 30, 1943), p. 8.
54. Slemp, John Calvin, "Does War Ever Settle Anything?" (Editorial) Biblical Recorder, CVI (May 8, 1940), pp. 3-4.

128   Social Ethics Among Southern Baptists

55. Masters, Victor I., "Anti-War Propaganda" (Editorial),
     Western Recorder, CVIII (August 30, 1934), p. 8.
56. Masters, Victor I., "The Christian and War" (Editorial),
     Western Recorder, CXV (March 6, 1941), p. 8.
57. McConnell, F. M., "When War is Right" (Editorial),
     Baptist Standard, LIV (April 23, 1942), p. 4.
58. Cody, Z. T. and Keys, J. C., "Persistent Pacifism"
     (Editorial), The Baptist Courier, XLIX (May 9, 1918),
     p. 4.
59. Winburn, H. L., "Conscientious Objectors" (Editorial),
     Baptist Advance, XLVIII (March 13, 1919), p. 4.
60. Ibid.
61. Ibid.
62. Report of the Committee on Social Service and Civic
     Righteousness, "Universal Military Training and
     Conscientious Objectors" Annual of the Baptist State
     Convention of North Carolina, November, 1946),
     p. 48.
63. Maston, T. B., "Baptists and Conscientious Objectors,"
     Religious Herald, CXIV (January 9, 1941), p. 17.
64. Ibid.
65. Macon, Leon, "Conscientious Objectors" (Editorial)
     The Alabama Baptist, 116, No. 7 (February 15,
     1951), p. 3.
66. Cody, Z. T. and Keys, J. C., "Peace at Last" (Edi-
     torial), The Baptist Courier, XLIX (November 14,
     1918), p. 4.
67. Edmonds, Richard H., "Not a Time for 'The Gospel of
     Reconciliation,'" The Baptist Courier, XLIX (Decem-
     ber 5, 1918), p. 1.
68. Ibid.
69. Pitt, R. H., "The German People," (Editorial), Re-
     ligious Herald, XCI (December 12, 1918), p. 10.
70. White, John E., "In Comfort of the Editor of the Bap-
     tist Courier," The Baptist Courier, XLIX (Decem-
     ber 5, 1918), p. 2.
71. Ibid.
72. Watterson, Henry, "Colonel Watterson on Peace," The
     Baptist Courier, XLIX (December 5, 1918), pp. 1-2.
73. Cody, Z. T., "Forgiveness vs. Paganism" (Editorial),
     The Baptist Courier, LII (February 10, 1921), p. 4.
74. Ibid.
75. Edmonds, R. H., "Mr. Edmonds on Forgiveness for
     Germany," The Baptist Courier, LII (February 24,
     1921), p. 2.
76. Cody, Z. T., "Mr. Edmonds' Article" (Editorial), The
     Baptist Courier, LII (February 24, 1941), p. 4.

77. Cody, Z. T. and Keys, J. C. , "The League of Nations"
     (Editorial) The Baptist Courier, L (March 6, 1919),
     p. 4.
78. Pitt, R. H. , "The League of Nations" (Editorial), The
     Religious Herald, XCII (July 17, 1919), p. 4.
79. Routh, E. C. , "The League of Nations" (Editorial)
     Baptist Standard, XXXI (January 2, 1919), p. 10.
80. Report of the Social Service Commission of the South-
     ern Baptist Convention, "World Court, " Annual of
     the Southern Baptist Convention (Nashville, Sunday
     School Board of the Southern Baptist Convention,
     1924), p. 114.
81. Edmonds, R. H. , "Against the League of Nations, " The
     Religious Herald, XCII (July 17, 1919), p. 9.
82. Jones, Maryus, "Mr. Edmonds and the League of
     Peace, " Religious Herald, XCII (September 18,
     1919), p. 5.
83. Thwing, Eugene, "The League of Nations as a Moral
     Issue, " (Advertisement from the Manufacturers'
     Record), Religious Herald, XCIII (October 21,
     1920), p. 12.
84. Ibid. , p. 13.
85. Ibid.
86. Ibid.
87. Smith, W. R. L. , "League of Nations, " Religious
     Herald, XCIII (October 28, 1920), p. 6.
88. Report of the Social Service Commission of the South-
     ern Baptist Convention, "Community and Peace, "
     Annual of the Southern Baptist Convention (Nashville,
     Sunday School Board of the Southern Baptist Conven-
     tion, 1943), p. 108.
89. Report of the Committee on World Peace of the Southern
     Baptist Convention, "Southern Baptists and World
     Peace, " Annual of the Southern Baptist Convention
     (Nashville, Sunday School Board of the Southern Bap-
     tist Convention, 1944), pp. 149-150.
90. "Committee on World Peace Urges Ratification, " Bap-
     tist Standard, LVII, (July 12, 1945), pp. 1, 5.
91. Brown, Joseph E. , "What Shall We Do with the Ger-
     mans?" (Editorial) The Word and the Way, 82 (May
     17, 1945), p. 2.
92. Brown, Joseph E. , "Christianity and the Atomic Bomb
     'Know-How'" (Editorial), The Word and the Way, 83
     (November 22, 1945), p. 2.
93. Gardner, David M. , "Atomic Bombs" (Editorial), Bap-
     tist Standard, LXII (August 23, 1945), p. 3.
94. Carver, W. O. , "America and Russia, " Baptist Stand-

ard, LVII (July 26, 1945), p. 13.

95. "Peace Time Military Training," Report of the Social
    Service Commission of the Southern Baptist Conven-
    tion, Annual of the Southern Baptist Convention (Nash-
    ville, Sunday School Board of the Southern Baptist
    Convention, 1945), p. 95.

96. "Universal Military Training and Conscientious Objec-
    tors," Report of the Committee on Social Service
    and Civic Righteousness, Annual of the Baptist State
    Convention of North Carolina, November, 1946, p.
    48.

97. "Recommendations," Report of the Christian Life Com-
    mission of the Southern Baptist Convention, Annual
    of the Southern Baptist Convention (Nashville, 1955),
    p. 334.

98. "World Peace and the United Nations Organization,"
    Report of the Committee on Social Service and Civic
    Righteousness, Annual of the Baptist State Conven-
    tion of North Carolina, November, 1946, p. 47.

99. "International Relations and Peace," Report of the So-
    cial Service Commission, Annual of the Alabama
    Baptist State Convention, November, 1950, p. 106.

100. Alley, Reuben E., "A Stronger United Nations" (Edi-
    torial) Religious Herald, (July 6, 1950), p. 10-11.

101. Stagg, Frank, "Christian Conscience and the War in
    Vietnam" Religious Herald, CXXXVII (May 22, 1969),
    p. 12.

102. Ibid.

103. Harwell, Jack V., "Do Baptists Have Something to Say
    on Vietnam?" (Editorial) The Christian Index, 148
    (June 12, 1969), p. 6.

104. "Peace," Report of the Christian Life Commission of
    the Southern Baptist Convention, Annual of the South-
    ern Baptist Convention (Nashville, 1967), p. 294.

105. Ibid.

106. It is interesting to note in this connection that the So-
    cial Service Commission of the Southern Baptist
    Convention set forth in 1943 lists of propositions
    on peace from two different American Christian
    groups as "worth our consideration." Annual of
    the Southern Baptist Convention (Nashville, 1943),
    pp. 108-109.

Chapter V

PROHIBITION AND THE RESTRAINT
OF THE LIQUOR TRAFFIC

The production, sale, distribution and consumption of
alcoholic beverages is the greatest of all social problems in
the estimation of Southern Baptists. They have constantly
and persistently fought for the establishment and maintenance
of prohibition; and, failing in this objective, have campaigned
for the reduction and limitation of the sale and distribution of
drinks containing alcohol. While they have been outstanding
in their refusal to cooperate with other religious groups on
issues other than separation of church and state, Southern
Baptists have not hesitated to cooperate with various and sun-
dry groups which were interested in prohibition and the limitation of the liquor traffic. So great an urgency and importance have been assigned to the liquor issue that Southern
Baptists have also abandoned in practice their own doctrine
of the task of the church in relation to the social order.
They do insist on preaching and teaching concerning the evils
of liquor. But they show little inclination to rely solely on
the regeneration of the individual through the preaching of
the gospel of salvation. In relation to this issue, Southern
Baptists have been thoroughly activist, concentrating heavily
on legislation and the power of the state. They have taken
their fight directly to the halls of legislation; they have appealed to the people to cast their ballots right; they have
voted as a bloc; they have exerted pressure on individual
public officeholders; and they have preached, taught, boycot-
ted, and propagandized.

1.   The Baptist Stand on Prohibition
     and the Liquor Traffic

Why do Southern Baptists lay so much stress on the
issue of alcohol? A hidden reason may be the fact that they
have so sadly neglected other social problems. The emphasis on prohibition and the restraint of the liquor traffic may

be partly compensatory. In addition to this psychological explanation, there may be another at the sociological level.
With its agrarian and slave background, the concept of the
"Big Boss" is deeply entrenched in the South. The "Big
Boss" consists of the Southern "Bourbons"--all of the people
of power and prestige. [1] It is these people who have given
shape to the Southern System. More than any other people,
they have been responsible for the patterns of race relations,
politics and economics. But since, in the "Big Boss" tradition, they are immune to criticism, southern Christianity
has not "dared" to speak with a prophetic voice about the
problems which they have largely created. On the other
hand, the "liquor interests" in the South have always been
men of marginal status and limited power. They could accordingly be attacked with impunity.

But Southern Baptists themselves have answers to the
question why they are such ardent prohibitionists. They are
convinced that their opposition rests solely on Biblical and
moral grounds. "The right of prohibition is based on the
inherent evil of intoxicating liquor, and fundamental Bible
teaching both as to this evil and as to human relations and
principles of government." The Bible everywhere teaches
that intoxicating liquor is evil and brings ruin. [2] Taking the
position that God Himself was the first prohibitionist and that
the Bible is a book of prohibitory statues and total abstinence,
George W. McDaniel cites the following Biblical "admonitions
to abstinence." "Look not thou upon the wine when it is red,
when it moveth itself aright: at the last it biteth like a ser-
pent and stingeth like an adder." (Prov. 23:31). "Wine is
a mocker, strong drink is raging, and whosoever is deceived
thereby is not wise." (Prov. 20:1). "Wine is treacherous."
(Hab. 2:5). McDaniel further points out that total abstinence
was a prerequisite of the Nazarites and Rechabites; and "of
the man upon whom Jesus pronounced a panegyric, the angel
said before his birth: 'He shall drink no wine nor strong
drink.'" (Luke 1:15). [3]

Many passages of Scripture are cited by Southern Baptist writers as condemnatory of the use of intoxicating beverages. But one passage alone should be sufficient. It is the
Pauline assurance that the drunkard cannot inherit the Kingdom of God. "Nor thieves, nor covetous, nor drunkards,
nor revilers, nor extortioners, shall inherit the kingdom of
God." (I Cor. 6:10). The editor of the Biblical Recorder
interprets this passage to mean that drinking destroys the
desire to enter the kingdom. It is not that God has shut

the gates. [4]

In addition to listing several passages which strongly condemn and prohibit the use of alcohol for beverage purposes, Wyatt R. Hunter finds Biblical foundation for the bad effects and consequences of drinking alcohol:

1. It is a mocker and deceives. Prov. 20:1

2. It produces woe, sorrow, contentious babbling and wounds. Prov. 23:29

3. It produces negligence concerning the law and perverts justice. Prov. 31:4, 5

4. It causes error in judgment and makes men useless. Isa. 28:7

5. The craze for it will cause people to sell their children. Joel 3:3

6. It makes people haughty and greedy. Hab. 2:5

7. It aids and abets adultery. Hab. 2:15, 16

8. It brings people to poverty and rags. Prov. 23:21

9. It defiles man. It is the greatest enemy to health and character. Dan. 1:8

10. It takes away the heart and makes man without compassion and feeling. Hos. 4:11 [5]

It is generally agreed among Southern Baptists that there is Biblical warrant for the medicinal use of alcohol. Paul commended its use to Timothy for his stomach's sake and his frequent infirmities. (1 Tim. 5:23). [6] But the Southern Baptist stand on alcohol is that of total abstinence. On this issue the Southern Baptist ethic is absolutist, compromising neither with the nature of man nor with the social culture. "Baptists fundamentally believe in total abstinence from evil for the individual. " Temperance is defined as "total abstinence from indulgence in evil and moderation in the use of that which is right. "[7]

Abstinence from the use of alcoholic beverages must

not be understood to apply only to "hard liquor." It applies
to any degree of alcoholic content that may induce drunkenness.   In opposing a bill in the House of Representatives of
the Mississippi Legislature legalizing the sale of wine (21%
alcoholic content), Joe T. Odle rejects the appeal to the
Scriptures on the part of some of the legislators.   He admits that Jesus made wine for the wedding feast in Cana of
Galilee and that Paul suggested wine to Timothy for his
stomach ailment.   "We can be absolutely certain, however,
because of what we know about Jesus, that he did not make,
nor give to the people, any drink which would cause drunkenness." Odle's contention is that the Bible condemns all intoxicating beverages, including wine. [8]

2.   The Evils of Liquor

It is enough for Southern Baptists that the Bible
should teach against liquor.   They need no other sanction.
But since the evils of liquor are so palpable, the use of alcohol is also condemned on other grounds.   The bad effects
of the liquor traffic and liquor consumption are moral (in
the broadly accepted terms of human well being), biological
and economic.

Speaking of liquor as a moral evil, Henry W. Tiffany
states that "liquor and vice have cut away the foundations of
every great civilization of the past and they are striking at
the vitals of America today." Since the return of the legalized liquor traffic, America has witnessed a greater measure
of moral debauchery of its citizens than ever before.   Pointing to the 36,000 who are killed annually and the 1,000,000
injured, Tiffany calls the highways "slaughter houses for
drinking driving."[9]   Gambling has swept over the land, and
crime is rampant.   America's crime bill, already
$15,000,000,000 [in 1940], is still increasing.   "The first
year of repeal showed an increase of 195 per cent in arrests
for drunkenness over the first year of prohibition.   Of 11,000
prisoners in 1935, 4,615 were committed for liquor violations."[10]   According to the testimony of J. Edgar Hoover,
there are four times as many bootleg stills as there were
unver prohibition.   Political and economic leaders are help-
less in dealing with the situation created by bootleggers,
highjackers, and racketeers.   Affirming that the liquor traffic is right now undermining America's entire political structure and destroying the citizens' freedom, Tiffany predicts
that the liquor interests will in the future run the government. [11]

Liquor is also a destroyer of personal and domestic
well-being. "We have scientific proof that alcohol is quickly
assimilated by the blood stream and attacks the brain first."
Once the brain is reached, mental confusion is created, self
criticism is blunted, and self control is weakened. [12] As a
habit forming stimulant, alcohol carries "its own inherent
demand for repetition, " and produces a false sense of well-
being followed by depression. [13] The discord, strife, confusion, and irresponsibility which result from its use destroys many homes and disqualifies parents in many others
as effective performers of their functions. [14]

As a biological evil, alcohol is a depressant, a de-
ceiver, and a destroyer. Being taken up from the blood, it
produces a depressant effect on the functioning of every organ of the body. Its most important effect is on the brain,
the various forms of which are insanity, the substitution of
phantasy for reality, and narcotization. Its depressant effect on the central nervous system is expressed through relief from worry and anxiety, and freedom from the restraint
of social conventions and self criticism. In their narcotized
state, the respiratory centers are less sensitive to acid
stimulation and, therefore, do not eliminate carbon dioxide
in sufficient amounts. [15] Alcohol also produces adverse dietary effects, introducing large quantities of calories into the
body while failing to provide "vitamins, minerals, or other
dietary requirements to offset the straight calories it puts
into the body." Due to a false sense of hunger satisfaction
vitamin deficiencies result, [16] susceptibility to certain diseases increases, resistance is weakened and recuperative
powers are reduced. [17]

The liquor interests have made much of the economic
issue in defense of their position. Their principal claim is
that the liquor industry increases the prosperity of the society. Henry W. Tiffany charges that the opposite is the
case. The liquor interests say that they are paying
$500, 000, 000 a year[18] to Federal and state treasuries, but
Federal and state governments are paying more than
$500, 000, 000 a year for relief to the unemployed who are
largely the liquor buyers. The drink bill for 1940 was
$5, 000, 000, 000, or one-half of the total food bill of Ameri-
ca. It was $880, 000, 000 more than the total bill for educa-
tion.

In the prohibition period, the wealth of the nation increased by $100, 000, 000, 000. The period from 1916 to

1929 was America's greatest era of prosperity. The enforce-
ments of prohibition yielded the nation a net balance of only
$264,000,000. And the enforcement of laws under repeal is
costing the Federal government more money and is requiring
a larger force of employees than at any time under prohibition.

On the other hand, "the liquor traffic returns the
smallest proportionate share of the value of the product to
the producers of the materials of any of the twenty-six leading industries of the United States," employs the smallest
labor force in relation to capital invested, and pays "the
smallest percentage of the value of the finished product" in
wages. [19]

3. Waging the Prohibition Fight

Southern Baptists disavow social action on the part of
the church and affirm preaching and social service. The
task of the church lies solely in the evangelization and regeneration of individuals, who, in the newness of their lives,
will transform all institutions and social relations. The
church may and must render succor to society in the form
of hospitals, orphanages, homes for the aged, etc.; but it
is not the function of the church as an organized body to
take a definitive stand on a social or political issue.

To all practical intents and purposes, the Southern
Baptists broke with this doctrine on the issue of prohibition.
In this struggle, they not only failed to rely exclusively on
the preaching and teaching ministry of the church, but went
so far as to become virtually a political party. The prohibition issue was regarded as being of such great urgency and
importance that its resolution could not wait on the slow process of evangelization and regeneration. "Spiritual means,"
otherwise deemed appropriate for the church, were inadequate to deal with this crisis without the help of force and
power. Consequently, Southern Baptists relied heavily upon
the state as a supporting agency in this "righteous cause."

In 1917[20] a Commission of the Southern Baptist Convention called on the president of the United States and presented a memorial to him "protesting against any increase
in taxes on intoxicating liquors for purposes of revenue, and
fervently petitioning the president to use the influence of his
high office for immediate and complete prohibition as a war

measure. "21

The significance of the state in this cause of righteousness may be seen in A. J. Barton's report of the inter-
view:

> This commission came away profoundly impressed
> and thoroughly hopeful as to his attitude. It is
> my sincere conviction, shared I think by the other
> brethren, that Woodrow Wilson has come to the
> Kingdom for such a time as this, and that in the
> right time and in the right manner he will fear-
> lessly do the right as he sees and understands the
> right. 22

In 1918, the Committee on Temperance and Social
Service of the Southern Baptist Convention conceived its task
against a victorious background. The number of states
which had enacted prohibition had reached twenty-eight. In
most of the states the prohibitory law was already in effect.
And in Washington, during the latter half of 1917, both the
Senate and Congress adopted a resolution proposing to the
several states, for their ratification, a Prohibition Amendment to the Constitution of the United States. 23

In the light of these facts, the Committee sets forth
"the task that remains to be done for the final and complete
destruction of the beverage liquor traffic":

> 1. In the states which have only statutory prohi-
>   bition it must be put into the Constitution. ...
>
> 2. With all possible dispatch we must press for
>   the ratification of the Amendment to the Con-
>   stitution of the United States by the necessary
>   three-fourts of the states of the Union, indeed
>   by all the states, for, while only thirty-six
>   states are required to make it effective, we
>   hope that every state in the Union may join in
>   putting the ban of the whole nation upon so
>   great an evil.
>
> 3. We must create and maintain, in every nook
>   and corner of every state, a healthy, robust,
>   aggressive sentiment for law enforcement that
>   will make prohibition effective; no law will en-
>   force itself and no law is stronger than public

> sentiment.   Besides, law has an educative
> value....

> 4.   With all possible promptness and oneness of
>   action we must bring pressure to bear upon
>   Congress for the enactment of national prohi-
>   bition by statute as an emergency war measure
>   to conserve the food and fuel supplies which
>   are now worse than wasted by the brewers and
>   which are needed by our army and navy and
>   by the armies and navies of our Allies....
>   Your committee would recommend that this
>   Convention approve this measure [Representative
>   Barkley's bill for national prohibition] and urge
>   its constituency to bring all possible pressure
>   to bear upon Congress for the enactment of
>   this bill into law. [24]

When final victory was achieved over the liquor traffic
in 1920, it was hailed by the Committee on Temperance and
Social Service as "the greatest victory for industrial economy,
moral reform and sound governmental policy ever won by any
people."[25] The Committee warns, however, that temperance
organizations must not be disbanded and efforts relaxed, for
the liquor traffic is heartless and lawless.   The task that
lies ahead now is to see to it that only honest friends of
law and order are elected to all offices, legislative and executive.   The temperance cause must also be supported on
a world-wide basis.   The Committee suggests that aid to
the temperance and reform forces of other lands can best
be given through cooperation with the Anti-Saloon League of
America and the Women's Christian Temperance Union.[26]

The main task of Southern Baptists in 1921 was to
give support to strengthening legislation.   Former Attorney
General Palmer had ruled that under the Volstead Law beer
may be prescribed as a medicine, but a bill had been intro-
duced in the House of Representatives which would nullify the
ruling of the former attorney general and strengthen the law
where it was weak.   Since the Commission on Social Service
favored total prohibition, it made the following recommendation:

> We recommend that by the adoption of this report,
> the Convention give its hearty approval to the
> measure [the amendment to the Volstead law] and
> urge upon the Committee on the judiciary an early

and favorable report upon the measure, and urge
upon the House of Representatives and the Senate
its prompt enactment; and, further, to this end,
we recommend that the members of the Convention
keep in close and constant touch with their congressmen and senators, and let them know fully our
wishes in this urgent and important matter. [27]

The Southern Baptists could hardly escape indefinitely
the charge of being in politics.   When the charge was
brought, W. B. Crumpton responded by saying, "Yes, Baptists are in politics, and have been for years against the
mightiest foe of humanity. "[28]   The charge of being in politics was brought by a reader of an account concerning a
pronouncement made by a body called together by A. J.
Barton, chairman of the Social Service Commission of the
Southern Baptist Convention.   The assembled body issued
solemn warning to all political parties in America against
nomination of wet candidates for high office. [29]   Actually this
action was not unusual, inasmuch as the Southern Baptist
Convention had issued this warning in the form of a formal
resolution for several years and many similar resolutions
were adopted by Baptist District Associations and State Conventions.   In his article on the "Baptist Stand on Prohibition,"
A. J. Barton quotes the resolution adopted in 1931 by the
Southern Baptist Convention:

That we affirm our purpose, repeatedly expressed,
as citizens to support for president of the United
States and all other important official positions only such candidates and nominees as believe in and
support prohibition as the established policy of our
governments, both state and national, and that we
will seek the defeat of any candidate or nominee
who may oppose prohibition regardless of any party
affiliations and labels. [30]

These warnings were not a mere empty threat.   In
the presidential campaign of 1928, Al Smith was unmistakably
identified and described in the Social Service Commission's
report as the candidate to be opposed. [31]   Although Smith was
opposed because he was a Catholic, his wetness was equally
a burning issue.   Ballot consciousness on the local scene
may be observed in an appeal to the voters of Arkansas by
the Quachita Associational B. Y. P. U. of Polk County, Arkansas:

Be sure to pay your poll tax and be ready to vote
on July 18th to retain the 18th Amendment. The
18th Amendment is God's Amendment and God's
people will retain it. It would be better for us to
go one week without food than to fail to vote for
sobriety and home protection on July 18th. God's
people must not give one inch of ground in this
fight. Preachers and laymen should speak in every
speaking place in Arkansas between now and voting
time. [32]

In no respect did Southern Baptists more nearly re-
semble a political party in the prohibition struggle than in
this practice of forming a voting bloc. But this important
party device was supported by other political techniques. In
addition to pressure, personal suasion through direct contact
was employed on political officials and candidates, and propaganda was constant. The pulpit, lay speakers, the religious
press, and some of the secular press all helped to spread
the word. Southern Baptists were not hesitant about going
directly to the seats of political decision. They also made
use of the well known pressure group technique of lobbying.

An outstanding case in point was the address of A. J.
Barton before the Ways and Means Committee of the House
of Representatives on December 14, 1932. Although he appeared before the Committee as Chairman of the Social Service Commission of the Southern Baptist Convention, Barton
did not preach a sermon, but spoke in the language of the
economist and political scientist. He stated, first of all,
that the entire constituency of the Southern Baptist Convention, with the exception of a few persons who seek their own
aggrandizement through politics, oppose legislation which
would legalize the manufacture, distribution and sale of beer
or any other intoxicating liquor. This statement was con-
firmed by a presentation of the pertinent resolution adopted
by the Southern Baptist Convention in 1932: "That we affirm
our devotion to the Eighteenth Amendment to the Constitution
of the United States and to its supporting legislation as the
greatest and most beneficient piece of social, economic and
human welfare legislation ever enacted by any free people. "[33]

Barton proceeds to attack the claims of the liquor interests that their industry is an economic problem solver.
He denies that the liquor traffic will solve the market problem for grain inasmuch as the industry used only 32. 8 million bushels of the 4, 749, 000, 000 bushels of grain produced

between 1913 and 1917, and during this period the traffic was
at its height. Moreover, when, in 1917, the prohibition forces were urging legislation to conserve food supplies, the
liquor interests themselves declared that they did not use
much grain. On the other hand, increased consumption of
grains at the dairy farms, due to the increased demand for
milk under prohibition, is much greater than the total amount
of grain used by the liquor traffic. It is also untrue that the
liquor industry will solve the unemployment problem. Between 9, 000, 000 and 10, 500, 000 persons are unemployed in
this country. When it was at its height, the liquor industry
employed only 499, 999 persons. [34] Barton offers similar
proportions in figures to show that the liquor industry will
not solve the tax problem. Furthermore, since the very
purpose of government is to promote human welfare, "to
license a recognized evil and attempt to derive profit or
revenue therefrom is a violation of the most sacred and
fundamental principles of government. "[35]

Barton finally attacks the contention that the 18th
Amendment is a violation of States' Rights. On the contrary,
it is the highest expression of States' Rights when the States
act and amend the Constitution of the United States. [36]

These resolutions, appeals, and political activities
constitute a thorough going piece of social action. Southern
Baptists left no stones unturned for the cause of prohibition.
In all probability, they have been about as politically minded
on the matter of alcohol as any American Christian group
has on this or any other issue.

4.   Defending Prohibition's
     Achievements and Denouncing Repeal

Once prohibition became law, its enemies rushed forward to take advantage of every opportunity to show that it
was a failure and unworkable. The claim was made that the
law was hastily put over on the people, that large quantities
of liquor were still being consumed, and since the government received no revenue from it, the people were subjected
to a high tax rate. But Southern Baptists, not to be outdone
by anti-prohibition propaganda, met these charges with counter claims of the success of the prohibition laws.

It is not the law that has failed, says J. H. Jones;
rather, the people have failed to do their part to help make

it a success.   Many judges, court officials and law enforcement officers have never ceased to drink, and officers have
taken bribes.   Due to the corruption of the courts, bootleggers employ shrewd lawyers, make free use of bribery, and
are consequently able to continue in their business because
they get off so lightly when caught.

Jones gains consolation from the fact that "one day
those judges, lawyers and criminals will stand before a judge
that cannot be bribed and will give each one justice...." He
suggests that, if prohibition should be repealed because it is
not being enforced, all laws should be repealed which are
not being enforced. "[37]

But the prohibition law is being enforced with gratify-
ing success, according to W. L. Poteat.   "The rational ex-
pectation of prohibition enforcement is that it approaches the
level of enforcement of other laws. " In North Carolina
judges and solicitors testify that "the prohibition law is better enforced" than other laws of the criminal code, and prohibition has succeeded in reducing the national consumption
of liquor by sixty-five per cent. [38]

Certain new conditions created by prohibition have
caused lowered consumption.   Reduction in consumption is
achieved by the increase in the price of liquor which in turn
results from scarcity.   It is also achieved by the barrier to
the acquisition of liquor.   Since the saloon is closed, liquor
is harder to locate. [39]

Turning his attention to the economic advantages of
prohibition, W. L. Poteat asserts that the closing of the
saloon by the Eighteenth Amendment turned its annual invest-
ment of five billion dollars into the channels of wholesome
productive business, thus effecting an economic revolution
throughout the country. [40]

Southern Baptists spokesmen believe that prohibition
has brought the greatest benefit to the laboring man because,
more than any other class, he was the saloon's most faithful patron.   Following this line of thought, J. M. Davis
states that the standard of living of the poor people has
greatly improved under prohibition.   They not only enjoy
the comforts and necessities of life, but many of the luxuries.   Many of the poor own automobiles, dress in style,
educate their children, and supply their homes with the best
literature.   Included among those who enjoy this new life

style are some families who were in rags and whose tables were scantily provided during the days of the saloon. [41]

In the area of personal well-being, prohibition has been a great boon. It has put young people under more wholesome restraints, and it protects the weak man who wants to live soberly but has a taste for liquor. [42] It has caused the disappearance of the derelict and old-time drunkard. [43] The Salvation Army of New York City reports that "under legalized liquor they had 1, 200 to 1, 300 intoxicated persons to care for each night. Under the Eighteenth Amendment the average was not even seven. "[44]

On the political plane, prohibition has reduced the corruption of officers and "divorced the government from the unholy union of law and liquor. "[45]

The inverse side of the defense of the achievements of prohibition is the denunciation of repeal. With the same gusto that the liquor interests attacked prohibition as a failure when it became law, the prohibition forces attacked repeal when it became law. "Repeal has brought none of the benefits promised. " Unemployment has not been reduced, "relief is still a national problem, " there has been no reduction of taxes and the budget has not been balanced, illicit trafficking in liquor continues and the enforcement of liquor laws is more costly than under prohibition. [46] "Instead of bringing the economic benefits which the liquor interests claimed, repeal has brought on conditions which are economic liabilities. According to Secretary of the Navy Knox the most serious cause of absenteeism is weekend dissipation."[47]

There has also been an increase in deaths from drinking. During the four years leading up to 1933, the death rate for each 100, 000 unit of population declined by 1. 5. "The record for 1933, the first year of legalized beer, turned the tide upward, though by only . 01 per unit. "[48] Furthermore, the view, held by many drys as well as wets, that the legalization of mild beer would decrease both drunkenness and alcoholic deaths has proved to be unsound. Both have increased instead. [49]

Not only is brew harmful to society, the brewers are themselves a great evil. W. T. Rouse affirms that the return of beer means the return of an industry greater in its corrupting influence than that of the distillers of liquor, even though their influences are the same kind. To substantiate

this contention, Rouse appeals to the record and sets forth
"nine reasons why we are not willing to give the breweries
another strangle-hold on our government":[50]

1. The brewing industry is foreign, un-American
   and anti-American, being primarily under the
   control of Germans.

2. The United States Brewers' Association has
   spent vast sums of money to combat prohibition
   sentiment. Much of this money was raised by
   extortion.

3. The United States Brewers' Association has
   blackmailed and discredited opponents, and
   used front organizations to disguise its activities.

4. The Brewers' Association has manipulated
   organized labor through a special bureau set
   up for that purpose.

5. The brewers have also employed the boycott,
   an alien institution which has no place among
   free men. [51]

6. The breweries have been a degrading influence
   in politics through fraud and misrepresentation.

7. The brewers have controlled the press through
   subsidization and the writing of articles.

8. The breweries have dishonored womanhood by
   opposing woman suffrage and by protecting
   vice.

9. The brewers have been defiers of the law. [52]

5. Prohibition and the Negro

For a long time, students of the sociology of the
South have understood that much of the stimulus behind prohibition arose from the fear of the intoxicated Negro.   It was
believed that under the influence of liquor the Negro became
dangerous and uncontrollable.   Perhaps the deepest dimension of this fear is the unspoken one, namely, the concern

that liquor may "inspire" the Negro to rebel against the system which oppresses and degrades him. Presenting twelve reasons why one should vote against the local option proposal in the regulation of alcoholic liquors, Jesse L. Murrell states as one of the twelve, the "moral obligation to the Negro." "The Negro is not as stable under the influence of liquor as the white man and when drunk may be dangerous."[53] Moreover, if liquor is legalized, the Negro quarters may be shamefully exploited by the liquor interests. The resulting health conditions from the attendant immoralities may be spread among the whites where the Negroes work. The flow of liquor must therefore be held to a minimum for the sake of the rest of the people.[54]

Making a special prohibition appeal on behalf of the Negro, W. B. Crumpton testifies that "when the agitation began in earnest in Alabama, it was mainly on account of the negro."[55]

The best farm laborer on earth when sober, when whiskey was accessible, became utterly unreliable, inefficient and uncontrollable. White women and children, in districts densely populated by the black race, came to be in imminent danger. Riot and bloodshed was [sic] liable to break out at any time.

These conditions came close to home to the white man on the plantations, and to their friends in the towns and cities. This state of affairs furnished arguments that were irresistible in favor of prohibition, when put before the legislature. Representatives from the white counties, to a man, were ready to come to the rescue of their white brothers in the black belt.[56]

Crumpton goes on to say that the race question put ginger into the fight and sent dry forces on to victory. Good effects were immediately forthcoming, and everybody was pleased except the Negro and the drinking element among the whites. Some whites despised the law because they could not easily deceive and rob the Negro when sober.

Crumpton calls for vigorous moral reform among the blacks through informal education, schools, and more rigid enforcement of the laws. Negroes are weak, he insists, but a great moral reform has not been attempted among them.

> Let the superior race pity the poor negro and help
> him to organize against his foe and ours.
>
> With the help of the whites, with the great advance
> they have made, it will be easy to free the negro,
> of the curse of the worse slavery that ever befell
> any race. [57]

6. Waging the Battle for Restraint and Limitation

When prohibition became the law of the land, most
Southern Baptists undoubtedly thought it was here to stay.
When repeal was enacted, the hope for the restoration of
prohibition came alive in Southern Baptists breasts. As
late as 1944, the Social Service Commission of the Southern
Baptist Convention was confident that the liquor business itself was helping to create a fresh prohibition sentiment. Accordingly, the Commission called on pastors and churches to
strengthen Christian conscience against drinking, and "to
promote the rapidly growing movement to deliver the nation
from this evil. "[58]

It is not possible to say how long prohibition sentiment lasted after repeal. It is perhaps right now the ideal
political strategy for many Southern Baptists. But cultural
and political realities gradually produced a shift of emphasis
in the Southern Baptist strategy. From the earlier hope to
restore prohibition, Southern Baptists shifted to an emphasis
on restraint and limitation. In relation to the liquor business, this approach aims to prohibit and/or limit the sale
and advertisement of alcoholic beverages in as many places
as possible. Places include states, counties, and munici-
palities as well as hotels, recreational and pleasure sites.
In relation to the consumer, restraint and limitation make
alcoholic beverages hard to get and locate.

The strategies for the achievement of restraint and
limitation are essentially the same as those that brought and
sustained prohibition. They of course include the preaching
and teaching work of the church, but a vigorous program of
political and social action is added.

The first aspect of the latter is the effective use of
the ballot. Baptists are urged to support candidates for office who "pledge their vote and influence in the cause of
prohibition, "[59] and "who demonstrate their sincerity and

determination to enforce law and order. "[60]

Once the candidate has reached office, he must encounter lobbyists and recommendations concerning specific
pieces of legislation. These recommendations disclose the
elements which constitute the content of the technique of restraint and limitation. The Baptist Convention of North
Carolina urged the senators and congressmen from that state
to support the Capper Bill, prohibiting the advertising of alcoholic beverages. [61] The Baptist General Association of
Virginia called upon the state legislature to devise a system
"that would prohibit the purchase of alcoholic beverages by
any person convicted twice in one year of menacing public
safety or unbecoming conduct due to the influence of intoxicating beverage. "[62] The Mississippi Baptist Convention recommended to the state legislature the repeal of the Black
Market Liquor Law and the beer and wine law. [63] The editor of The Baptist Courier claimed a victory for Baptists
and The Baptist Courier when the state Department of Parks,
Recreation and Tourism restored signs in the state parks
forbidding the consumption or display in public of any beverage of alcoholic content. [64] The Social Service Commission
of the Southern Baptist Convention offered a series of legal
recommendations to the Convention in 1950. Included among
these were vigilance in relation to law enforcement, the
"enactment of laws which prescribe instruction in public
schools on the effects of alcohol, " keeping alive the local
option question, and the urging of both state and national
representatives "to support such legislation as will regulate,
control and ultimately eliminate the liquor traffic. "[65]

In addition to this distinctively political action, Baptists are urged to and do engage in selective buying, and to
cooperate in the various activities of the Anti-Saloon League
and other temperance groups.

The vigorous program of social action pertaining to
the alcohol question does not mean that Southern Baptists
reduce their use of "spiritual means. " Preaching, teaching,
and prayer are continuously applied to the problem. Almost
all appeals for political action also call for church discipline
--total abstention and dedication within the religious community. The peculiar feature of the Southern Baptist approach to alcohol is their lack of confidence in the sufficiency
of "spiritual means. " In this one case, they demand a sort
of "Christian unity of civilization. " The whole society must
be transformed. And the transformation of the whole society

requires law.   The gospel cannot alone achieve it.

Notes

1. In recent decades, they are the men of power in cities.
    The phrase "Big Boss" does not refer merely to the
    old agrarian South.
2. Barton, A. J., "The Baptist Stand on Prohibition,"
    Religious Herald, CVI (January 19, 1933), p. 4.
3. McDaniel, George W., "Practicing Prohibition," Re-
    ligious Herald, XCV (February 9, 1922), p. 6.
4. Carpenter, L. L., "Should a Christian Indulge in Al-
    coholic Beverages?" (Editorial), Biblical Recorder,
    119 (February 7, 1953), p. 5.
5. Hunter, Wyatt R., "The Liquor Problem as Seen From
    the Bible," The Baptist Record, LXXXV (January
    16, 1964), p. 3.
6. White, W. R., "Public Enemy Number One" in Chris-
    tian Faith in Action, compiled by Foy Valentine
    (Nashville, Broadman Press, 1956), p. 69.
7. Barton, A. J., "The Baptist Stand on Prohibition,"
    Religious Herald, CVI (January 19, 1933), p. 4.
8. Odle, Joe T., "The Bible and Legalized Wine," (Edi-
    torial), The Baptist Record, LXXXIV (May 17, 1962),
    p. 4.
9. Tiffany, Henry W., "The Liquor Traffic: Moral Ene-
    my No, 1," Religious Herald, CXIV (May 29, 1941),
    p. 4.
10. Ibid., p. 24.
11. Ibid.
12. Myers, Donald G., "The High Cost of Drinking," Bibli-
    cal Recorder, 123 (April 6, 1957), p. 3.
13. White, W. R., op. cit., p. 73.
14. Ibid., pp. 71-72.
15. Tiffany, Henry W., "The Liquor Traffic: Biological
    Enemy No. 1," Religious Herald, CXIV (May 15,
    1941), pp. 4-5.
16. Oates, Wayne E., Alcohol In and Out of the Church
    (Nashville, Broadman Press, 1966), p. 6.
17. White, W. R., op. cit., p. 69.
18. This claim was made in 1941.
19. Tiffany, Henry W., "The Liquor Traffic: Economic
    Enemy No. 1," Religious Herald CXIV (May 22,
    1941), p. 4.
20. This is the first year of the period covered by this
    study.   The prohibition struggle began many years

prior to 1917.
21. Barton, A. J., "A Visit to Washington and National
    Prohibition," Baptist Standard, XXIX (July 12, 1917),
    p. 7.
22. Ibid.
23. Report of the Committee on Temperance and Social
    Service of the Southern Baptist Convention, Annual
    of the Southern Baptist Convention (Nashville, 1918),
    pp. 130-131.
24. Ibid., pp. 132-133.
25. Report of the Committee on Temperance and Social
    Service of the Southern Baptist Convention, Annual
    of the Southern Baptist Convention (Nashville, 1920),
    p. 94.
26. Ibid., pp. 94-96.
27. Report of the Commission on Social Service of the
    Southern Baptist Convention, "Additional Legislation
    Needed," Annual of the Southern Baptist Convention
    (Nashville, 1921), pp. 78-79.
28. Crumpton, W. B., "Baptists in Politics," The Alabama
    Baptist, LVII (January 26, 1926), p. 8.
29. Ibid.
30. Barton, A. J., "The Baptist Stand on Prohibition,"
    Religious Herald, CVI (January 19, 1933), p. 4.
31. See Chapter I.
32. Quachita Associational B. Y. P. U. of Polk County, Ark-
    ansas, The Arkansas Baptist, XXXII (May 18, 1933),
    p. 1.
33. "Statement of Arthur James Barton, D. D., LL. D.,
    Chairman, Social Service Commission of the Southern
    Baptist Convention, before the Ways and Means Com-
    mittee of the House of Representatives, Washington,
    D. C., December 14, 1932," Religious Herald, CVI
    (January 12, 1933), p. 4.
34. Ibid.
35. Ibid., p. 5.
36. Ibid.
37. Jones, J. H., "Is Prohibition a Failure?" The Baptist
    Courier, LXIV (October 27, 1932), p. 16.
38. Poteat, W. L., "Thirteen Points," Religious Herald,
    CV (July 14, 1932), p. 3.
39. McDaniel, George W., "Anti-Prohibition Propaganda,"
    Religious Herald, XCIX (April 15, 1926), p. 11.
40. Poteat, op. cit., p. 3.
41. Davis, J. M., "Prohibition not a Failure," The Baptist
    Courier, LVIII (September 15, 1927), p. 11.
42. McDaniel, George W., op. cit., pp. 11, 14.

43. Davis, J. M., op. cit.
44. Report on Temperances, Minutes of the Columbia Baptist Association of Alabama (1933), p. 14.
45. McDaniel, George W., op. cit., p. 14.
46. Gaines, W. W., "The Liquor Traffic," The Christian Index, CXVII (January 7, 1937), pp. 6, 20.
47. Report of the Committee on Social Service, "Drink and the War," Annual of the Mississippi Baptist Convention, (1943), p. 142.
48. Tinnin, Finley W., "Deaths from Drink on Increase" (Editorial), The Baptist Message, LII (March 28, 1935), p. 2.
49. Ibid.
50. Rouse, W. T., "Nine Reasons Why We Are Not Willing to Give the Brewers Another Stranglehold on Our Government," Baptist Standard, XLV (August 10, 1933), p. 6.
51. Ibid.
52. Ibid (August 17, 1933). Rouse gives the first five reasons in an article appearing on August 10, 1933, and the remaining four in an article appearing on August 17, 1933.
53. Murrell, Jesse L., "Why Vote Dry on November 6," Florida Baptist Witness, XLVII (October 18, 1934), p. 5.
54. Ibid.
55. Crumpton, W. B., "Pity the Poor Negro," Alabama Baptist, XLVIII (February 13, 1918), p. 7.
56. Ibid.
57. Ibid.
58. Report of the Social Service Commission of the Southern Baptist Convention, "The Liquor Problem," Annual of the Southern Baptist Convention (Nashville, 1944), pp. 133-134.
59. "Liquor Traffic," Report of the Committee on Social Service and Civic Righteousness, Annual of the Baptist State Convention of North Carolina (November, 1947), p. 39.
60. "Suggested Patterns for Action," Report of the Social Service Commission of the Southern Baptist Convention, Annual of the Southern Baptist Convention (Nashville, 1950), p. 374.
61. "Liquor Traffic," Report of the Committee on Social Service and Civic Righteousness, Annual of the Baptist State Convention of North Carolina (November, 1947), p. 39.
62. "Alcohol," Report of the Social Service Committee,

The Virginia Baptist Annual (November, 1953), p. 88.

63. "Temperance Report, " Report of the Social Service Committee, Annual of the Mississippi Baptist Convention (November, 1946), p. 146.

64. Roberts, John E. , "A Victory - No Beer or Wine in the Parks, " (Editorial) The Baptist Courier, 100 (November 7, 1968), p. 3.

65. "Suggested Patterns for Action, " Report of the Social Service Commission of the Southern Baptist Convention, Annual of the Southern Baptist Convention (Nashville, 1950), pp. 374-375.

Chapter VI

THE FAMILY

In no sphere of institutionalized life has the Christian
religion more profoundly influenced the West than in that of
the family. The moral ideals and judgments of western
civilization are more rigoristic as they bear upon the family
than on any other sphere. While traditional Christianity has
made some concessions to human weakness and has been influenced by culture patterns in this area as well as in others,
the compromises have been less in number and degree. In
the ethic of the family, the churches have maintained a high
degree of consistency in making the New Testament their
starting point. They have not set out to find the best possible compromise; rather they have sought to make human
situations meet the demands of New Testament teaching.
The result has been the formulation of the most demanding
phase of the ethic of the churches. The effectiveness of
this rigorism has been historically evident in the divorce
legislation of some of the states of the United States of
America. Even in dealing with divorce, the greatest problem of the familial ethic for American Christianity, several
of the states have sought to formulate their laws directly
from the Bible.

There are two reasons which perhaps explain why the
churches have stubbornly remained with the New Testament
in the ethic of the family. First, the family is the only major institution which has experienced no basic change in pattern and structure during the Christian era. Prior to the
Christian era, the monogamic family had already crystallized
among the Jews, and had a fair measure of stability among
the Romans. The coming of Christianity gave additional stability to the monogamic family, and this structure has continued until the present almost wholly unchallenged. On the
contrary, Christianity has witnessed a variety of economic
systems--Roman imperialism and slavery, feudalism, capitalism, democratic socialism, fascism and Marxism. Since,
in the case of the family, the basic structure of our time

is much the same as that found in the New Testament period, it is a simple matter to republish New Testament teaching concerning the family.

The second reason why the churches have strongly ad-
hered to New Testament teachings on the family is the fact
that these teachings are more specific in their bearing on
the family than in relation to any other social unit. The
family is unique among the institutions in that the relations
and forces at work within it are largely interpersonal, while
those operating within other institutions are primarily inter-
groupal. The teachings of the New Testament are set forth
in interpersonal terms. This conjunction of the nature of
New Testament teachings and the unique character of the
family results in more specific words of address to the
family than to other institutions.

In their ethic of the family, Southern Baptists are in
harmony with traditional Christianity. Here their claim concerning remaining with the New Testament gains its fullest
justification in the field of institutional ethics. This does
not mean that there are no influences from culture, but adherence to the New Testament is strong and determinant in
most aspects of the ethic.

1. Marriage

The institution of marriage was created by God Himself in paradise. It was given in the period of man's innocence, before sin came. [1] "And the Lord God said, It is
not good that a man should be alone; I will make him an
help meet for him.... Therefore shall a man leave his father
and his mother, and shall cleave unto his wife; and they
shall be one flesh." (Gen. 2:18, 24).

Not only did God create the institution of marriage,
He also brought the first couple together in marriage:[2]
"And the rib, which the Lord God had taken from man, made
he a woman, and brought her unto man." (Gen. 2:22).
Monogamy was thus established by God.

The strong Biblical orientation of Southern Baptists
produces a heavy stress on marriage as an ordinance, but
marriage is also interpreted theologically. Following Karl
Barth, Thomas A. Bland states that the male-female co-
existence of humanity reflects the image of God. "As the

triune God is Being-in-Relation, even so has God projected
this being-in-relation in the male-female constitutive parts
of humanity. "[3] In Christian marriage, this representation
of the unity of God is more than accidental and symbolic.
"There is the dynamic and volitional expression of that
unity. For in Christian marriage man and woman express
in terms of mutuality the unity of those different facets of
the divine nature with which each has been implanted. "[4]

Marriage also completes creation. Since God created
humanity male-female, the creation of humanity remains in-
complete when male and female are separated. Male and
female not only need each other biologically and psychologically, they also need each other ontologically. [5]

As a divinely ordained institution, marriage is a
sacred union. The sacral character of marriage is neither
dependent upon the subjective states of men, nor is it elimi-
nated by their violations of its character. "It is a sacred
union according to the laws of God or according to the will
of God. "[6] "Wherefore they are no more twain, but one
flesh. What therefore God hath joined together, let no man
put asunder. " (Matt. 19:6)

Man is by nature a social creature. Marriage is designed to provide companionship or mutual society. [7] "And
the Lord God said, It is not good that a man should be
alone. " (Gen. 2:18). Thomas A. Bland sees the ordinance
of marriage as "God's remedy for human loneliness. "[8] He
thus introduces, perhaps inadvertently, one of the agonizing
problems of a fallen existence into the creation itself.

In marriage there is a mutual sharing of all things;
it "is a complete union, involving both physical and spiritual
factors. " Husband and wife become "one new life existent
in two persons. " Accordingly, they go about their duties
and activities in community of purpose and concern for one
another's welfare. If complete union is to be experienced
in the life of a particular couple, commitment must be added to consent. [9]

Marriage "is intrusted with the sacred office of parenthood. "[10] The reproduction of offspring is fundamental to
the purpose of marriage. "The creative plan of God is not
complete until new life is born as a result of the one-flesh
union. " The propagation of the race is a divine commandment to all married couples. "Be fruitful and multiply and

replenish the earth. " (Gen. 1:28). Intentional childlessness
is a violation of the divine will. [11]

The connection between marriage and the fall of man
is given only scant attention by Southern Baptist writers.
Amos Clary asserts that the institution of marriage was ordained in the time of man's innocence and given "to repress
irregular affections. " But he does not explain how it was
that irregular affections existed during the period of inno-
cency or what happened to produce them. [12] Thomas A.
Bland, however, sees the fall as "a radically changed situation" in which marriage becomes God's ordinance for the
restraint of sin. [13]

It may appear from what has been said above that
marriage is purely a religious matter, but this is not the
case.   Like other Protestant groups, Southern Baptists recognize the authority of the state over marriage.   In committee
reports adopted by the Southern Baptist Convention several
years apart, two forms of explanation of the relation of the
state to marriage, not thoroughly consistent with each other,
are presented.

In 1918 the Committee on Marriage and Divorce asserted the following:

> The relation itself is both religious and moral.
> With its religious phase the state has nothing to
> do, and if all who enter upon the relation observed
> the law of God governing the relation the state
> would have no need to enact laws concerning it.
> The celebration and regulation of marriage have
> become civil because the state, the organized au-
> thoritative unit of society, has exercised very
> properly its right to legislate concerning the mat-
> ter in the interest of public morality.... [14]

These statements obviously mean that the marriage relation
is in its essential nature religious and moral, and only becomes civil when those who enter it fail to observe the law
of God.   Those who do observe the law of God are, therefore, beyond all state regulation.   Their marriage is in no
sense civil.

In 1932, the Social Service Commission of the Convention approached the issue in quite a different manner:

> Marriage has both a religious and a civil aspect.
> Religiously marriage is simply the union of two
> lives and destinies upon the basis of absolute and
> unquestioning love. The form of ceremony by
> which this union is consummated and made public
> is of small moment, if the union is genuine and
> to be maintained in the fear of God.... Baptists,
> along with all other non-Catholic Christians and
> citizens, freely recognize the authority of the state
> over marriage as a matter related to and involving
> public morality. Marriage then is a civil matter.
> The state has power and authority to say what
> classes of persons shall marry and what shall not.
> This applies to race, age, physical and mental
> health and all matters affecting the peace and hap-
> piness of those who enter the marriage relation,
> their probable offspring and the public. To deny
> or question the right of the state in this matter
> would be to take the position of the Vatican or to
> favor 'common law' marriage. 15

Here the civil nature of marriage is treated as just as essential and original as the religious aspect. Marriage does
not become civil because of failure to observe the law of
God in the relation, it is civil at the outset. All marriages
are civil as well as religious. This view of marriage is
based on a sharp division between private and public morality.
In its private aspect, marriage is religious and an expression
of spiritual quality at the highest possible human level. It
is based on "absolute and unquestioning love." But in its
public aspect, marriage is civil and an expression of the socially accepted morality and conventions.

        Since the family is the most basic social institution,
society must exercise some controls over it including regulations pertaining to marriage. In this respect, marriage
is a social contract. It has the quality of a merely legal
institution. 16 In its civil aspect, marriage can only be a
social contract. But a truly Christian marriage is a union
of male and female under God. It "is both a sacred union
and a social contract. "17

        In dealing with the question of the choice of a mate,
Theodore F. Adams advises that certain qualities be sought
in the mate and cultivated in the self. One should strive to
be a person and find a mate who is a person of Christian
commitment, integrity, consideration and consecration. 18

In addition to community of interests and ideals, C. W.
Scudder stresses good health and equality in age, ability
and education as factors which must be considered in choosing a life companion. [19]

Placing all of the emphasis on marriage between
equals, Amos Clary states that every factor of human life
must be counted in the equation, and he makes no distinction
between matters of character and morality and matters of
convention. Race, social standing, wealth, personal habits,
personal aspirations, etc. should equally be considered.
And no indication is given that the yardsticks for measuring
these various factors may vary. In fact, race, nationality
and culture are hopelessly confused, and the impression is
left that a marriage across racial lines is a great sin since
it is a violation of the fundamental nature of reality.

> It is particularly risky to marry outside one's own
> race. The reason for this is that every nation of
> people possesses certain racial peculiarities. It
> is hard for the people of one nation to understand
> the peculiarities of another and harder to sympa-
> thize with them when they are understood. A dog
> and a cat may live together very beautifully and
> peaceably in the same home until they are tied to-
> gether. Then something happens. Every person
> manifests certain racial dispositions with which the
> members of other races have no patience or toler-
> ance. Think well, think many, many times before
> you marry one of another nationality. [20]

Since there is much theological and ecclesiastical
rigidity among Southern Baptists, the question of mixed religious marriages is heightened. Marriages between Protestants and Catholics are "nothing else than a token of weakened
faith. They manifest great indifference in religious matters.
They evidence religious incongruity."[21] Even marriages between "sincere members of different Protestant groups" are
highly questionable. They bring serious theological and ethical differences into one intimate community. [22] Offering a
summary of "what's wrong with mixed marriages," Roy L.
Johnson states that they produce inequality of yoke-fellowship,
lose the adhesive power of religion, rob the family of a common church home, and "prove to be yokes of bondage un-
pleasant to the victims and unpleasing to God."[23]

Addressing himself to the real situation--the fact that

marriages between Protestants and Catholics do occur and
will continue to occur--Edwin T. Dahlberg presents four
possible decisions which may be made to solve the religious
problem. The spouses may decide to practice nonreligious
neutrality and leave religion out of the home. They may effect a friendly compromise, marrying outside the church,
each leaving the other to his own religious views. They
may be united in the Catholic faith; or the home may be
united in the Protestant faith. The fourth choice--a home
united in the Protestant faith--is the one which a Protestant,
who is staunch in conviction, will and ought to make. He
must make this choice because "the protestant church, particularly in its Baptist expression, is most nearly like the
simple and democratic Christian fellowship of the New Testament believers. "24

The fact that the Roman Catholic Church imposes certain rules and regulations on mixed marriages which favor
Catholicism increases the complications of such marriages. 25
In an editorial, the Biblical Recorder agrees with the Southern Presbyterians that the requirements of the Catholic
Church are "harsh and unfair. "26   The Committee on Relations with Other Religious Bodies of the Southern Baptist
Convention also designates the demands of the Roman Catholics in regard to marriage as unfair and unjust, and concludes its report with the charge that the church substitutes
its authority for that of Christ.

> The requirements of the Roman Catholic Church
> in regard to the pre-nuptial agreement are foreign
> to the spirit of Christianity and are worse than
> physical slavery because they bind the conscience.
> The Lord Jesus Christ, and not the Roman Catho-
> lic Church, is the only Lord and Master of the
> conscience of a Christian. 27

2.   Courtship and Engagement

Since marriage is a sacred thing, the relationships
that are allied to marriage ought to be considered as sacred
as marriage itself. 28   Courtship accordingly should be carefully cultivated, with the note of seriousness running through
it.   Parents ought to be careful about the social environment which they provide for their children. "If they do not
want their children to marry among the Philistines they
must keep them out of Timnath. "29   And the young peo-

ple themselves must be careful in the formation of social
relationships.

Courtship should be "an open-eyed, level-headed,
sensible affair. If love is blind that is no reason that it
should be crazy, too. If love cannot see, it is all the more
important that it have a sound mind."[30] Samson fell in
love with a beautiful girl, but this was not his great mistake.
His tragic mistake was the fact that he fell in love with the
wrong kind of beautiful girl. In choosing a wife, one must
take into account purity and lovingness of heart, not merely
a beautiful face and attractive figure.

"If courtship is a sacred thing, the marriage engagement is far more sacred. An engagement should not be the
product of a mere vacation flirtation or a mere act of sport,
such as is expressed in making two engagements or wearing
two engagement rings at one time.[31] The engagement is "a
period designed to test the satisfaction derived from being
devoted solely to each other... a time for adjustments to be
made in the light of fuller knowledge of each other... a time
for making lifetime plans."[32]

One should know about the mental and physical well-
being and the family background of his prospective spouse.
During the engagement period, all matters pertaining to marriage should be frankly discussed. There should especially
be detailed discussions of money matters, children and
sex.[33] The roads which lead to unhappy marriage lie precisely in these areas. They are sensuality and lust, the
desire for money, and the thoughtless and frivolous marriage
in which the two persons hardly know each other.[34]

It is not possible to state in specific terms how long
an engagement period should last. The length of time varies
with need. If two people have known each other for many
years or almost all their lives, they will in all probability
not need a long engagement. "One year is probably the
ideal length with eighteen months the maximum beyond which
it is seldom advisable to go."[35] Amos Clary believes that
location and environment are important aspects of time exposure, and accordingly makes a plea for the teaching and
practice of the "good orthodox doctrine of love-making":

> ...there must be more of the old-time love-mak-
> ing-in-the-parlor matches. Benches in the park
> and automobile seats are poor places for such

match-making. The latter do not allow sufficient
time in the process. In picture-making those
secured by snapshot are never as satisfactory as
those secured by time exposure. [36]

3. Sex and Birth Control

The union of male and female in marriage is a complete union. It involves the two persons in the totality of
their beings. "Male and female made he them. For this
cause shall a man leave his father and mother, and shall
cleave to his wife; and the two shall become one flesh."
(Mark 10:6b, 7, 8a). The sex factor is God given. [37] It
is entrusted to man as a steward of God. [38] But, unlike
money and property, the sex factor is a part of man's
stewardship from which he can never detach himself. The
"one flesh" principle of sexual relations describes "the in-
terior ontological aspect of sexual union. "[39]

In the mutual self-giving of sexual intercourse, a
genuine knowledge of the self and of the other is conveyed.
The Bible uses the phrase "to know" in referring to the
sexual act to express the communication of personhood that
is involved in coitus. This becoming one flesh by means of
"the mutual surrender of the depth of being" takes place no
matter how detached or commercial the relationship may be.
"There can be no casual, 'natural,' or promiscuous sexual
intercourse without affecting the total person. "[40]

In the life of the faithful, agapeic love takes up human sexual love and transforms it. Under the power of
this self-giving love, the mutuality of self-giving is intensi-
fied and finds expression in "kindness, concern, consideration, and justice. "[41]

The gift of sex is rightly used when it is employed
in accordance with the purposes for which it has been given.
It is a source of pleasure, the means of reproduction, and
an experience of intimate togetherness which gives strength
to marriage. [42] In addition to the fulfillment of purpose,
sexual activity must be exercised according to the nature of
sexuality. The "one flesh" principle is grounded in creation
and "indicates a monogamous pattern of marriage for life. "
"Chastity before and after marriage is the norm of sexual
relations" and "adultery is the violation of the 'one flesh'
unity, the ontological aspect of marriage. "[43]

Chastity and monogamy are also implied by love. Agape motivates the spouses toward monogamy because it drives each toward the full acceptance of the other in the fullness and uniqueness of his being. [44] Emil Brunner affirms that human love itself is in its very essence monistic. [45] Henlee Barnette agrees with this, but the cross-cultural studies of anthropology do not substantiate it.

All sexual deviation from the monogamic ideal is sinful, [46] and this includes the lustful look:

> There is nothing wrong in looking at a woman and admiring her womanly charm, personality, beauty or character, provided it is not allowed to go further or stimulate lust. This is the crime condemned by Jesus, and this teaching should put one on his guard at all times and cause him to bring every desire under control and subordinate it to the living of a pure, clean life in his inner being as well as outwardly.... [47]

Since God made them male and female for companionship and mutual society as well as procreation, the restriction of sexual activity to procreation alone is unjustifiable. Male and female are complementary beings from the hand of God. Their companionship reaches "its climax of completeness and perfection in the sexual union." The Catholic point of view, which makes the sexual union sinful when it does not aim at reproduction "destroys the beauty and joy of sexual union as the highest expression of love and companionship. "[48]

The Pope's ruling on birth control is psychologically wrong in that it generates sexual inhibitions and guilt feelings about sex as an expression of love and companionship; but it is morally wrong in that it often undermines the physical and mental well being of women by encouraging continual and repeated pregnancies. [49]

The use of birth control devices accords with the Divine commission to man to subdue and have dominion over the earth. God willed that man should discover the secrets of the universe through exploration and experimentation. One of these secrets constitutes the devices of birth control. [50]

By the proper application of this secret, planned parenthood can be practiced and the population explosion

controlled. The alternative to such control is the birth of
multitudes of "unwanted, uncared for, undernourished and
underprivileged" children[51] and the starvation of millions of
people in the future. [52] Planned parenthood practices in
Christian conscience may fulfill rather than violate the will
of God. "[53] The decision for or against planned parenthood
properly belongs in every case to the couple involved.

In the thought of Leon Macon, support for the practice of birth control is based on a fundamentalist dispensa-
tionalist interpretation of the Scriptures. Macon contends
that it is morally wrong to bring more children into the
world than can be properly fed, clothed, and educated. In
the early history of mankind, God permitted polygamy to
populate the earth. "We can see no difference in permitting
polygamy to populate the earth and systems of birth control
to restrain over-population. It is the same identical problem, only in the other direction. " Macon concludes that
God's admonition to multiply and replenish the earth has
been met. [54]

4.   Relations in the Home

The home is the community in which the love idealism
of the gospels is lived out most fully. In this respect, it is
the Protestant equivalent of the Catholic monastery. The
family is an intense fellowship which surpasses the structures of "mine" and "thine" and in which self-denying, self-
giving, and other-regarding love is expressed. Its categorical imperative is: "So act that the fellowship of the family
becomes an advance demonstration of the heavenly kingdom. "[55] The Christian home has its foundation in a happy
marriage in which God is feared and Christ is imitated. "[56]

There is of course no such thing as a faultless
spouse. Many things must be endured in marriage and
many concessions made. Every marriage calls for the disposition to bear and forbear, for "no man and no woman
will ever find a mate who has not faults that will need to be
tolerated cheerfully. "[57] But spouses who have the spirit of
Christ can make these adjustments because each has the capacity and the willingness to adapt himself to the other.
The home which has Christ as its center is one in which
the spirit of service overcomes the spirit of being served.
In it, each of the spouses is solicitous of the happiness and
well-being of the other. [58]

The husband is the head of the house. According to the Scriptures, "wives should be subject to their husbands 'in everything,' just as the church is subject to Christ."[59] (Eph. 5:24). But this does not mean autocratic control. It is a "joint partnership" of which the husband is the head.[60] The individuality of the wife is in no way reduced by the arrangement; her submission is in fact voluntary, flowing "from reverent respect for her husband."[61] The submission of the wife is not a demand on the part of the husband; rather, it is a response in accordance with the Divine intent and the wife's basic need. "She was created for just such a life."[62] The place of culture and the nature and shape of the economic apparatus in giving character to the husband-wife relationship is not considered in Southern Baptist literature. It is assumed that woman is fitted by nature to be subordinate in a beneficent patriarchal structure.

The system must be recognized as beneficent because of the demands which the Bible lays on the husband. While the husband, along with his wife, should acknowledge her subordinate place in the home, he should nevertheless honor and show deference to her.[63] He should love her "as Christ loved the church and gave himself up for her." (Eph. 5:25). This is to love her as though she were a part of his own body.[64] (Eph. 5:28).

In the Christian home, the child stands at the center as the object of concern and care. The primary task of the home is the nurture of the child;[65] the twain "become one flesh in reality first and only in the child."[66] The assumption of parenthood means the taking up of very special obligations. Parents owe the child the privilege of being well-born, the right to be well nourished, the right to happy recreation, the discipline of suitable and productive work, and an education "adapted to its physical, mental and religious needs."[67] To meet these needs, parents must themselves be emotionally, socially, and spiritually mature, but they must also work at the business of achieving good family relations.[68] Basic to the well-being of the child are the sense of security and the sense of belonging. When the child is surrounded by love and a clear manifestation that he is wanted, these sentiments are insured. Such a home is characterized by mutual sharing as well as by discipline and authority. Chores, play and recreational activities are shared, and a democratic fellowship is achieved. The democracy of the home is "based upon the principles of discipline, mutual understanding, helpfulness, and shared authority."[69]

In addition to these obligations, parents have religious duties. The home is a religious institution; it is "God's finest and best institution for Christian education and training, " and "a godly parent will pass on to his child his faith in Christ. "[70] J. A. Rucker believes that children will intuitively grow and develop along proper lines if their parents live exemplary Christian lives, but suggests specific religious teachings and practices for the home. Emphasis ought to be placed "on Church and Sunday-school attendance as a means of worshiping God and living closer to Him. " Systematic giving to the Lord must be taught, the family altar established and maintained, and the Catechism brought back into the home. Pictures and literature for the children should be well chosen with a view to building their lives; and parents should exercise authority and keep the young busy doing Kingdom work. [71] Similar suggestions are offered to parents by Henlee Barnette. Parents must cultivate the devotional life in the home, provide direct religious instruction, and interpret the Christian faith by the personal example of their lives. [72]

Children also have obligations to their parents. They must listen to receive the knowledge and wisdom which the parents provide, and "exercise respect and obedience. "[73] Paul Caudill suggests four duties of children to their parents. First, they must "honor" them. To honor parents means to hold them in high esteem. Second, children must "be subject to the counsel of their parents in all things, " trusting the wisdom and understanding which their parents have acquired. (Ephesians 6:1). Third, children should minister to the material needs of their parents. And fourth, they should care for them in old age. When Jesus committed his mother to the care of the beloved disciple, John, He gave all children an example of their duty. [74]

The possibility that responsibility to Christ and responsibility to parents may come into conflict is raised by C. W. Scudder. In Ephesians 6:1, the Apostle Paul admonishes children to obey their parents "in the Lord. " Obedience is evidently set forth in this passage as a Christian responsibility. In agreement with Ray Summers, Scudder concludes that "wherever responsibility to parent and responsibility to Christ would come into vital conflict, it is doubtful that Paul would advise the child to obey the parent. "[75]

5. Divorce

There is unanimity among Southern Baptists that marriage as a gift of God is a permanent union. [76] Wherever
one turns in the Scriptures he finds that "God's original purpose and his ultimate ideal for the home was and is the union of one man and one woman as husband and wife for life."
Since this is the purpose of God for an institution which He
has ordained, "divorce on any grounds involves sin. "[77] The
original divine intent is clearly stated by Jesus when the
Pharisees asked him about the bill of divorcement granted
by Moses. [78] Jesus answered them by saying, "For your
hardness of heart Moses allowed you to divorce your wives,
but from the beginning it was not so. " (Matt. 19:8).

The words which follow this utterance in the Gospel
of Matthew contain the traditional Christian "exception
clause. " "And I say unto you: whoever divorces his wife,
except for unchastity, and marries another, commits adultery. " (Matt. 19:9). The majority of Protestants have accepted the Matthewean exception as the legitimate ground for
divorce; and, even Roman Catholics, who reject divorce,
permit separation from bed and board on account of fornication. Southern Baptists likewise are generally agreed that
the Gospel of Matthew has recorded the exact words of Jesus in offering this one exception. "The only possible exception is mentioned in Matthew 19:9, that is, where one
party to the marriage contract is guilty of unfaithfulness and
has been untrue to the other. "[79]

The fact that Mark 10:11-12 does not include the exception clause is noted by Ray Summers as a complicating
factor in the teaching of Jesus concerning divorce. [80] To
this complicating factor, there is the added fact that Paul
does not give any sanction to divorce. [81]

> Whenever a divorce in marriage is allowed, it is
> permitted, not as a moral right, only as a social
> privilege. (Deut. 1:4). Such privileges are al-
> lowed, not because there is any moral right in
> marriage divorcements, but because of the evil in
> the lives of those who practice such divorcements
> .... (Matt. 19:8). Jesus further taught that 'Who-
> soever shall put away his wife, except for fornica-
> tion, and shall marry another, committeth adultery.'
> (Matt. 19:9)

> 'But unto the married I give charge, yea, not I but
> the Lord, that the wife depart not from the hus-
> band, but should she depart, let her remain un-
> married, or else be reconciled to her husband;
> and that the husband leave not the wife. ' (I Cor.
> 7:10, 11). [82]

Although Clary includes Matthew 19:9 among his Biblical
references, he does not modify his original assertion that
divorce is only a social privilege. And since the words of
Paul concerning departing not from one's spouse are placed
after the Matthewean reference, it seems that Clary is seeking to clinch his argument that there is no moral right to
divorce.

Richard Brannon agrees that "there are no Christian
grounds for divorce" inasmuch as divorce is always less
than the Christian ideal. "But it is a Biblically approved
way out of a bad situation. "[83] Sexual infidelity was not presented by Jesus as the ground for divorce but as an illustration "to teach men that they should not look for easy reasons to divorce. "[84] In some cases involving infidelity, the
parties should remain together; on the other hand, in some
cases of absolute sexual loyalty, the marriage is hopeless.
"Not even God expects people to stay together and destroy
themselves and those around them. "[85]

Theo Whitfield accepts the prevailing view that the
Bible allows divorce for fornication only, but adds that the
Bible permits separation whenever necessary and for many
reasons. For example, a woman is not obliged to live with
a drunkard by God's law or man's. "The Bible says in
such cases that you do not know that you will ever be able
to save him and that you are not bound to him in such a
case. Now it does not command you to leave him, but says
that you may do so. "[86] Whitfield does not offer any Biblical passages to substantiate this interpretation.

Under the provocative title, "The Divorce Question--
New Statement, " E. R. Carswell claims two Scriptural
grounds for divorce. In a quoted statement, he affirms that
the "Divorce Question has never been given a truly Scriptural statement. Failure to do so has been due to the false
assumption 'that our Lord in the Gospels, meant to give,
and in fact, did present the whole question of divorce. ' "[87]
But Jesus did not present the whole question of divorce. He
only answered one question about it. The disciples asked

Him if a man could put away his wife for every cause. Jesus answered that a man can put away his wife for only one
cause--adultery, sexual impurity.

> 'Put-away,' means 'forcible separation.' A man
> can force the separation between himself and his
> lawful wife, only if he can prove her guilty of
> sexual sin.
>
> But, we go over to First Corinthians, seven, and
> we find the opposite question came before Paul for
> settlement: This time it is 'going-away,' voluntary
> abandonment on the part of either party to the mar-
> riage compact. Here the wife is supposed to de-
> part from her husband, in the instance cited, for
> religious cause.
>
> . . . . o . . . . o . . . .
>
> Thus we see that Jesus and Paul gave answers to
> reverse sides of the same problem. Jesus judged
> on the case of 'putting-away,' and Paul on the case
> of 'Going-away.'
>
> In both cases the innocent party is free: in each,
> the guilty party is bound while the other lives.
>
> There are therefore, two Scripture (sic) causes
> for divorce, and not one only--adultery and aban-
> donment. It is easy to see that the principle of
> justice is the same in the two instances. [88]

Concerning the question of the right of divorced persons to marry again, the dominant view among Southern Baptists is that this right belongs to the aggrieved party only.
This is an issue, of course, on which there is no Scriptural
statement. Like other Christians, Southern Baptists are
therefore obliged to reach their conclusion by interpreting
inferences and implications. The writer of the Sunday
School lesson in The Baptist Courier is noncommittal on the
issue, saying, that, in the case of unfaithfulness divorce is
permitted to the aggrieved party, but it is not stated whether
the aggrieved party has the privilege of marrying another.
But he concludes the discussion of the remarriage question
with two statements that seem to cancel each other: "Many
hold that this [the right of the aggrieved party to marry
another] is implied as a logical consequence, but this [un-

faithfulness] is the only possible exception.   Only death sev-
ers the marriage tie. "[89]

Scott L. Tatum believes that Matthew 5 and Matthew
19 imply the permissibility of the remarriage of the innocent
party and that Jewish history validates it.   He also asserts,
in effect, that if Jesus' words, "Whoso marrieth her which
is put away doth commit adultery, " are taken literally, their
true meaning is missed.   Jesus utters these words in a context of thought.   "Inasmuch as Jesus did not recognize divorce except for sexual immorality and assumed that divorce
reflected it, " to marry a divorced woman was to commit
adultery. [90]

If the phrase in Matthew 19:9, "except for fornication,"
modifies both verbs ("put away" and "marry another"), Jesus
is granting the right of remarriage to the innocent party.
There is a strong implication from grammatical construction
that the phrase does modify both verbs. [91]   It is clear in the
thought of Paul that if the spouses are separated "they are
to remain unmarried or be reconciled one to another" (I Cor.
7:10-11). [92]

Clyde L. Breland finds two reasons for supposing that
Jesus would endorse the right of remarriage by the aggrieved
party.   First, it was commonly understood among the Jews
that divorce severed the marriage relationship entirely, and
the right of remarriage followed.   If, then, Jesus had intended to forbid remarriage for the innocent party in the case of
fornication, He would have made the matter explicit.   Second, to grant the right of remarriage to the innocent party
is in harmony with Jesus' spirit.   "Jesus loves His own, He
would not have one of His little ones doomed for the years
ahead to deprivation of the blessings of the matrimonial state
because of an unfaithful spouse. "[93]

6.   Dealing with Marriage and Divorce

Marriage and divorce are both religious and civil
matters.   The improvement of the relationship between
spouses whose marriage has fallen into difficulty, the reduction, and wherever possible, elimination of divorce must
therefore be accomplished by both religious and civil means.

The religious means for dealing with marital difficulties virtually include the whole range of ministry--preaching,

teaching, worship, counseling, and the application of ecclesiastical policy. The Committee on Marriage and Divorce of
the Southern Baptist Convention of 1918 urges the ministers
of the Convention to preach more frequently on the subject
with dignity and solemnity, and to refrain from performing
the rite of marriage for divorced persons "except for the
unoffending when the divorce shall have been granted upon
scriptural grounds. "[94] The policy of remarrying only the
innocent party when a divorce has been obtained on scriptural grounds is supported by O. W. Taylor,[95] but K. Owen
White will perform the marriage rite for no one who has
been divorced.[96] The sure cure for the divorce evil, in
the thought of J. B. Cranfill, is found in the erection of
the family altar. He testifies that he knows of no case of
the filing of a divorce suit by husband or wife in a home in
which there is daily reading of the Scriptures and family
prayer. Cranfill also suggests the return to the large family as a way of diminishing the evil. "Given children to
bless a home and the likelihood of divorce suits is greatly
diminished. ... We need to hark back to the old days when
motherhood was woman's crown and fatherhood was the glory
of man. "[97]

    The approach to divorce and remarriage "on scriptur-
al grounds" is legalism, albeit religious legalism. Southern
Baptists are not unanimous in this definition of ministry.
Proceeding from the conviction that divorce on any grounds
is sin, T. B. Maston places the reconstitution of life after
divorce under grace and the forgiveness of sins.[98] He thus
implies a pastoral rather than a legalistic approach to the
subject of remarriage. The same outlook is espoused by
W. Y. Henderson, who rejects the idea that there is no
pardon or forgiveness for those who have remarried after
divorce unless they separate from the new spouses and that
such persons should be kept outside the church. Divorced
persons should be granted church membership "on the
grounds that they themselves would renounce and repudiate
divorce as a violation of God's ideal of the marriage relationship. And further that they renounce all past double relationships and repent and give their sanction to the Christian
standards of moral and social purity. " This process, Henderson asserts, would bring the divorced persons up to the
norms of the church rather than having the church descend
to their level, and would be far more desirable than that of
treating the whole class of divorced persons as beyond the
reach of mercy and forgiveness.[99]

The plea for state action in dealing with marriage
and divorce is for stricter and better guarded marriage and
divorce laws and for uniformity in the laws.   Southern Baptists believe that federal action will eventually be required
to bring about uniformity, but fear federal action for the
reason that federal control of marriage and divorce may
also bring about the intermarriage of the races.   In its
1932 report, the Social Service Commission of the Southern
Baptist Convention sought to dispel this fear.   It is perfectly
safe to assume, t he Commission states, that interracial marriage will be prohibited, so the constituency may continue to
strive for uniformity in the laws regulating marriage and divorce "even if it requires some forms of federal action."[100]

In the matter of marriage and divorce regulations, as
already seen in the case of prohibition regulations, Southern
Baptists believe that their duty as a Christian group is more
than the preaching of the gospel.   Their responsibility is not
merely to educate and create the right attitudes but also to
secure proper enactments.   Moreover, they feel called upon
and qualified to present the specific terms of the enactments.
The following recommendations were included in the report
of the Committee on Temperance and Social Service adopted
by the Southern Baptist Convention in 1920.

> 1.   The enactment of a uniform code on the sub-
> ject of marriage and divorce by the several States
> which shall be carefully prepared so as to safe-
> guard the health and morals of the people and the
> sanctity and permanency of the home.

> 2.   That touching marriage this code should pro-
> hibit the marriage of males under 21 and females
> under 18 without the consent of parents or guardi-
> an, with a reasonable prohibition as to age with
> parental consent.

> 3.   That such code should require not only the
> securing of a license, but also the publishing of
> the bans for at least 30 days before the rite can
> be celebrated.

> 4.   That such a code should require a physical ex-
> amination of each party by a regularly authorized
> physician, who shall give certificate of health,
> with the provision that those afflicted with infectious
> disease or other maladies disqualifying them for

marriage and threatening the health, happiness and usefulness of offspring shall be prohibited from marrying.

5. That as nearly as possible this code should come to the basis of Bible teaching concerning the ground of divorce with the right of remarriage and that in all other cases when divorces be granted it be without the right of remarriage. [101]

7. Woman

The Southern Baptist familial ethic contains a strong patriarchal strain, as seen in the discussion of the relation between the spouses. Appeal is made to Paul as the New Testament justification for this train; but the influence of a period of slavery and feudalism is undoubtedly also at work.

In his attack on the feminist movement, J. W. Porter suggests: "God created us male and female, and the determined effort to abolish sex distinction bodes no good for the present and less for the future." Woman has a distinct sphere, no less limited or honored than that of man. "The fact of motherhood sanctifies her existence and magnifies her mission." The ideal woman will be content with her God-given destiny. [102] Porter declares that he does not believe in the equal rights of woman, but in her superior rights. To illustrate "superior rights" he points to various acts of chivalry which are appropriately exercised on her behalf. Finally, he demonstrates the impact of Southern culture upon his attitude toward woman by attacking the feminist movement as antithetical to the southern social system:

> The truth is, and we may as well speak it, this contention about equal rights for women is a by-product of a civilization that is antithetic to the genius of our Southern social system. Susan B. Anthony, one of the leading advocates of the sexless woman, was also an ardent advocate of the social equality of the races.

> In view of the fact that several of the early agitators of woman's rights were committed to the equality of the races, it might be well for some of the present leaders of the movement to make a deliverance on this subject.... "[103]

The feminist movement is also repudiated by W. O.
Carver on the ground that the movement has been untempered
by Christian ideals, motives, and aims, and is lacking in an
essentially Christian method. Jesus and the early church
did not encourage the oppressed and suppressed elements of
society to go forth crusading for their rights. "Christianity
calls upon its followers to serve, not to assert themselves;
to proclaim God's grace for all, and themselves ever bear-
ers of blessings to others. " It is through the demonstration
of efficiency in service that woman's freedom of action within Christianity has been achieved. 104   (Carver does not discuss woman's opportunities and responsibilities outside of
Christianity).

Taking his stand on the proposition that God did not
intend for man and woman to be equal in all things, W. I.
Hargis opposes political suffrage for women. He finds Biblical authority for his political conclusion in Genesis, I Timothy, and Paul:

> Did God in the beginning intend that man and
> woman should be equal in all things? If so why
> did He say to the woman thy desire shall be to
> thy husband and he shall rule over thee. Gen.
> 3:16. In I Tim. 2:12-14. 'I suffer not a woman
> to usurp authority over the man. ' Then the rea-
> son follows: 'For Adam was first formed, then
> Eve. And Adam was not deceived, but the woman
> being deceived was in the transgression. ' And
> again in another place Paul says, in speaking of
> Christ and the church: 'For the husband is the
> head of the wife, even as Christ is the head of
> the church. Therefore as the church is subject
> unto Christ, so let the wives be to their husbands
> in every thing. ' Does this sound like God intended
> that man and woman should be on a parity in every-
> thing, civil, religious, social and everything else?
> Then follows an admonition to husbands: 'Husbands
> love your wives, even as Christ also loves the
> church and gave himself for it. ... 105

Hargis concludes that woman's two greatest missions are to
bear children and make a home, and the emergence of political suffrage for women is a menace to homes. Disintegration already characterizes American homes in which mothers
are too busy about other things to look after the home in a
proper manner; and with the additional rights, duties and

ambitions brought by woman suffrage, further disintegration is inevitable. [106]

Mrs. C. L. Billington agrees that woman suffrage laws are contrary to God's laws. When women go beyond building homes and mothering children, for which they have the greatest wisdom, they are overstepping the authority which God gave them. [107]

Livingston Johnson opposes woman suffrage in principle, but advises that it is woman's moral obligation to vote if given the ballot. [108]

Southern Baptists are not unanimous in restricting women to the home. A modified endorsement to woman's going beyond the home is provided by J. J. Wicker. The endorsement is modified inasmuch as the specified outside-the-home activities are all forms of Christian service.

> Of course the home is the throne of the woman, but it never was meant for a woman to wear herself out on the throne. She is capable and deserves to carry her queenliness outside the home, and thank God for all the missionary, philanthropic, charitable and other enterprises she is carrying on. [109]

A. T. Robertson makes a complete break with the idea of subordinating woman and restricting her to the home. He accepts the fact that woman is winning her freedom, declares that she will get the ballot because she is entitled to it, and that the forces of evil have made the chief fight against her suffrage. [110] In agreement with Henry C. Vedder's The Gospel of Jesus and the Problems of Democracy, Robertson denounces the double standard in wages, and calls on the men of America to ponder American treatment of women. "Ponder it well men of America. We are the most backward country on earth that pretends to the possession of a Christian civilization, in the protection of womanhood. "[111]

The question which arises from this discussion of woman's place is whether her subordination means inferiority of person. J. W. Porter responds with a clear "no." Woman was created for man and made subject to him, but this does not mean inferiority. In many respects, woman is superior to man; her place in the world is "not a whit less

important" than man's. [112] "Even more than man, her hand
is potent in moulding the character of man.... It is the
mission of woman to fashion the world, but not rule it.
With her heart, more than her hands, she is to shape the
lives of her loved ones. "[113] Porter evidently intends to say
that God has made woman subordinate to man, but her subordination does not mean that her historical role is less important or that she is essentially inferior. It does not seem
to occur to Porter that to say that woman is created for man
is to ascribe an end-quality to man which woman cannot enjoy for the very reason that her essence is a means-quality.
Contemporary evangelical theology for the most part understands the passage, "Male and female he created them, " to
refer to mutual society.

The question of woman's subordination to man often
takes another form in Southern Baptist thought. It is discussed under the heading of whether a woman should speak
in mixed assemblies. P. J. Lipsey ably summarizes the
prevailing Southern Baptist position in an article opposing
the view taken by E. B. Pollard of the Crozer Theological
Seminary. Lipsey contends that Paul explicitly forbids wom-
en's speaking in mixed assemblies: "Let your women keep
silence in the churches: for it is not permitted unto them
to speak; but they are commanded to be under obedience, as
also saith the law. And if they will learn anything let them
ask their husbands at home: for it is a shame for women
to speak in the church" (I Cor. 14:34-35). This prohibition,
says Lipsey, was not a mere temporary expedient, as the
advocates of the freedom of women to speak in public assemblies claim.

Furthermore, Dr. Pollard is incorrect in his interpretation of the statement from Paul--"There is neither Jew
nor Greek, there is neither bond nor free, there is neither
male nor female: for ye are all one in Christ Jesus. " Pollard understands this as a "statement of a general principle
which was intended eventually to wipe out all temporary re-
strictions and distinctions. " This is a serious error. On
this passage, Paul is speaking of the way of salvation; he
is saying that there is but one way, and that way is applicable to all alike. [114]

Paul had several reasons for giving this prohibition.
First, man was created before woman. Second, woman was
the first to sin. Third, because of the law which cannot be
broken as expressed in I Cor. 14:34. Fourth, because the

"prohibition was not local but universal--'As in all churches
of the saints, let your women keep silence in the churches. '
(I Cor. 14:33, 34 Rev. Version). "[115]

In a reproduction of a commentary on the subject of
women speaking in mixed assemblies by John A. Broadus,
the Western Recorder presents an additional reason why they
should not. It is that Paul prohibits woman's speaking in
mixed assemblies because she is thus undertaking to "teach"
men and "have dominion" over them. On the contrary, she
should be "subjected" to man. While the Bible does not
teach the precise nature and exact limits of this subjection,
it does teach subjection. [116]

A modified version of the right of women to speak in
public is presented by Z. T. Cody. He asserts that the
Scriptures do not have in mind "mixed assemblies" and "before man, " but the church of God. "The Apostle's instruction concerning women is wholly in the interest of preserving
or setting forth this ideal of government" (that of God's family). The Apostle is "dealing with the formal governmental
meetings of the church of God, in which high ideals are to
be observed in what can be called ritual conduct. " His admonitions do not refer to any other meetings. [117]

Even this modification is not enough for Amos Clary.
He rejects completely the view that women should be silent
in church, and even affirms their right to preach. It is a
masculine superiority complex crystallized in social custom
which denies Christian women freedom of speech and activity. The view that woman is inferior is an oriental opinion
and a fiction of the masculine mind. Actually, she possesses
no handicap so far as preaching is concerned which man does
not also possess. [118]

The patriarchal strain in the Southern Baptist ethic of
the family is strongly influenced by cultural patterns and beliefs. These influencing patterns and beliefs are those of a
bygone day and exist alongside democratic cultural elements
with which they are incongruous. The result is, many of
the same people who talk about woman's staying in her place
--in the home--also proclaim equality of opportunity for all
people, and support college, university, and at least some
professional education for women.

Notes

1. "Concerning Marriage and Divorce," Report of the
     Committee on Marriage and Divorce, Annual of the
     Southern Baptist Convention (Nashville, 1918), p.
     107.
2. Caudill, Paul, "The Christian View of Marriage," The
     Christian Index, CXXII (October 28, 1942), p. 22.
3. Bland, Thomas A., "Toward a Theology of Marriage,"
     The Review and Expositor, LXI (Spring, 1964), p. 7.
4. Cale, Franklin, "Christian Marriage - An Interpreta-
     tion," Religious Herald, CXXX (August 1, 1957),
     p. 8.
5. Scudder, C. W., The Family in Christian Perspective,
     (Nashville, Broadman Press, 1962), p. 30.
6. Ibid., p. 23.
7. Caudill, op. cit., p. 22.
8. Bland, op. cit.
9. Scudder, op. cit., pp. 24-25.
10. Caudill, op. cit.
11. Scudder, op. cit., p. 32.
12. Clary, Amos, "Marriage I," Religious Herald, CIV
     (July 16, 1931), p. 6.
13. Bland, op. cit., p. 8.
14. "Concerning Marriage and Divorce," Report of the Com-
     mittee on Marriage and Divorce, Annual of the South-
     ern Baptist Convention (Nashville, 1918), p. 107.
15. "Marriage and Divorce," Report of the Social Service
     Commission of the Southern Baptist Convention, An-
     nual of the Southern Baptist Convention (Nashville,
     1932), pp. 92-93.
16. Scudder, op. cit., p. 28.
17. Ibid., p. 29.
18. Adams, Theodore F., "Christian Love and Marriage"
     in Christian Faith in Action, compiled by Foy Valen-
     tine (Nashville, Broadman Press, 1956), pp. 54-55.
19. Scudder, op. cit., pp. 54-55.
20. Clary, Amos, "Marriage II," Religious Herald CIV
     (July 23, 1931), p. 3.
21. Morse, W. H., "Mixed Marriages," Religious Herald
     XCIV (August 4, 1921), pp. 6-7.
22. Scudder, op. cit., pp. 55-56.
23. Johnson, Roy L., "Mixed Marriages... Unequal Yokes,"
     Baptist Standard, 60 (April 1, 1948), p. 7.
24. Dahlberg, Edwin T., "Marriage and the Home," The
     Arkansas Baptist, XXXIII (May 17, 1934), p. 7.
25. Reference is being made to pre-nuptial instructions

and the performance of the marriage ceremony by the priest, the requirement of the promise that children will be reared in the Catholic Church and the promise that they will attend parochial schools.

26. Carpenter, L. L. "Southern Presbyterians Condemn Mixed Marriages" (Editorial), Biblical Recorder, 112 (May 22, 1946), p. 3.

27. "Mixed Marriage," Report of the Committee on Relations with other Religious Bodies, Annual of the Southern Baptist Convention (Nashville, 1952), pp. 461-462.

28. Clary, Amos, "Marriage I," Religious Herald, CIV (July 16, 1931), p. 6.

29. Ibid.

30. Ibid.

31. Ibid., p. 15.

32. Scudder, op. cit., p. 57.

33. Adams, op. cit., p. 56.

34. Mullins, E. Y., "The Cause of Happy and Unhappy Marriages," The Christian Index, CI (August 25, 1921), p. 3.

35. Scudder, op. cit., p. 58.

36. Clary, Amos, "Marriage III," Religious Herald CIV (July 30, 1931), p. 12.

37. Denham, W. E., "Sex Education and the Church," Review and Expositor, LXX (November 17, 1938), p. 10.

38. Noffsinger, J. R., "The Christian View of Sex" in Christian Faith in Action, compiled by Foy Valentine, (Nashville, Broadman Press, 1956), pp. 40-42.

39. Barnette, Henlee H., The New Theology and Morality (Philadelphia, The Westminster Press, 1967), p. 65.

40. Ibid., pp. 66-67.

41. Ibid., p. 67.

42. Elder, Lyn, "The Sanctity of Sex," Baptist Training Union Magazine, XXXI (June, 1956), p. 12.

43. Barnette, op. cit., p. 68.

44. Ibid., p. 69.

45. Brunner, Emil, The Divine Imperative (New York, The Macmillan Company, 1942), p. 347.

46. Odle, Joe T., "The Sex Revolution," (Editorial), The Baptist Record, XC (July 24, 1969), p. 4.

47. "The Sacredness of the Home," Sunday School Lesson, The Baptist Courier, LXX (November 17, 1938), p. 10.

48. Cowling, Dale, "The Pope is Wrong, " Arkansas Baptist, 67, (August 8, 1968), p. 5.
49. Ibid.
50. Ibid.
51. "Planned Parenthood, " Report of the Christian Life Commission, The Baptist General Convention of Texas, Texas Baptist Annual, 1968, p. 105.
52. Lester, James A., "The Papal Ban on Birth Control (Editorial) Baptist and Reflector, 135 (February 6, 1969), p. 6.
53. "Planned Parenthood, " Texas Baptist Annual, 1968, p. 106.
54. Macon, Leon, "Birth Control" (Editorial), The Alabama Baptist, 125 (January 7, 1960), p. 3.
55. Scudder, op. cit., p. 91.
56. Mullins, E. Y., "The Cause of Happy and Unhappy Marriage, " The Christian Index, CI (August 25, 1921), p. 3.
57. Ibid.
58. Ibid.
59. Scudder, op. cit., p. 93.
60. Hill, John L., "Family Life in Christian Homes, " Baptist and Reflector, 116 (May 11, 1950), p. 4.
61. Scudder, Ibid.
62. Ibid., pp. 94-95.
63. Ibid., pp. 96-97.
64. Ibid., pp. 97-98.
65. Dawson, J. M., "Calm Talks on Home Building--The Child in the Midst, " Baptist Standard, XXXVIII (January 28, 1926), p. 12
66. Poteat, Edwin M., "Thine Only Son" or "The Steward-ship of Family Life, " The Baptist Courier, L (October 16, 1919), p. 1.
67. Dawson, J. M., op. cit.
68. Barnette, H. Henley, "Strengthening Family Foundations, " Arkansas Baptist, 56 (March 7, 1957), p. 8.
69. Ibid.
70. White, J. R., The Role of the Home in Christian Education, " The Alabama Baptist, 133 (July 4, 1968), p. 14.
71. Rucker, J. A., The Christian Home, " Religious Herald, CVI (September 7, 1933), p. 18.
72. Barnette, Henlee, op. cit., p. 9.
73. White, J. R., op. cit.
74. Caudill, Paul, "Honoring Our Parents, " The Christian Index, CXXIII (October 14, 1943), p. 22.
75. Scudder, C. W., op. cit., p. 101.

76. Sunday School Lesson, "The Sacredness of the Home, "
    The Baptist Courier, LXX (November 17, 1938),
    p. 10.
77. Maston, T. B., "Divorce and Sin, " Baptist and Reflec-
    tor, 135 (February 20, 1969), p. 3.
78. Scudder, C. W., op. cit., p. 42.
79. Sunday School Lesson, "The Sacredness of the Home, "
    The Baptist Courier, LXX (November 17, 1938),
    p. 10.
80. Summers, Ray, "Marriage and Divorce According to
    Jesus, " Baptist Standard, 60 (October 28, 1948),
    p. 12.
81. Summers, Ray, "Marriage and Divorce According to
    Paul, " Baptist Standard, 60 (November 4, 1948),
    p. 6.
82. Clary, Amos, "Marriage III, " Religious Herald CIV
    (July 30, 1931), p. 12.
83. Brannon, Richard, "Marriage and Divorce, " The Bap-
    tist Courier, 100 (July 11, 1968), p. 9.
84. Ibid., p. 8.
85. Ibid., p. 9.
86. Whitfield, Theo, "A Sermon on Marriage, " The Baptist
    Record, XXIII (June 16, 1921), p. 6.
87. Carswell, E. R., "The Divorce Question - New State-
    ment, " The Baptist Courier, LIX (March 22, 1928),
    p. 9.
88. Ibid.
89. Sunday School Lesson, "The Sacredness of the Home, "
    The Baptist Courier, LXX (November 17, 1938),
    p. 10.
90. Tatum, Scott L., "The Christian Attitude Toward Di-
    vorce" in Christian Faith in Action, compiled by
    Foy Valentine (Nashville, Broadman Press, 1956),
    p. 66.
91. Summers, Ray, "Marriage and Divorce According to
    Jesus, " Baptist Standard, 60 (October 28, 1948),
    p. 12.
92. Summers, Ray, "Marriage and Divorce According to
    Paul, " Baptist Standard, 60 (November 4, 1948),
    p. 6.
93. Breland, Clyde L., "Shall a Minister Marry Divorced
    Persons?" Western Recorder, CXIV (February 1,
    1940), p. 4.
94. Report of the Committee on Marriage and Divorce,
    "Concerning Marriage and Divorce, " Annual of the
    Southern Baptist Convention (Nashville, 1918), p.
    108.

95. Taylor, O. W., "The Marriage of Divorced People" (Editorial), Baptist and Reflector, 116 (July 27, 1950), p. 2.
96. White, K. Owen, "What Christ Said About Divorce and Remarriage," Arkansas Baptist, 52 (April 2, 1953), p. 16.
97. Cranfill, J. B., "Dr. J. B. Cranfill's Chronicle," Religious Herald, XCIII (August 26, 1920), p. 11.
98. Maston, T. B., op. cit. See also Scott L. Tatum, op. cit., pp. 66, 67.
99. Henderson, W. Y., "The Churches and the Divorce Evil," The Baptist Courier, LXIV (October 27, 1932), p. 6.
100. "Marriage and Divorce," Report of the Social Service Commission of the Southern Baptist Convention, Annual of the Southern Baptist Convention (Nashville, 1932), p. 92.
101. "Marriage and Divorce," Report of the Committee on Temperance and Social Service of the Southern Baptist Convention, Religious Herald, XCIII (May 27, 1920), p. 16.
102. Porter, J. W., "No Sex, No Shirks, No Simpletons in Citizenship" (Editorial) Western Recorder, XCII (February 14, 1918), p. 8.
103. Ibid.
104. Carver, W. O., "Christ's Gift to Women and His Gift of Women to the Human Race," Review and Expositor, XXXVIII (July, 1941), pp. 254, 255, 258, 259.
105. Hargis, W. I., "Woman Suffrage," The Baptist Record, XXIV (August 10, 1922), p. 6.
106. Ibid.
107. Billington, C. L. (Mrs.), "Woman's Place," Western Recorder, CXVIII (October 12, 1944), p. 4.
108. Johnson, Livingston, "Must Women Vote?" Biblical Recorder, LXXXV (March 31, 1920), p. 7.
109. Wicker, J. J., "Chips - Women," Religious Herald, CXI (July 7, 1938), p. 5.
110. Robertson, A. T., The New Citizenship (New York, Fleming H. Revell and Company, 1919), p. 73.
111. Ibid., pp. 74-75.
112. Porter, J. W., "What is Woman? (Editorial), Western Recorder, 94th year (January 30, 1919), p. 8.
113. Ibid.
114. Lipsey, P. I., "More About Women" (Editorial), The Baptist Record, XX (May 16, 1918), p. 4.
115. Ibid., p. 5.

116. Broadus, John A., "Should Women Speak in Mixed Pub-
      lic Assemblies," Western Recorder, 93rd Year
      (March 21, 1918), p. 6.
117. Cody, Z. T., "Women in the Church (Editorial), The
      Baptist Courier, LXI (June 27, 1929), p. 2.
118. Clary, Amos, "Why Should Not Women Preach?" The
      Baptist Courier, LXIII (January 30, 1930), pp. 7,
      19.

Chapter VII

THE ECONOMIC ORDER

The Southern Baptist economic ethic is largely a product of the puritan tradition, as it found expression in the United States. Its main features are the essential puritan and Calvinistic elements, such as the duty and ascetic character of labor, the trusteeship of property, the connection between prosperity and righteousness, the teaching concerning class and calling, and the duty of generosity.

In the southern context, this puritan ethic has been modified by and accommodated to an agrarian civilization. The cultural influence is evident in the following ways: First, it is seen in the large amount of concern given to the duties of laborers and, to a less extent, to their rights and needs, as against a small amount of concern for the duties of employers. Second, it appears in a generally conservative attitude toward the existing economic conditions. Third, there has been an incredible insensitivity to the great agrarian problems of the South, even during the decades when they were most grievous and most publicized. [1]

1. Viewing the General Situation

In the 1930's, when the capitalistic system in America was being widely criticized in both religious and secular circles, the prevailing notion among Southern Baptists was that by and large all is well on the American economic front. The system was praised for having produced the most prosperous civilization in the world; and, despite the awful conditions of the depression years and some admitted abuses, it was hailed for having made prosperity more widespread and the common man better off than in any other country. By the test of history American economic practice was said to be the best. Therefore, the correction of whatever abuses had arisen lay in a continued affirmation of the American economic ways of doing things.

182

In its report of 1938, the Social Service Commission
of the Southern Baptist Convention denied that we live under
a "capitalistic" system in America. The Commission called
it, instead, "a system of Constitutional freedom, providing
for individual and personal initiative and prowess, " and proceeded to sing its praises:

> We are grateful for the material prosperity of our
> nation, which has resulted in the accumulation of
> large fortunes, both individual and corporate.
> While there are great fortunes accumulated it is
> equally true that by and through such accumulation
> labor finds its best and most remunerative employ-
> ment. It is equally true that we have a greater
> distribution of wealth than any other nation, and
> that the so-called 'average man' is better situated
> and has a better income and a more adequate liv-
> ing than in any other nation in the world.
>
> We are not contending or even suggesting that
> there have not been abuses or that there are not
> now abuses. We are not even hinting that there
> is no poverty, no unemployment, no bad housing
> conditions, indeed there are such, but the facts
> are as stated and whenever and wherever conditions
> are not what they should be they are to be cor-
> rected and improved in the American way and
> within the letter and spirit of American free-
> dom.... [2]

In an article on "Labor and Capital, " the obvious
purpose of which is to advise labor to be Christian, efficient,
and avoid agitators, John J. Wicker describes present social
and economic conditions in terms that border on utopianism:

> Labor and capital ought to be in closer relation to-
> day than ever before. They should understand each
> other better. All men everywhere of every caste,
> class and color enjoy the best day in history.
> There are more material comforts for the rich
> and poor than ever before. There are better edu-
> cational advantages than in any period in history.
> Social recognition has a better basis--a man is a
> man, if he is a man.... The hand of capital was
> never so generous. The heart of the rich was
> never so tender. The brotherhood of man was
> never so real. Men are giving, yes, giving with-

out thought of return, millions of dollars just for
the joy of giving and the good of society. The
meaning of life is better interpreted than at any
previous period.

There have been days when the world resented the
ambition of the poor. Today wealth welcomes ambition on the part of any man. Any young man
who wants to be something will find not only open
doors, but helping hands and smiling faces. The
rich men of this country are hunting for poor boys
with ambition and ability. A capitalist would rather meet such a boy than to stand before kings.

What has brought this condition in our country?
Christ and the Church. Christianity is the father
of all. The Carpenter of Nazareth is coming into
His own.... [3]

Giving his attention to the North Carolina industrial
situation, J. S. Farmer states that until recently cotton mill
workers have been contented with the really good wage of the
cotton mills, and strikes among them were almost unknown.
He attributes the General Textile Strike of 1934 to unassimi-
lated foreign elements in the American population and accuses
northern cotton mill owners of welcoming it. [4]

In suggesting that it would not be advantageous for
southern cotton mill workers to join the C. I. O., Farmer
states that "nearly all the cotton mills in the South are already paying as high wages as they can afford to pay if they
are to compete for the sale of their production in the mar-
kets of the world."[5] Since laborers and owners alike understand this, it is hardly probable that laborers will demand
such high wages as to injure the sales possibilities of their
products. "In our North Carolina mills, mill owners and
laborers are on the best of terms and working in harmony
with one another."[6]

Even during the 1920's and 1930's, some Southern
Baptists were dissenters from the prevailing point of view
which praised and even glorified the existing economic order.
Pointing to the great wealth of production on the one hand
and poverty on the other, J. Elwood Welsh calls the present
arrangement of the social order anti-Christian and pagan.
He infers that the Southern Baptist Convention has nothing
to say to the situation since, in the last meeting of the Con-

vention, "this whole matter was rudely, discourteously, un-
baptistically, and in a most unchristian manner shelved without the semblance of a serious consideration. "[7] Capitalism,
says Welsh, is selfish and unchristian. The root difficulty
of our economic troubles is the profit motive, for which Jesus would have us substitute the service motive. The existence of slum areas under the shadow of towering Baptist
Churches, and of pellegra-ridden workers who labor for
those who live in comfort and luxury, constitute "an indict-
ment of the church and its interpretation of Christianity for
this generation. "[8]

Speaking in terms similar to those of Welsh, Amos
Clary says that the man who produces wants more of the
necessities, and some of the comforts and luxuries for himself and his family.

> He has seen capital enjoying those things even to
> surfeiting. But when he asked for more bread
> capital gave him a stone. When he asked for a
> fish he was given a serpent. When he asked for
> a better home and a little more time to spend in
> his home with his family he was sent away to
> make bricks without straw. He was denied even
> the crumbs that fall from capital's table. All
> these things happened before the days of unionized
> labor. Now labor demands the right to carry the
> keys to the storehouse, or some of the keys at
> least. He demands it in the interest of his home. [9]

In a minority report of the Social Service Committee
of the North Carolina Baptist Convention made in 1935, the
competitive economic order is condemned as the root of the
war system. Only two members of the Committee, E. Mc.
Niell Poteat and L. E. M. Freeman, signed this report.
The other five members felt that they could not conscientious-
ly sign it. [10]

The industrial strife which immediately followed
World War II evoked responses from Southern Baptists that
were quite different from those of the preceding decades.
As we have seen, during the previous period the interpretations of the economic scene were in the main accommodation-
ist; but since World War II they have been prevailingly critical.

From the perspective of an overview of the relationship of Christianity to all of the major economic systems,

E. Earl Joiner rejects the notion of a completely Christian
economic system and the identification of Christianity with
any system. All economic life, even in its most favorable
manifestations, "is dominated too largely by a pagan, grasp-
ing, jungle philosophy of life." Christianity is true to its
essence when Christians are obedient to the Divine sovereignty. Christian ideals accordingly transcend all historic
programs--political, economic or cultural--but must be in-
jected into them. [11]

Speaking directly to the manner of operation of the
capitalistic economy, the Social Service Commission of the
Southern Baptist Convention criticizes the system as being
too exclusively management and investor conscious. Full
recognition must be given to "the part played in industry
and the equity rightfully claimed by the producer, laborer
and the consumer." The Commission also reminds the organizers and managers of labor that they, too, in claiming
their rights, must recognize the rightful claims of all other
parties in the economic enterprise. [12]

The Social Service Commission of the Alabama Baptist Convention designated the labor situation of 1945 as dangerous to peace and economic stability. Pointing to the fact
that both labor and capital made substantial economic gains
during the war, the Commission concludes that the present
pressures and conflicts between them "seem to justify compulsory arbitration, through a fair, just, and unpolitical
commission appointed by the government for the purpose of
keeping the peace and administering justice and equity to
both parties to the existing contention and strife. "[13]

In its report of 1946, the Committee on Social Service of the Baptist Convention of South Carolina reflected on
the Convention's own uncritical past by saying, "We should
no longer welcome the efforts of Chambers of Commerce to
get imported industries with the offer of cheap labor which
will not organize. "[14] In 1948, the Committee expressed
satisfaction in the progress that had been made in American
industrial life toward implementing the principle of mutual
concern. But the Committee also recognized the significance
of the coercive power of legislation and the pressure of organized labor in bringing about the better day. [15] The great
need for the future is the intensification of mutual concern
on the part of both capital and labor and their recognition of
their mutual responsibility to the public. [16]

2. Property

The Southern Baptist doctrine of property is the traditional Christian understanding of stewardship. A human property owner is a trustee who has been put in charge of a portion of God's property. Ownership belongs to God only. "The earth is the Lord's and the fulness thereof, the world and they that dwell therein. " (Psalms 24:1). The ground of human possession of property is the dominion over the earth which God bestowed upon man in the creation. Accordingly "no man is qualified to hold property according to the Christian idea unless he accepts it as a trust from God." It may be said "that the basis of property in the Christian conception is Sonship to God. And there is no other basis for it. "[17]

T. Clagett Skinner is convinced that the basis of property lies in human creatureliness, whether sonship is recognized or not. "Proprietorship does not depend upon confession. God's property rights in us and in the things committed to our care do not depend upon our acknowledgement or consent. They are his, not by human consent, but by right of creation.... Confession is only the recognition of divine property rights in human personality. "[18] Every man then is a steward of God; but when one becomes a spiritual son as well as a creature, he enters consciously and joyously unto the service of God.

James A. Stewart also finds the basis of property in the Divine Creative Act, but in agreement with Emil Brunner in his Justice and the Social Order, places the emphasis upon the nature of the creature as a free, responsible being. "In the divine order of things man has a right to his own life, to freedom. " The liberty which is inherent to personal being cannot be expressed without some private property because being free involves having something at one's own disposal. [19]

The ground of private property is Divine law according to Ray Summers[20] and B. H. Duncan. [21] Summers calls Exodus 20:15, "Thou shalt not steal, " God's basic law; but Duncan adds to it Exodus 20:17, "Thou shalt not covet. " The interpretation that is given to Exodus 20:15 makes it a double affirmation. The commandment, "Thou shalt not steal" is saying that it is wrong for one to take the property of another; but it is also saying by inference that it is right for the other to own the property which the one must not take.

B. H. Duncan takes a strongly Biblicist or literatistic point of view in his interpretation of private property, rejecting all state ownership of land on the ground that the Bible does not mention it. His reference to the apportionment of land to the individual families within the twelve tribes of Israel, "which constituted twelve federated states," indicates some recognition of difference between the socioeconomic circumstances of the ancient and contemporary worlds and some recognition of the pragmatic and dynamic nature of the forms of ownership. But he concludes that the "government exists to protect the people in their rights of ownership as well as other rights, " and has no right "in the field of business and ownership to compete with private enterprise. "22

The question of how property is acquired is, of course, as ethically important as how it is used. In Christian ethics, says McNiell Poteat, there are three factors of production, namely, God, society, and the individual. God contributes all the original materials--the human being and his intelligence, the earth, and the law of nature. Society contributes to the individual's accumulation the character of wealth and the increment in the value of the accumulation. The individual contributes industry and some forethought. Production is always a cooperative enterprise. 23 The manner in which property is acquired is of great moral significance "because of what it develops within the individual if acquired in the right way and because of what results in the life of the individual and others if it is acquired the wrong way. "24

In view of the fact that all production is a joint enterprise, the distribution of property and goods is also an ethical concern. James A. Stewart sees the distribution problem as a process in constant practical resolution between Scylla and Charybdis. On the one hand, the concentration of wealth and the means of production in a few hands or in state ownership makes slaves of the majority of men; on the other, the abolition of private property "might well make man a slave of the state. " The church must take its stand against both these perils. "Private property widely diffused is man's surest barrier against tyranny. Private property is the guarantee of his liberty. "25

McNiell Poteat proposes the Christian ethical principle of service as the only sure and adequate basis for the determination of a just distribution of property and goods:

> Our conclusion then is--Since love is the Christian
> law, and service is the Christian life, a man may
> have all that is necessary to maintain him in full
> efficiency as a servant of the general good; and
> that means that all the property he has must be
> good for him while he has it, and <u>at that time a</u>
> <u>good for every other member of the race</u> within
> his possible influence. [26]

3. Prosperity and Righteousness

It is not possible to determine to what extent the Depression shook the old puritan idea of the connection between
righteousness and prosperity among Southern Baptists.   But
the clearest evidence of this idea is found only before and
during the early days of the Depression.

J. P. Williams is thoroughly convinced that "righteous
living has the promise of material prosperity. "[27]   This is
the meaning of Jesus' words when He said: "Seek ye the
kingdom of God and his righteousness and all these things
(food and raiment) shall be added unto you. "   (Matt. 6:33).
Williams testifies that he is convinced of the truth of this
statement by experience in praying for rain.   "Any community needing rain to make a crop, and their desire for a good
crop is that they may the better serve God, may ask Him
for rain with assurance that the rain will come.... "[28]

Since God rewards righteousness, the church has more
to do with material prosperity than any other agency.   And
since the financial collapse of the present time (1931) is the
result of the moral collapse of society, the chief task of re-
turning financial prosperity lies with the churches.   They
must "humble themselves and pray, and pay the Lord what
they are due Him and there will be a return of financial
prosperity. "[29]

Testimony is added to this position by F. F. Brown
who states that "it would be a truism to say that Christianity
is the basis of permanent progress and prosperity.   More
vitally associated than the economic law of supply and demand
are the principles of righteousness and the stable progress of
society.   God Himself has united them in indissoluble wed-
lock, and man dare not divorce them. "   Even periodicals are
emphasizing "the fundamental place of righteousness in all
progress and warning us against the neglect of it. "[30]   The

difference between North America and South America in material progress is due to the "different life ideals that moved
the hearts of the original settlers. "31

In presenting reasons why tithing should be the normal pattern of giving, J. H. Hildreth states among other
things that "tithing would prevent many of the disasters
which overtake us" on the one hand, and "will bring temporal and spiritual blessings" on the other. 32   The many
troubles which beset us, such as unemployment, strikes,
bank failures, whiskey making, whiskey selling, etc. , are
due to unbelief and ingratitude.   On the contrary, those who
tithe in faith and love reap both temporal and spiritual blessings.   Hildreth clinches his argument with two illustrations,
one of which is as follows:

> Years ago three brothers living in the same house
> had banks in which they deposited their savings.
> Upon an appointed day they opened up their banks
> and found that each one had about the same amount
> of money.   One of the boys said, 'Well, I am get-
> ting along all right, so I am going to give my
> money to the church. '   Another one of the boys
> said, 'I am going to give half of mine to the
> church. '   The other boy said, 'I cannot give any-
> thing at this time to the church.   I have been
> wanting a watch for some time and I have just
> enough money to get it. '   Within a few years the
> boy who gave all of his savings to the Lord was
> worth two hundred and fifty thousand dollars, the
> boy who gave half was worth fifty thousand and the
> boy who gave nothing is now being supported by
> his two brothers. ... 33

P. L Lipsey believed that the whole problem of the
Depression was analyzable in terms of personal righteousness and its solution amenable to personal generosity and
benevolence.   Rejecting the notion that society is suffering
from a lack of proper distribution, Lipsey declares that the
solution to the financial distress created by the Depression
is the Christian principle of sharing with those in need.   He
advises against changing laws, socializing industry, or striking a balance between capital and labor.   The thing needed
at this time is a revival "that goes down to the roots of our
being and permanently changes our attitude toward one another and our conduct as it affects the welfare of others. ... "34

4. Calling and Work

The Christian doctrines of the Divine call and the Divine appointment of work have been greatly confused in modern Christianity. "The calling is the call of Jesus Christ to belong wholly to Him. " It is directed to the person himself; it is only indirectly related to his functions. "In response to God's call, the total life of the believer comes under the Lordship of Christ. This includes his daily work. "[35] When one responds in faith and obedience to the Divine call, this act necessarily "embraces all that he is and does. " On the other hand, both the Old and New Testaments speak of work as God-appointed, which is the lot of every person whether he is conscious of God or not.

Human work as such is not "divine vocation" in the New Testament, as it became in Protestant and Puritan circles. "God does not call people to be doctors, lawyers, truck drivers, etc. , " as a secularized version of the Biblical doctrine of the calling has led us to believe. "Rather God calls doctors, lawyers, truck drivers, etc. , to be Christian ministers. "[36] The occupational role which one chooses is the "means by which one serves God and neighbor. The Christian calling to serve God and neighbor takes concrete form in vocation or job. "[37] And since the calling embraces all that a person is or does, response to God in the calling includes the whole range of human responsibility in society--citizenship, all institutional tasks and opportunities, and occupation.[38]

It has been said that work is the God-appointed lot of every man. It must be added that God also calls every man. But every man does not respond: The call is not an objective, institutionalized condition as is work; it is rather a personal-spiritual relation, involving response. When there is no response to the Divine sovereignty, the call cannot be effective. But when men do respond to the Divine call, the priesthood of all believers becomes a reality in the lives of those who respond. All are priests, ministers, or servants of the Word of God through their callings, no matter what their occupations are, so long as they are amenable to the service of God and neighbor. Thus there are no "higher" or "lower" callings.[39]

"There are three distinct meanings of calling in the Bible, and each applies equally to ministers and laymen. ... The primary meaning is the call to salvation, " the second

is service to God in one's station, and the third is God's
call of the individual to a specific task. [40] It is the second
and third of these meanings, brought together by erroneous
interpretation, that have been the bases of the misunderstanding of the doctrine of the calling, especially in modern Christian history. When the words of Paul in I Corinthians 7:17-
24, concerning serving God in one's station, are taken out
of their eschatological context, the stress is placed on service in rather than through one's station, and calling is closely identified with class. And when calling is identified with
work, the idea of a call to a specific task is given a totally
deterministic meaning from which all choice and deliberation
on the part of the one allegedly called are excluded. The
combination of these two ideas is overwhelming in the direction of determinism.

Ransom[41] and Price[42] reject the notion that God assigns people to tasks wholly without reference to their personal tastes and talents. But the idea that men are called
to specific work and spheres is found in Southern Baptist
circles. In such circles it is assumed that it is the duty of
every man to fulfill earnestly the demands of the work and
sphere which God has given to him. In dealing with the laborer, the employer must exhibit the Christian spirit; in giving work and in giving directions for work, he must do so
as one who is acting for Christ. Threatening the laborer is
a denial of Christ and brotherhood. [43]

In using wealth, the rich must not be "high-minded, "
depending on their riches. Rather, they must be liberal,
giving their lives in good works, depending on God and recognizing Him as the source of their wealth. [44]

Laborers ought to recognize the authority of their employers, for real authority does inhere in them. If the laborer does his work as the work and sphere that God has
given him, "this spirit would give that work a power to lift
the worker to where the Lord one day would say to him,
'Thou hast been faithful over a few things, I will make thee
ruler over many. ' "[45] This is a Calvinistic affirmation of
the dynamism of the calling. Even though God does assign
one a specific task, God's reward for service in one's calling
may come in the form of an elevation in status. H. C.
Moore seems to agree with this view. After affirming that
servants must obey their masters in sincerity and goodwill,
he says: "Finally, they may expect to receive their reward
from the Lord whom faithfully they have served under the

handicap of adverse social conditions.... "[46]   But since this
is all that Moore says on the subject, it is impossible to
determine whether God's rewards are understood in the form
of higher status or eternal life.

Z. T. Cody is careful to point out that the acceptance
and fulfillment of the demands of one's status must not breed
class consciousness.   Class consciousness unfits members
for seeing members of other classes in a true light.   When
a class of society obtains its political, social, economic and
religious ideals from itself, the evil of class consciousness
is inevitable. [47]   Only the cross of Christ can save us from
the evils of class consciousness.   It "breaks down the middle wall of partition between classes.... At the same time,
it maintains all men in their rights and respective callings
and spheres. "[48]

As we have already seen, work is not a mere necessity; it is a duty.   Before the Fall, God commanded man to
labor.   "And the Lord God took the man and put him in the
garden of Eden to dress it and keep it" (Gen. 2:15).   In this
act, F. M. McConnell sees three elements: (1) "God put
the worker in a beautiful garden, " in the midst of beautiful
and pleasant working conditions.   Contemporary employers
should follow God's example.   (2) The man was given a
pleasant occupation--that of dressing the garden, of improving and adding to the beauty of plants, trees, and scenes at
all times.   (3)   There was to be no unemployment since man
was commanded to "keep" the garden, to maintain its beauty
indefinitely.   Labor as a God-appointed task was thus a
pleasant enterprise.   It was changed into grinding toil by
sin. [49]   "When man rebels against God all things are seen
differently and nothing is quite the same anymore.   Those
things meant for human joy become meaningless disappoint-
ments, and only after a restoration to fellowship with God
can these Divine gifts be seen again as opportunities for
human fulfillment. "[50]   Only the man who is rightly related
to God can see his work as Divine gift and experience it as
fulfilling.

Not only is work Divinely commanded, it is also appointed that man shall work with his hands.   "Let him that
stole steal no more, but rather let him labor, working with
his hands the thing that is good, that he may have whereof
to give him that hath need. " (Eph. 4:28).   P. I. Lipsey believes that this commandment makes it dishonorable not to
work with one's hands.   Manual labor is, moreover, "a

necessary exercise for the mind, " developing mental elasticity and versatility, while helping to save the body from nervous and physical wreck. [51] This is of course an excessive Biblical literalism, which fails to take into account the context in which the Apostle Paul spoke and which makes the Christian doctrine of work inapplicable to wide contexts of productive work in the contemporary world.

T. B. Maston speaks meaningfully to the contemporary situation in his plea for honor and respect on behalf of manual labor. Modern technology has greatly decreased the number of manual laborers and has contributed to the false notion of "high" (non-manual) and "low" (manual) work. An important task of the churches is to recapture the dignity of manual labor or common toil. [52]

A serious limitation of the Southern Baptist work ethic in the pre-World War II period was the apparent puritan conviction that the only alternative to work is idleness. There was no theory of leisure. Quoting from Charles Kingsley's sermon on "Work, " J₀ S. Farmer says that work is a blessing to the soul and character. It brings temperance and self control, diligence and strength of will, cheerfulness and contentment and other virtues. But idleness brings restlessness, discontentment, greediness, and licentiousness. [53] M. E. Dodd states that demagogues, agitators, idlers and strikers should be informed that if they will not work they cannot eat. "Idleness is wasteful and destructive of everything that is worth while in life. To be unemployed is a sin. Jesus said, 'My Father worketh hitherto and I work. ' Labor has been glorified and dignified by the touch of His hand. Work is honorable in all. To be idle is a shame. "[54] Victor I. Masters deplores the anti-work infection that has gripped America, a land that has gloried in work in the past. He suggests [in 1920] that if everyone does his part, stops bickering and organizing to gain more, America will swing back to normal conditions. [55]

These sentiments are expressed without any manifest awareness of the emergence of the corporation age and capitalist-technological unemployment. They assume that the decision to work or not to work is totally private and a reflection of the character of the decision maker. The doctrine, simply stated, is "Thou shalt work. " The vicissitudes of history, amidst which the worker is obliged to live, are either misunderstood or judged to be absolutely irrelevant to individual decision.

Another case in point is an attack on the "idleness"
of the employees of area farmers by the Greenville Association of South Carolina:

> God has ordained that 'six days thou shalt labor'
> but it appears that many of our millions out of
> employment today don't want to work. Farmers,
> for instance, who have heretofore relied upon hired
> help for the busy seasons in their crops are being
> seriously handicapped today by former employees
> who are now on relief and will not work on the
> farms. 56

The real issue in this case is without doubt unstated.
It is not "idleness"; it is the matter of working for wages at
lower rates than relief. While it is true that the crops need
to be harvested, it is also true that the workers need income
as near to the health and decency subsistence minimum as
they can obtain. Given all the economic realities of the
time, relief became another form of "occupation" for the
workers, which, despite its meagerness, provided for some
of them a better livelihood than they had ever had.

In contrast to these views, the Christian Life Committee of the Baptist General Association of Virginia in its
1966 report saw the shortening of the work week and the increase in leisure time as a major labor problem, but one
offering opportunities. The thought of the Committee was
not bound within the traditional work-rest rhythm. Leisure
was seen as a third reality with creative possibilities. The
Committee bore witness to the Scriptural condemnation of
idleness, but added that "leisure hours must be constructive
and good hours.... It is not that man must keep himself
busily occupied, but it is that his leisure should be a complement to his work, an equally fulfilling and maturing experience. "57

5. Labor's Rights, Demands and Duties

During the 1920's and 1930's, American labor was
still struggling for the right to bargain collectively; and, in
many cases, this amounted to the right to exist. Religiously sensitive people across the nation accordingly laid heavy
stress on the legitimate rights of labor. At no point in
Southern Baptist economic doctrine did Southern Baptists
more effectively speak to the contemporary conditions than

in this phase which pertains to the rights and demands of labor. In this aspect of the ethic, spokesmen demonstrate a clear awareness of the presence of the corporation age and the impersonal quality of much economic activity. Consequently, they speak in terms of the right to organize, bargain collectively, the elimination of the "stretch-out" system, etc.

In 1929 there was widespread unrest in the textile industry in the South. Against this background, the Social Service Commission of the Southern Baptist Convention made its report to the Convention of 1930.[58] This report is outstanding in its sharp departure from traditional economic ideas in the South as they pertain to labor. At this very time, northern textile mills were being lured into the South on the promise of cheap and docile labor, and even sizeable periods of tax exemption. In the Commission report, the traditional idea of cheap and docile labor is repudiated, and an "underwage" is described as "a fruitful mother of poverty, disease, immorality and crime." A health and decency subsistence wage is affirmed, and a wage below this level is declared to be "a social wrong." To organize and bargain collectively is judged to be "the inalienable right of labor," and the helplessness of the lone workman in the trade relationship is recognized. Shorter hours, better wages, the elimination of the "streth-out system," the protection of older children, and "the gradual and complete elimination of night work for women and children" are supported as goals. And finally, organized labor, traditionally unpopular in the South, is praised for its achievements.[59]

Approaching the labor problem under the aspect of freedom, J. J. Wicker supports the right of labor to collective bargaining, but affirms the right of individual bargaining alongside collective bargaining. The employer, a collective body of employees, and the individual employee should all alike be protected in their freedom to make their respective bargains.[60] How this can be achieved at the same time and in the same place is not stated.

The oppressiveness of the capitalistic system is emphasized in the thought of Amos Clary. "The state must protect the lambs of society from the wolf of avaricious greed...." and "destroy organized capitalized evil...."[61] Some of the blame for this evil, however, must be laid at the door of society. Driven to desperation, "organized labor rightly holds all of society responsible for the evils that oppress labor, since society allows one of its groups through wealth and political prestige to oppress another. " Clary concludes that the heart of labor's demand is for better homes, and warns labor to do what capital failed to do, that is, discriminate carefully between justice and injustice, always favoring the former. [62]

One of the issues which arose in the textile labor conflicts was the unjust use of the police by the capitalistic powers. In the late 1930's, the Committee on Public Morals of the Fairfield Association of South Carolina made a plea for the police protection of the rights of both labor and capital, opposed the hiring and clothing of police officers with the power of the state by the mills, and expressed satisfaction that South Carolina, along with other states, was taking steps to put an end to such abuses of public power. [63]

With the judicial validation of the National Labor Relations Act in 1937 as a landmark victory in the background, and war time prosperity as a contemporary aid, organized labor reached the peak of strength during World War II. In the bargaining encounters with management labor was now as nearly equal as at any time in American history. This new situation was reflected in the ethical teaching and analyses of Southern Baptists, as well as of other denominations, in the post-World War II period. Instead of the previous emphasis on the rights and demands of labor, the stress was now placed on mutuality and the duties of both labor and management.

As in all cases of serious group conflict, a matter of major moral concern was that of the strategies and procedures of the contending parties. In 1946, the Southern Baptist Convention urged the managers of labor and the managers of capital to "seek, in the name of patriotism, humanity and basic morality, peaceful methods of adjustment and cooperation. "[64] In the same year, Brooks Hays deplored the extreme positions sometimes taken by management and labor-- that of management being the morally indefensible view of the absolute ownership of property without social obligations, and that of labor being a power take-over of authority based on the false view that labor is the sole unit of production. [65] The Committee on Social Service of the Baptist Convention of South Carolina was thankful for the gains already made in industrial relations through the efforts of management, labor, state and federal laws; but looked ahead to greater progress

through improved laws and especially by means of the application of the Golden Rule on the part of management and labor. [66] The newly experienced power of the labor unions
soon found expression in internal as well as external corruption, racketeering and gangsterism. W. C. Fields warns
union leaders against this tendency and notes the disastrous
effects of such conduct on both labor and the nation. [67]

6. The Strike

        Southern Baptists have given almost no attention to
the issue of the labor strike during the post-World War II
period. The reason for this may be that the legality of collective bargaining and the strike has been a settled issue
during these decades. An exception to this "no comment"
pattern is an article by Weston W. Ware, who analyzes the
strike and demonstration against melon growers in the area
of Rio Grande City, Texas. Ware never comes to a specific ethical conclusion about this strike or about strikes in
general, but urges both strikers and owners not to forget
their social obligations. He also manifests the tendency to
resort to privatized solutions of institutional and systematic
problems in pointing out that unions "are only as good as
the ideals and purposes of their members and leaders" and
that the task of the churches is "to stimulate men to see
the vision of love for others that includes concern for their
economic needs. "[68]

        During the period between the World Wars, Southern
Baptists unrelentingly opposed the strike. It was assumed
that labor had a right to organize and bargain collectively,
but that labor had absolutely no right to strike.

        Testifying that although he has recently seen the
strike in perhaps its most innocent form, Z. T. Cody is
nevertheless convinced that it should be outlawed. Since
there are courts in the country for labor as well as for
others, the strike is not a right that is essential to labor.
The strike is in its essence an effort to force a business
or industry to agree to labor's terms. To force a business
agreement ought forever to be against the law in this country. The ultimate logic of the strike is Bolshevism. [69]

        Having already declared the availability of the courts
to labor as well as all others, Cody qualifies his position by
suggesting the need of courts and laws "which have super-

vision of labor problems, and to which all disputes could be
referred, and whose decision finally settled the points at issue. "[70]

In an article thirteen years later, Cody further developed the theme that the strike leads to Bolshevism.   There
is no stopping place between the two because the strike is
war; it is an appeal to force.   As a part of government, labor has no right to appeal to force, but should appeal to reason. "The whole is greater than the parts. "   The government, as a whole, should control all of the parts, else it is
not the government. [71]   "That is why we say that strikes
lead to Bolshevism.   Bolshevism is where labor has become
the whole thing. ...   And the argument that is against strikes
is also against the lockout. "[72]

As an opponent of the steel strikes of 1919, J. W.
Porter is convinced that they are the revolutionary work of
people who are already aliens and Russian Bolshevists.
"This tribe cannot be satisfied with better pay and shorter
hours, nothing less than the destruction of the American
government will gratify their diabolical ambition.   They are
anarchists at heart and Bolshevists in practice. ... "[73]

Several other reasons are advanced against the strike
and against particular strikes by Southern Baptist spokesmen.
J. D. Moore opposes strikes as a deprivation of the personal liberty of union members who do not wish to strike. [74]
Applying the parable of the vineyard laborers to contemporary labor problems, P. I. Lipsey states that "the way to
get more wages is to be worth more, to be worth so much
that an employer cannot afford to lose his service, and will
be personally attached to the workman. "   Trouble will continue to exist in industry until all deal with one another "according to the disposition of God and the direction of his
word. "[75]   Livingston Johnson calls the threatened strike of
ship carpenters of 1918 "unpatriotic conduct, " especially
"when wages are phenomenally high. "[76]   Opposition to
strikes on the ground that the public pays is voiced by many
spokesmen.   Looking over the strikes occurring during
World War II, Chaplain Roy O. McClain appraises them as
acts of sabotage.   He decries the "double standard" which
America allows to exist between the striker and the soldier.
The striker can do what he will but the soldier must do what
he is told. [77]

Concerning the matter of what should be done when

strikes do occur, there is general agreement among Southern
Baptists that the power of the state ought to be brought
against the strikers.   Speaking of the Russian Bolshevists as
the leaders of the steel strikes of 1919, J. W. Porter says,
"they have wrought ruin in their own land and are attempting
to repeat in our land their destructive deviltry.   They are
enemies of God and man and short shift should be made of
this Bolshevistic band. " As concrete suggestions, Porter
recommends that the authorities immediately "arrest every
alien enemy in our country and promptly deport them, " de-
naturalizing every one who has been naturalized, and that
the next Congress "pass stringent laws that will prevent this
terrible tribe from coming to our country.   We have already
had enough to convince the most skeptical that the very life
of our nation is imperiled by the presence of these human
hyenas. "[78] In a similar vein, P. J. Lipsey designates the
threat of a strike held over the president and Congress by
the railroad trainmen as the spirit of anarchy, affirms that
the moral sentiment of the nation ought to condemn it, and
the civil and military power of the nation should be prepared
to forestall it. [79] Expressing his agreement with the plan of
Governor Hoffman of New Jersey to use the resources of
the state against sitdown strikes, J. S. Farmer states that
few in North Carolina would disagree with the general proposition that labor unions and organizers have no more right
than others "to break the law wantonly and intentionally and
flout the duly constituted authorities. "[80] Later, Farmer
praised the management of the cotton mills of North Carolina
for "doing all they can for their workers" and claimed that
"the workers know it. " He further expressed the conviction
that Governor Hoey has the united support of the people in
his warning that the state will not tolerate sit-down strikes.[81]

          It may be seen from the expression of these senti-
ments that Southern Baptist thought had not caught up with
some of the harsh realities of the nation's economic life.
During the 1920's, for example, judges were still handing
down decisions that organization for collective bargaining
was a conspiracy.   During these very decades when the
strike was stubbornly opposed by Southern Baptists, virtually
all of the power of the legal and judicial forces was weighted
on the side of capitalistic interests.   Judges and legislators
were the allies of capitalists, shared their ideology, and
rendered decisions and made laws accordingly.   The strike
was frequently the only instrument left to labor.   These
facts are not evident in Southern Baptist literature.   Perhaps "cultural imprisonment" explains the Southern Baptist

spokesmen themselves.   They spoke out of an environment
in which some workers had been slaves, many were "hands,"
and persons of privilege and respect were still boasting of
the cheap and docile labor which the environment afforded.
It is undoubtedly difficult for the children of such a culture
to think of mere workers as wielding power of the proportions which the strike often contains.

Notes

1.   For his Th. D. dissertation, Hugh A. Brimm of the
     Southern Baptist Theological Seminary made a study
     in 1944 of hundreds of district association and state
     convention minutes, and found in them practically no
     concern for migratory workers and sharecroppers
     except as "objects of missionary effort. "
2.   "Industrial Relations" Report of the Social Service Com-
     mission of the Southern Baptist Convention, Annual
     of the Southern Baptist Convention (Nashville, 1938),
     p. 104.
3.   Wicker, John J. , "Labor and Capital (Editorial), Re-
     ligious Herald, CX (July 1, 1937), p. 10.
4.   Farmer, J. S. , "Current Topics - One Aspect of the
     Strike, " Biblical Recorder, C (October 3, 1934),
     p. 7.
5.   Farmer, J. S. , "The C. I. O. and Textiles, " Biblical
     Recorder, CII (April 28, 1937), p. 10.
6.   Ibid.
7.   Welsh, J. Elwood, "Jesus and our Economic Problems,"
     The Baptist Courier, LXIX (January 21, 1937), p. 6.
8.   Ibid. , p. 7.
9.   Clary, Amos, "The Heart of Labor's Demand, " The
     Baptist Courier, LII (September 15, 1921), p. 3.
10. "Resolution of the Committee on the Subject of War--
     Minority Report, " North Carolina Baptist Annual
     (1935), p. 41.
11. Joiner, E. Earl, "What Economy Should Christian Sell?"
     Florida Baptist Witness, LXXX (December 5, 1963),
     p. 5.
12. "Industrial Relations, " Report of the Social Service
     Commission of the Southern Baptist Convention,
     Annual of the Southern Baptist Convention (Nash-
     ville, 1946), p. 122.
13. Report of the Social Service Commission of the Ala-
     bama Baptist State Convention, Annual of the Ala-
     bama Baptist State Convention (1945), p. 109.

14. Report of the Committee on Social Service of the Bap-
    tist Denomination in South Carolina, Annual of the
    State Convention of the Baptist Denomination in
    South Carolina (1946), p. 121.
15. "Industrial Relations," Report of the Committee on So-
    cial Service of the Baptist Denomination in South
    Carolina, Annual of the State Convention of the Bap-
    tist Denomination of South Carolina (1948), p. 109.
16. Ibid., p. 110.
17. Poteat, Edwin McNiell, "The Christian Doctrine of
    Property," The Word and the Way, LIII (March 22,
    1917), p. 6.
18. Skinner, T. Clagett, "Property and Personality," Re-
    ligious Herald, CVI (June 1, 1933), p. 4.
19. Stewart, James A., "Christianity and Industrial Strife,"
    The Review and Expositor, XLIII (July, 1946), p.
    307.
20. Summers, Ray, "Persons and Property," Baptist Stand-
    ard, 64 (June 5, 1952), p. 20.
21. Duncan, B. H., "The Right of Personal and Private
    Ownership," Arkansas Baptist, 47 (February 12,
    1948), p. 3.
22. Ibid.
23. Poteat, Edwin McNiell, op. cit.
24. Summers, Ray, op. cit.
25. Stewart, James A., op. cit., p. 308.
26. Poteat, Edwin McNiell, op. cit.
27. Williams, J. P., "The Church and Property," The
    Baptist Record, XXXIII (April 2, 1931), p. 5.
28. Ibid.
29. Ibid.
30. Brown, F. F., "Material Prosperity and Soul Prosperi-
    ty," The Baptist Courier, LVII (May 13, 1926), p. 5.
31. Ibid.
32. Hildreth, J. H., "The Way to Peace, Prosperity and
    Plenty," The Christian Index, CXI (January 1, 1931),
    p. 8.
33. Ibid., p. 27.
34. Lipsey, P. I., "Inequitable Distribution (Editorial) The
    Baptist Record, XXXVI (June 7, 1934), p. 4.
35. Barnette, Henlee, Has God Called You? (Nashville,
    Broadman Press, 1969), p. 66.
36. Ibid., p. 67.
37. Ibid., p. 71.
38. Price, Richard E., "The Meaning of Christian Voca-
    tion," Religious Herald, CXXIX (March 14, 1957),
    p. 5.

39. Ibid., p. 4.
40. Ranson, Guy H., "The Christian Understanding of Vo-
    cation," The Baptist Student, 38 (January, 1959),
    p. 4.
41. Ibid.
42. Price, op. cit., pp. 4-5.
43. Cody, Z. T., "The Christian Spirit in Industry," (Sun-
    day School Lesson), The Baptist Courier, LXI (De-
    cember 12, 1929), p. 11.
44. Ibid.
45. Ibid., pp. 10-11.
46. Moore, H. C., "The Christian Spirit in Industry,"
    (Sunday School Lesson), The Baptist Record, XXXI
    (December 12, 1929), p. 10.
47. Cody, Z. T., "Class Consciousness" (Editorial) The
    Baptist Courier, LXII (September 4, 1930), p. 1.
48. Ibid., p. 2.
49. McConnell, F. M., "The Case of Labor" (Editorial),
    Baptist Standard, XLIII (September 3, 1931), p. 4.
50. "A Christian View of Work and Leisure," Report of
    the Christian Life Committee of the Baptist General
    Association of Virginia, Virginia Baptist Annual,
    1966, p. 78.
51. Lipsey, P. I., "Working with your Hands," (Editorial),
    The Baptist Record, XXII (January 22, 1920), p. 3.
52. Maston, T. B., "The Dignity of Manual Labor," Bap-
    tist and Reflector, 134 (November 7, 1968), p. 3.
53. Farmer, J. S., "Work" (Editorial), Biblical Recorder,
    102 (February 24, 1937), p. 6.
54. Dodd, M. E., "Work" (Editorial), The Baptist Message,
    XXXIII (October 9, 1919), p. 4.
55. Masters, Victor I., "The Primacy of Work," The Bap-
    tist Courier, LI (August 12, 1920), pp. 1-2.
56. "Idleness," Report of the Committee on Public Morals
    of the Greenville Association of South Carolina, The
    Baptist Courier, LXX (August 25, 1938), p. 5.
57. "A Christian View of Work and Leisure," Report of
    the Christian Life Committee of the Baptist General
    Association of Virginia, Virginia Baptist Annual,
    1966, p. 79.
58. The Social Service Commission of the Southern Baptist
    Convention reproduced as its own the report of the
    Georgia Baptist Commission on Social Service to the
    State Baptist Convention of Georgia.
59. "Industrial Relations," Report of the Social Service
    Commission of the Southern Baptist Convention,
    Annual of the Southern Baptist Convention (Nash-

ville, 1930), pp. 68-69.
60. Wicker, J. J., "Chips--Freedom, " Religious Herald, CXI (July 21, 1938), p. 9.
61. Clary, Amos, "The Heart of Labor's Demand, " The Baptist Courier, LII (September 15, 1921), p. 3.
62. Ibid.
63. Report of the Committee on Public Morals of the Fairfield Association of South Carolina, The Baptist Courier, LXIX (January 7, 1937), p. 12.
64. "Industrial Relations, " Report of the Social Service Commission of the Southern Baptist Convention, Annual of the Southern Baptist Convention (Nashville, 1946), p. 122.
65. Hays, Brooks, "Industrial Strife, " Arkansas Baptist, 45 (September 5, 1946), p. 5.
66. "Industrial Relations, " Report of the Committee on Social Service of the State Convention of the Baptist Denomination in South Carolina, Annual of the State Convention of the Baptist Denomination of South Carolina (November, 1948), p. 110.
67. Fields, W. C. , "Morality in Labor Unions" (Editorial), The Baptist Record, LXXX (September 5, 1957), p. 4.
68. Ware, Weston, W. , "What About the Strike?" Baptist Standard, 78 (September 14, 1966), p. 7.
69. Cody, Z. T. , "Let the Strike be Made Lawless" (Editorial), The Baptist Courier, LII (April 14, 1921), p. 4.
70. Ibid.
71. Cody, Z. T. , "The Strike, " (Editorial), The Baptist Courier, LXVI (September 13, 1934), p. 2.
72. Ibid. , p. 3.
73. Porter, J. W. , "Strike Leaders, " (Editorial), Western Recorder, 95th year (October 30, 1919), p. 8.
74. Moore, J. D. , "Strikes, " Baptist and Reflector, LXXXVIII (July 13, 1922), p. 1.
75. Lipsey, P. I. , "The Vineyard Laborers--The Wage Question" (Editorial), The Baptist Record, XXII (September 30, 1920), p. 4.
76. Johnson, Livingston, "Unpatriotic Conduct, " Biblical Recorder, LXXXII (February 27, 1918), p. 1.
77. McClain, Roy O. , "A Chaplain Looks at Strikers, " The Baptist Courier, LXXVI (July 6, 1944), p. 9.
78. Porter, J. W. , "Strike Leaders" (Editorial) Western Recorder, 95th year (October 30, 1919), p. 8.
79. Lipsey, P. J. , "Threat of the Strike" (Editorial), The Baptist Record, XXL (January 23, 1919), p. 4.

80. Farmer, J. S., "Sit-Down Strike," <u>Biblical Recorder</u>, CII (February 24, 1937), p. 7.
81. Farmer, J. S., "Strikes," <u>Biblical Recorder</u>, CII (April 14, 1937), p. 7.

Chapter VIII

RACE

From the beginning of the period of abolition agitation (about 1830) to the present, race has been an obsession in the Southern states of the United States. Everything is made different by the impingement of the "race question."[1] Whenever any other problem--political, economic, educational, religious, etc.--bears on race relations, it takes on an intensity far out of proportion to its expression as a nonracial issue. There are no interests in the South that have not been "colored" by the color problem. Race is as pervasive and determinative of attitudes and behavior as any other cultural force, if not more so. It is to be expected therefore that this force has had a greater impact over the generations on the understanding and practice of religion than religion has had on attitudes and practices in race relations.

Despite this tragic history, we can no longer look at the decades since World War I as one uninterrupted cultural continuity. Southern Baptist thought on race must be divided into two periods, from World War I to the end of World War II, and from the end of World War II to the present. Of course, no sharp boundaries can ever be established in history, but new cultural forces were let loose by World War II which had been developing for some time, and the one which became most pronounced in the United States was new thought and new policy on race. Southern Baptists, like other religious bodies, manifest the effects of this cultural transformation. While the old ideas continue to persist alongside the new after World War II, there is an increase in the prophetic criticism of racist attitudes and practices, of such proportions as to constitute a new historical period. In addition to this decisive fact, the period after World War II brought new racial issues.

1. From World War I to the
    End of World War II

(1) The Origin of the Negro

A generation ago, many well trained Southern Baptists
turned to Genesis to explain the origin of the races rather
than to physical anthropologists. According to Noble Y.
Beall, the Negro is the son of Misraim, the second son of
Ham, who was the second son of Noah. Popular belief is
incorrect, however, in holding that the Negro bears a closer
family relationship with Canaan, upon whom Noah pronounced
a curse, than do other nations of the East: Babylon,
Persia, Media, India, and probably China and Japan. Beall
does not indicate what Noah's curse was, whether his curse
was also God's curse, or what significance it has for the
present status of those who are close to Canaan in family
relationship. [2] At any rate, the curse does not destroy the
possibilities of the faith experience in the Negro. In fact,
it does not even seem to affect it. Although the Negro has
"absorbed much that is purely American, " he is well fitted
for the Christian religion, since the Christian religion is an
oriental religion and the Negro still has an oriental mind. [3]

R. L. Breland disagrees with Beall concerning the
line of descent from Canaan (Ham), stating that only the
people of Africa belong to this line.

Noah and his wife, his three sons (Shem, Ham and
Japheth) and their wives were the only survivors of the
flood. All other people were destroyed. After his experience in the flood, Noah took too much wine. Having become drunk, he took off his clothes and "acted the fool. "
Ham came along and made fun of his father, but the other
two sons rebuked Ham and proceeded to cover their father.
When Noah awoke from his wine, he said, "Cursed be
Canaan (Ham); a servant of servants shall he be unto his
brethren. ' Thus Ham seems to have been demoted in the
family relationship. He was still a son, destined to become
the head of a great race but that race was to be the servant
class. How true that has been fulfilled. "[4]

In the days of Peleg, God willed to divide the world.
Ham was given Africa; Shem was given the western part of
Asia and perhaps Europe; and Japheth was given the eastern
part of Asia. But these people would not separate as God
had indicated. Instead they stayed together and sought to

build a great tower as the way to God. Being displeased, God confused their language, giving each a different language and thus accomplished the threefold division originally intended in the days of Peleg.

Just when and why a large per cent of the children of Ham became black is not known. Not all of them are black. Egyptians and some other groups of a fairer complexion belong to the race of Ham also. [5]

Breland concludes his story of the origin of the Negro with an account of God's providential dealings with the American Negro. "It seemed practically impossible for the Christian 'Sons of Japheth, '[6] whose sons and daughters we Christians are, to reach the millions of Africans, so we Americans went down there and brought thousands of them as servants." Just as Noah had predicted, they made good servants; and, "while they served us, we preached to them the gospel of the Son of God." Thousands were converted, becoming faithful servants of the Lord and, fittingly, Baptists. "For as the old Negro explained why so many Negroes were Baptists, 'The average Negro has not got sense enough to splain away the Scriptures, so he takes it just like it reads and is a Baptist.' There is more truth than poetry in this homely philosophy of the old Negro."[7]

(2) The Alleged Harmony of the Races

The period between World War I and World War II was a long, dark night for the Negro of the South. The soldiers of color who returned from World War I were made to understand swiftly that the war in which they had fought "to make the world safe for democracy" was not designed to secure democracy for them. They were to return to the same disfranchisement, the same wage differentials based on race, the same menial jobs, the same deprivations of share-cropper life, the same judicial injustice, and the same exclusions from institutional and cultural life. They were to witness the resurgence of the Ku Klux Klan and their night-riding, of which they would be the chief victims. And to them the panic of 1922 and the depression of 1929 would mean the loss of even the servile and menial type jobs which they had gained.

Despite the oppressiveness of a system which could produce conditions of this kind, Southern Baptist spokesmen

proclaimed and even extolled the peaceful and harmonious relationships that allegedly existed between the black and white
races of the region.

In attacking the false rumors of riot in Richmond,
Virginia in 1918, R. H. Pitt gives several reasons for ignoring such rumors, all of which are indicative of the harmonious relations between the races. He asserts that we
have the best Negroes in the land. "Of course, there is
occasional lawlessness among them, " as among white people,
but "we have never had any serious or widespread or permanent race difficulties in our fine community. "8 Pitt attributes this in part to the fact that Negro leaders are in the
main "wise and sensible. " They have taught their people to
bear with patience whatever wrongs they suffered or imagined
they suffered. The splendid character of this community is
also due "to the fact that the white people of the city of Richmond, with, of course, some exceptions, have dealt kindly
and justly with the colored folk. The sensible negroes of
Richmond know that if they are in trouble and need the counsel and help of their white neighbors they can always secure
it. "9 Ten years later, Pitt stated that the two races in Virginia were "separate in blood and in ordinary social relations,
but united in the love of Christ and in a common Christian
hope and faith.... "10

The black man's receptivity of the Christian faith at
the hands of the whites is explained by Victor I. Masters as
being due to the spirit and conduct of the missionaries. The
black man accepted the Christian faith and continues to do so
because the master showed kindness and love to his slaves
across the racial line and the landlord has done the same
thing since slavery. There have been many unhappy abuses,
but the main line has been in the opposite direction. 11

The race problem is virtually dismissed as a major
issue by J. S. Farmer; he speaks of it in the same category
with the "many things that tend to set white people in groups."
He accuses Drs. Mordecai W. Johnson and John Hope of
being the only speakers in the World Baptist Alliance of 1928
to sound discordant notes, and virtually convicts them for
being "almost white. " Both Johnson and Hope claimed that
the Negro was not getting a fair deal in the world. Farmer
decries this sentiment, charges Johnson and Hope with ingratitude for all the fine things white people have done for the
blacks, and contrasts their attitude with that of an African
girl and Dr. C. H. Parrish of Louisville, "a real Negro. "12

Answering accusations brought against the South by
the Presbyterian Witness, P. I. Lipsey brands them all as
untrue.   The Presbyterian Witness had charged the South
with denying the Negro an education, fair trial in the courts,
and an opportunity to work.   To each of these charges, Lipsey issues a counter claim.   He asserts that "millions of
dollars are spent every year in the South from taxes on
white people to educate the Negro. "   The Negroes are always
afforded an opportunity to work in the South "and considerable
pressure is brought to bear on some of them to get it done. "
The fact that Negroes do not always get a fair trial in the
courts is admitted by Lipsey, but he adds that their chances
are about as good as that of the average poor man in any
country. [13]   In a later statement, Lipsey states that "there
is as little of race prejudice in Mississippi as in New England and far less sectionalism. "[14]   Speaking in similar
terms, J. W. Porter says that Negroes are treated better
in the South than in the North, but adds that their treatment,
of course, would not satisfy the advocates of social equality.[15]

The concept of the harmony of the races in the South
is rejected by the Racial Commission of the Columbia Baptist Association of Alabama.   The Commission states that
Southerners living in 1944 are not responsible for the in-
heritance of racial conflict "from Reconstruction Days, 'Car-
petbagger Days, ' "   But "to shut our eyes and say it is not
here, is to be blind or dishonest.   To shrug our shoulders
and say it is none of our affairs, is to ignore a responsibility placed on us by the Word of God. "[16]

Taking his stand on the principles of the Kingdom of
God, E. A. McDowell denies that there is peace and harmony on the racial front, even among Christians.   "Far too
many Christians go with Christ as far as the color line, but
stop there. "   At the color line, they reject love as the fundamental motive of the Christian life and "accept the standards and traditions of the world in preference to the principles of the kingdom of God. "[17]   McDowell proceeds to
point out ways in which Southern white Christians conduct
themselves in an unchristian manner toward Negroes.   He
cites the use of the contemptuous epithet, "nigger, " the low
wages and long hours to which the Negro servant is subjected, the low wages of Negro men on farms and in businesses,
the inequalities in educational appropriations, the injustices
in the courts, and the inequalities in parks and playgrounds
and often the total absence of such facilities for Negroes.
McDowell warns that Southern white Christians must realize

"that the color line was not made by Christ but by the
world. " As his followers they must not "conform to the
world but be transformed by Christian principles and Christlike actions. "[18]

(3) Caste[19] Accepted as the Ideal

The fact that Southern Baptists could talk about peace
and harmony in race relations during the period between the
two World Wars was due to their acceptance of the racial
caste system as the ideal pattern for relating the races.
For most Southern Baptists, caste stood in a position of
priority to Christ in racial matters. It never occurred to
them to examine the caste system in the light of the teaching and spirit of Christ, for the caste system had its own
absolute foundation. This does not mean that no efforts
were made to justify caste; it means that there were few
efforts to examine and evaluate it.

The "right" relation between the black and white
races is clearly set forth by the Committee on Temperance
and Social Service of the Southern Baptist Convention in the
following statement:

> There has not been nor indeed can there be, any
> change in the fixed separation of the two races in
> the matter of individual social relation. No change
> here is possible, nor is any change desired by the
> thoughtful of either race. If any member of either
> race desires or cherishes hope of any change in
> this respect he is doomed to disappointment. But
> in the broad matters of better education and more
> complete Christianization of the negro, or better
> housing conditions, or a better economic and in-
> dustrial opportunity, or a more evenhanded justice
> in the courts for the race and of a better under-
> standing between the two races and a more sym-
> pathetic attitude of each toward the other there is
> urgent need and an open door.... [20]

As has been suggested, the caste system is not cri-
tically evaluated by its defenders, but it is justified. And
among the grounds of justification is to be found the Christian religion itself. There are values in religious, racial,
national and class distinctions, says Z. T. Cody, and these
must be preserved. The problem, he continues, is how to

preserve necessary distinctions and, at the same time, show real Christian brotherhood. Only Christ has solved this problem perfectly. In the case of the Samaritan woman he overcame prejudice and antipathy, but did not deny that the Jews were superior to the Samaritans or hide his own superiority. Rather, he brought these out in the conversation. There is nothing wrong with the sense of superiority. "It is pride rather than superiority that does the evil work." Authentic superiority "is a gift of God and not of man; and a man who has this gift ought always to be humble, even while genuinely prizing the gift."21

Declaring that both races must bring the religion of Christ to bear upon their dealings with one another, P. I. Lipsey hastens to indicate that this does not mean the destruction of racial lines; rather, it means their preservation. God Himself has appointed racial boundaries. "He made one of every nation of men to dwell on the face of the earth, having determined their appointed seasons, and the bounds of their habitation." (Acts. 17:26) But God who separated men into races is Lord of all, and has given the races reciprocal duties and obligations. Their duties to one another and to God are the same. Therefore, to fulfill their obligation to God is to do right by one another. 22 Within this specific context, Lipsey does not make clear what the God-given reciprocal duties of races are, and how these duties relate to the duties of other definable groups within or between races.

Taking issue with Russell Conwell Barbour's23 criticism of segregation at the 1938 assembly of the World Baptist Alliance in Atlanta, George, W. C. Allen expresses the hope that "Negro leaders will realize that Christian principles can be applied in all their relations with other races without necessarily violating the social customs and conventions which prevail in different sections of America, and of the world." Allen also labels as unjustified the action of the Negro ministers of Richmond, Virginia, who refused to attend the sessions of the Southern Baptist Convention because they were segregated. The action of the local committee which made the arrangements, he says, are but "natural" under all circumstances. 24 Joining in the discussion of Christian principles and the segregation of the assembly of the Southern Baptist Convention, Victor I. Masters expresses regret that Negro Christians are confronted "by what are essentially Russian Communistic theories," and states that "Christian fellowship is not a

matter of eating and drinking. " It can and does exist without conventional social intermingling, and to assume otherwise is to manifest "spiritual infancy or complete blind-
ness. "25 In a later editorial, Masters points out that
"there are many white people in America who, for one reason or another, go to different kinds of hotels and do not
mingle or eat together. "26 This descriptive statement is
evidently presented as the ethical norm for interracial conduct. Despite the presence of the phrase "for one reason
or another" in this "normative" statement, Masters demonstrates a total incapacity to discern the central spiritual issue in segregation, namely, the pride and contempt which
prompt it.

An unusual twist is given to the discussion of Christian principles and segregation by R. W. Lide, who calls
the spirit of the Negro Baptist ministers "glaringly unchristian" in their refusal to attend the segregated Southern Baptist Convention. Jesus "made Himself of no reputation, but
took upon Him the form of a servant, humbled Himself and
did not claim for Himself special privileges. " Further, Jesus taught humility: "When thou art bidden of a man to a
feast, sit not down in the chief seat; lest haply a more honorable man than thou be bidden and he that bade thee and
him shall come and say to thee, give this man place, and
thou begin with shame to take the lowest place, etc. " (Luke
14:8-11). It apparently does not occur to Lide to apply this
example and teaching to the prideful spirit of the one who
segregates, for he goes on to say that in all the years since
freedom "colored friends have invited their white friends to
special services, " and have reserved seats for them. White
people have done the same thing, "and there has been mutual
satisfaction and pleasure in this arrangement. "27

Alongside the religious justification of the caste structure, J. B. Gambrell places the democratic justification. In
effect, he calls segregation the voluntary principle at work
in race relations. That no person or group shall be allowed
to intrude upon another person or group in social life is an
inherent principle of right. "All social relations are formed
on the voluntary principle, both parties agreeing. " It is the
duty of government, therefore, to regulate race relations so
as to avoid conflicts and injury to one side or the other. 28
Two erroneous assumptions are inherent in this line of
thought. The one is that "race relations" are always identical with voluntary social relations, having no major institutional and public domain aspects. The other is that racial

encounters are and must always be "intrusions" in the absence of a rigid system of segregation.

The most influential and widely accepted ground of justification for the caste system is the anti-amalgamation doctrine. The fear of intermarriage is overwhelming, and it is assumed that social equality leads directly to it. Consequently, the anti-social equality and the anti-amalgamation doctrines are thought of together. The concept of the Negro as a sub-human being which developed in the cultural matrix of modern imperialism and slavery is the foundation of these doctrines. The dichotomy of the human race comprising men (white people) and sub-men (black people) is assumed by most spokesmen who talk about improving the economic, political, educational, and religious status of the Negro, or even of giving him equality in these areas. Livingston Johnson typifies this point of view when he says that Negroes should not be discriminated against in the courts or in the business world, they should enjoy equality of educational advantages so far as they are prepared to make use of them, and they should be invited to participate in interracial conferences for the improvement of interracial understanding.

> But when it comes to receiving them on terms of
> social equality, of eating with them at the same
> table, or receiving them in the homes of white
> people at social functions, the South will never
> permit the color line to crumble. This is not
> prejudice, but in the opinion of Southern people,
> it is absolutely necessary in order to prevent the
> possibility of inter-marriage, or further miscege-
> nation of the races. [29]

The reason most frequently offered for opposing inter-marriage is that it "would prove disastrous to both races."[30] George W. Paschal resorts to a simplistic interpretation of history to "prove" that intermarriage is disastrous. He calls attention to the "superiority" of society and culture in the United States and other English-speaking countries, in which amalgamation is prohibited, over the societies and cultures of those countries in which amalgamation is the rule. In the light of this comparison, he asserts that "it seems ordered of heaven that the races in our country have been kept separate" and ordered of God that the colored people establish their own churches after the Civil War.[31]

In an attack on a position taken by the Southern Bap-

tist _Home Missions Magazine_, Finley W. Tinnin unashamedly
defends the caste system on impulse.

> We are ready to defend, even with our life, the
> negroes' rights, in his [sic] rightful place, but we
> are equally determined to oppose social intermin-
> gling and intermarrying between negroes and whites
> even with our life. If Home Missions consider
> this 'racial prejudice, ' we then confess the guilt.[32]

On this issue, on which unanimity seemed assured
during the period between the World Wars, one voice called
out for a reexamination of the idea in terms of the Kingdom
of God. E. A. McDowell asserted that reconciliation between
the white man and the Negro is only partial, being based on
the white man's terms expressed in the phrase, "the Negro
is all right in his place. " Such a relation, McDowell affirms, violates the principles of the Kingdom.

> Neither race, creed, nor social position determined
> the value of a person for Jesus. All persons were
> priceless to him. In subjugating the Negro, in fix-
> ing for him a menial place, in thwarting his growth
> individually and as a race, we are violating one of
> the first principles of the Kingdom of God. [33]

McDowell goes on to say that putting and keeping the
Negro "in his place" is a violation of the principle of reconciliation and a rejection of the Golden Rule. Reconciliation
does not and cannot take place between those of an exalted
posture and those whose lowly posture they have created.
"We are not reconciled to our 'brothers in black' so long
as we extend our hands downward to grasp his. We shall
clasp his hand as our brother in the Kingdom of God when
we are willing to acknowledge him as our brother indeed. "[34]

(4) Paternalism and Control

The caste system, long accepted as the ideal pattern
of race relations in the South, does not leave the races without reciprocal obligations. It is not merely a rigid structure; it is also a rigid prescriptive system. There is a
proper nexus between white and black people. In all things,
the Whites must be above and in authority and the Blacks below and in submission and dependence. In short, the proper
relation of the white man toward the Negro is paternalistic.

The obligations of the white man in his position are kindness, benevolence, helpfulness and direction. These sentiments are never directed toward the Negro as an equal or potential equal; rather they are directed toward him as one who is permanently subordinate and inferior. They are expressions of noblesse oblige. On the other hand, it is the duty of the Negro to accept this state of affairs in joyful gratitude, loyalty, obedience, and diligence in the menial tasks which are set before him.

The racist, stereotypical system provides ample justification for the paternalistic arrangement. In the first place, the Negro is said to be naturally childlike. "The greatest virtue of the Negro, when the Negro is at his best, is his childlikeness; and I am sometimes almost inclined to believe that God created the Negro in order that the Negro might embody this great truth for all mankind. "[35] Since the Negro is naturally childlike, he is equipped for a permanent, subservient role. In caring for him and guiding him, the white man is, as it were, meeting the demands of the Negro's very being.

In the second place, the Christian religion justifies the position of major and minor, of which the racial caste system is an expression:

> Our common religious faith lends itself to a proper adjustment, not extinction, of dissimilar racial or personal characteristics, and recognizes the place of the major as well as that of the minor and obligates the stronger to help the weaker, and requires each to respect the position and personality of the other.... [36]

An illustration of the principle of the major and the minor is the letter of Paul to Philemon concerning the latter's runaway slave. [37]

A third ground of justification for paternalism and control over the Negro is the fact that the Negro can be depended upon to leave the control of affairs in the hands of white people, provided he is kept free of agitators. Livingston Johnson presents this idea while accusing both political parties of "agitation" in the form of bidding for the Negro vote in the national campaign of 1928. The result of this "agitation" was the creation of "prejudice in the hearts of many members of the white race" and the illusion in many

"ambitious Negroes" "that there is a possibility of having
their race represented in the affairs of government. ... "38

In their ideological justifications, men always manage
to hide their real motivations. In the statements above,
there are appeals to God and nature; but, as in every system of oppression, the real motivations are the political and
economic interests of the oppressors. Although men avoid
clear presentations of such interests, their presence as motivations is not entirely hidden even in public defenses of the
system.

The motive of self-interest is found in the language
of B. D. Gray in his address before the Southern Baptist
Convention in 1919. Among other things, Gray said, "we
must care for our Negroes. They are worth more to us
than a hundred million others. "39 Gray does not indicate
the nature of the Negro's worth, but, given the cultural context in which the statement was made, it yields much meaning in terms of the aims and values of a slave-feudal society.
As a matter of fact, Negroes were in servile roles in large
numbers at the time. Many others were employed at the
same tasks also performed by white people, but the Negroes
performed these tasks at lower wages. All over the South,
the Blacks were the victims of "taxation without representation. " And, although they were counted in the population of
the South in the allocation of Congressional seats in Washington, most of them could not vote for the Congressmen who
allegedly represented them. Phrases like "care for" and
"our Negroes" reflect this system perfectly, and "worth"
takes on an instrumental meaning.

The influence of the motive of self-interest is reflected in the thought of W. J. McGlothlin in his stress on the
importance of controlling the Negro's thinking. McGlothlin
complains that the education of the Negro has been left to
the state and the people of the North.

> Knowing this, it would seem that we Southern
> whites would have desired above all things else
> to have the education of the Negro leaders in our
> own hands; whereas we have relegated it entirely
> to the hands of others. It seems to me high time
> that we should be bestirring ourselves to recover
> our influence over the ideals and ideas of the South-
> ern Negro. 40

McGlothlin continues by pointing out why the Negro's
thinking should be controlled by southern Whites. He states
that many Negroes in the South are reading inflammatory
literature from the Negro presses of the North. This social
poison is dangerous to the peace and happiness of the southern people. The way to meet the situation is "to train Negro leaders who can counteract its baneful influence among
their own people. "[41]

By setting it within the framework of the doctrine of
stewardship, the paternalistic system gains religious motivation. "If one race has advantage over another, it should be
accepted as a stewardship, and every effort should be made
to faithfully discharge the obligation. "[42] This judgment, of
course, sanctifies racial "advantage over another, " but it
calls for the meeting of the obligation that is correlated with
the Divine gift. The idea of a racial stewardship is also
set forth by the Social Service Commission of the Southern
Baptist Convention as it reminds the constituency of the Convention that the strong must bear the burdens of the weak.
But the Commission tones down the paternalistic element by
adding the phrase "without any spirit of patronizing or air
of condescending. "[43]

What specifically are the white man's obligations to
the Negro? How can he and should he aid the Negro? Several "ways to aid the Negro" are presented by W. W. Leathers.

First, certain things ought to be done for the Negro's
economic salvation. The white employer should demand the
Negro's best service, thus engendering pride in him in his
own labor. White employers should pay their Negro labor
honest and living wages, and inculcate habits of thrift. This
will lead the Negroes to relative economic independence
which is essential to healthy character, and "will help to
stop stealing, which is so prevalent among this race. "[44]

Second, the Negro must be given justice in the courts
and must be free from mobs. If a Negro steals a few dollars, he gets a heavy sentence of several years "while the
white man makes away with his thousands and escapes with
a much lighter sentence. This is most unjust. " Lynching
should be stopped; it tends to increase rather than curb rape.

Third, Negro housing and home surroundings must be
improved. White ladies employing Negro servants should

take a sympathetic interest in their homes giving them flow-
ers to plant and making helpful suggestions to them. [45]

Fourth, Negro education must be improved. It
"should be largely technical and vocational looking toward
fitting them for their actual life. "[46]

The Negro, like all men, is religious. "Yet it is
sadly true that his religion does not affect his life to any
great extent. " The white man can help at this point by
leading an exemplary life before the Negro, who is very
imitative of the white man and susceptible to his influence.
Whenever the opportunity arises, the white man can and
should teach the Negro. He can help in the Negro's church
life through teaching a Sunday School class, speaking at
some service, or assisting with money. White ministers
should meet and counsel with Negro ministers occasionally,
and they may personally assist them in many ways. [47]

It is evident from these suggestions that Leathers believes that he is describing all Negroes, that all are children
who can never grow up; and therefore, that he is unable to
conceive of "aids to Negroes" that are truly developmental
and which would enable them to do for themselves the things
that need to be done in any and all areas of life.

Even during this period when caste and paternalism
were taken for granted by the overwhelming majority, a few
voices to the contrary could be heard beneath the din.
David Morgan represents a small group when he says,
"alongside us Caucasians there is in America another culture worthy to be reckoned with. " To give point to his contention, Morgan cites statistics on the number of Negroes
enrolled in colleges and universities, on Phi Beta Kappas,
Ph. D. 's, etc. [48] Quoting from Clarence Jordan, Morgan
suggests a plan of procedure for a white local church worker which represents a repudiation of paternalism:

> Find a Negro pastor. Don't say, 'We want to
> bring a program'; just go worship. Call at his
> home; call him 'Mister. ' Sit in on a deacon's
> meeting when you are invited. Once a quarter
> arrange a joint deacon's meeting with the deacons
> of your own church. Avoid emphasizing differen-
> ces by too much talk. Persuade parents not to
> make derogatory statements about other races be-
> fore their children. Read books giving the Negro's

point of view. Arrange occasional interracial ex-
changes of pulpit. Pronounce 'Negro' with a long
e and a long o, taking care not to slur the second
syllable. When speaking to colored groups, do not
begin by telling how much an old Negro mammy
meant to you. The new Negro knows little and
cares less about the old 'mammy.' It is usually
safer not to mention race at all. Remember that
the Negro has his own customs, and do not try to
run his church on your favorite plan. [49]

(5) The Good Negro and Negro Leadership

It has been seen that segregation in the South is not
a parallelism. Segregation does not mean two mutually independent and self realizing racial societies, although this is
precisely what some of the defenders of the system claim
for it. Racial segregation means subordination as well as
separation; it is a system involving a dominant and a sub-
ordinated caste. Yet there is a nexus between the races;
each race has its obligations to the other. There is a racial ethic, that is, the right racial way of doing things. As
we have seen, the white man must rule, direct, employ,
punish when necessary, etc. He is good when he carries
out his functions in a paternal kindness, benevolence and
helpfulness.

What are the Negro's obligations and when is he good?
During the period between the World Wars, the good Negro
was generally described as one who embodies the ideals of
the "old-time darky." In fact, the good Negro and the "old-
time darky" are one and the same person. His virtues are
humility, servility, docility, reverence, kindness, patience,
and obedience. Such virtues as courage, bravery, and ambition, commonly proclaimed as American, do not apply to
him and do not become him.

The Southern Negro is a good citizen "when untam-
pered with by unprincipled white schemers." The Negro
who has been free from such tampering is "most thoughtful
and kindly toward his white neighbor and most appreciative
and responsive to every help and kindness extended to him."[50]

After pointing out that there have been many great Negroes, such as Booker T. Washington, George Washington
Carver, John Jasper, and Maggie Walker, J. J. Wicker

proceeds to tell the stories of Robert Booker, head waiter
in the William Byrd Hotel of Richmond, Virginia, and "Aunt
Martha," the washwoman of his school days. These two
persons are designated as "great Negroes."

As a resident of the William Byrd Hotel for about a
year, Wicker was served his breakfast in his room every
morning by Booker. This created the occasion for a rich
fellowship. "I have had no finer fellowship in my life than
I had with Robert Booker.... To talk with Robert Booker
opened my mind and soul in a most delightful way." Wicker
proceeds to describe Booker as a very religious and ethical
man. At the time of Wicker's writing about him, Booker
had become head waiter in the John Marshall Hotel and official chaplain for all guests. On Saturday mornings he gave
lectures to his waiters on ethics. He never cursed and
never shouted at one of his waiters, but explained the waiter's error when the latter had completed his chores. 51

The second part of Wicker's account has to do with
"another wonderful 'colored person.'" He never learned her
surname, but knew her as "Aunt Martha," her relation to
him having been that of his washwoman. Despite her lowly
estate, she had somehow bought and paid for "a nice little
brick home." During Wicker's ministerial student days,
"Aunt Martha" did his washing for twenty-five cents a week,
never receiving a cent of pay until the summer months.
"Yet she did the washing as perfectly and as joyfully as
though she was being paid right on the spot. To me she
is one of the most wonderful characters I ever knew."52

"Fortunate is the college that numbers among its
servants an 'old-time darky.' Such a college is Limestone."
These words introduce a eulogy of "Old Joe," a servant of
Limestone College of South Carolina. "Old Joe" is described
as having good common-sense, and as being thoroughly dutiful
and loyal. 53

When Lee Battle, a servant of Mercer University,
died, the president of the university lauded him in a special
supplement to his annual report to the trustees. He spoke
of him as one who had been "a faithful, trusted, and increasingly influential Mercerian," and affirmed that "more
alumni had known and loved him perhaps than any other
member of our institutional family and nobody ever felt
other than kindly and affectionately of him." At Battle's
funeral the president said "there had been no finer influ-

ence on the Mercer campus during his administration than
Lee Battle. "54

The portrait of the good Negro is continued in that of
the good Negro leader.   The good or "wise" Negro leader is
conservative, quietistic, and a staunch opponent of social
equality.   He is a strong support for the "peaceful and harmonious relations" already existing between the races.   He
is a "true friend of his race, " and knows what will make
for the "peace and happiness" of all the people of the South,
being very careful in his own personal life to show the proper deference to white people.

"The two greatest Negro leaders in this country--
Booker T. Washington and Dr. Carver--discouraged all aspirations among their people toward social equality.   They
knew that, in the South where most of the Negroes live,
segregation of the races would make for peace and happiness and understanding by both whites and colored. "55

Designating the Booker Washington type of Negroes,
who do not demand social equality, as wise leaders, Livingston Johnson advises his colored friends "to adopt Tuskegee
policies rather than those which come from New York. "56
In comparing Oscar De Priest, an "unwise" Negro leader,
with Robert Moton of Tuskegee, Johnson says, "the Moton
type is the real friend of his race, and such a leader is
worth far more than a cow pen full of inflated De Priests."57

Victor L. Masters deplores the emergence of bad and
unwise Negro leaders who are seeking to displace "the conservative race leaders":

> Racial leadership's most prominent exponent is Dr.
> W. E. B. DuBois, of New York, editor of the
> Crisis and author of certain books as bitter as the
> Crisis is.   He is half-negro, one fourth Dutch,
> and one-fourth French--'Thank God, no Anglo-
> Saxon!' to quote DuBois.

> This man and others of his ilk, through radical
> papers and in other ways, are seeking to take
> away from the conservative race leaders... the
> prestige and leadership they have had.   DuBois
> preaches revolt, revolution--anything to get back
> at the whites for real or fancied race grievances. 58

(6) Improving Race Relations and
Solving the Race Problem

In spite of the zealous clinging to the status quo in
race relations and the many testimonies concerning "our
peaceful and harmonious race relations, " Southern Baptists
believed even a generation ago that something needed to be
done in this sphere. All was not really quiet on the racial
front after all. In every area of the relationship between
the races improvements needed to be made. But Southern
Baptists insisted that all changes be made within the existing cultural framework and pattern of race relations. There
was by and large no vision of democratic equalitarianism and
Christian brotherhood.

In its report of 1940, the Social Service Commission
of the Southern Baptist Convention makes an appeal for the
removal of inequalities and injustices suffered by the Negro
in the courts of justice, in industry, and in education. [59]
But the Commission qualifies its appeal at two points, thus
effecting an accommodation to existing social realities and
sanctioning the very inequalities which it pleads against.
Concerning the industrial wage differential based on race,
the Commission says: "We would not be arbitrary or dogmatic; we would not assert that no differential in wages paid
could ever be justified because of social position and living
requirements. "[60] And concerning the differential in teacher's
salaries based on race, the Commission says:

Here again we would guard our statements and
would keep them well within the boundaries of a
reasonable and a just program. We recognize the
fact that absolute equality in the distribution of
public funds for education would perhaps not be
feasible. [61]

To illustrate this point, the Commission refers to the necessity of large appropriations for advanced and technical education, serving a comparatively small number of people, as
against the proportionately smaller appropriations to the lower phases of education, serving comparatively large numbers
of people. [62] This illustration contains a built-in handicap;
it fails to illustrate. It fails because it cannot be applied
to Whites and Blacks alike; it says nothing about disparities
based on race. In 1940, Negroes were not only the victims
of unequal appropriations and facilities from the first grade
through college; they were also totally excluded from all pro-

grams of advanced and technical education.   There were no
public graduate, professional and technical schools, worthy
of the name, open to Negroes.

Just why the Commission would call for the removal
of inequalities based on race, and at the same time sanction
inequality, even though of a diminished measure, becomes
evident from the Commission's statement of its goal in race
relations, in its report of 1943.   The Commission states
that there is no final solution of the race problem and a
final solution is not "what we seek":

> What we seek is a modus operandi that will di-
> minish friction, eliminate injustices and promote
> friendly cooperation.   We would be unable to blue-
> print a final framework.   We are not that far
> along.   But we can 'seek justice, love mercy and
> walk humbly' in the Spirit of Jesus Christ. [63]

Why cannot the race problem be solved?   Why must
we be content with a mere modus operandi in which friction
is diminished and cooperation increased?   Several answers
are given to these questions.

Ryland Knight says that the two races differ in heredi-
ty, background and aptitude.   "To say that there should be
identity of treatment for the two races is to ignore these
differences. "[64]

Charles L. Leek states that the barrier between the
races is not altogether a color barrier.   There is a "definite barrier" between them, which appears to mean a cultural barrier.   "The greatest barriers are sanitation, clean-
liness, character, habits, and the like. "[65]   Since Leek says
that the white man will be unwilling to share his full privileges with the Negro until the latter shows "a desire, an
aptitude, and an effort worthy of his objective, " the racist
confusion between nature and culture is manifestly a part of
his thinking.

Since there can be no ideal race relations for all concerned apart from social equality and intermarriage, "it is
folly ever to talk about ideal race relations. "[66]   While the
Christian religion may have the power ultimately to solve
the race problem, "at present the sociological principle of
'consciousness of kind' draws deeper than the Christian religion itself. "   This basic biological difficulty in race re-

lations is "deep as life itself. "[67]

Accepting the idea that the two races cannot live together on equal footing, R. M. Hunter suggests that the clock be turned back on the Negro. He announces himself to be "a strong Southerner, " adding, "and that means the Negro's best friend, one who is willing to do him good, and not harm. "[68] With this introduction, Hunter proceeds to set forth a "fair" program for the Negro. He affirms that the creation of a condition without creating something to satisfy that condition is cruel, and testifies that this is precisely what the Whites of the South are doing in the case of the Negro. They are educating Negroes to occupy the highest places politically, socially, and religiously; yet they are failing to create a place for them. Thus the Whites create a condition that can never be satisfied without a revolution that will establish black supremacy. "One race that is supreme can exist beside another that is inferior. But two races equal to each other, so much unlike, each striving for supremacy, cannot long exist. "[69] It is cruel to give a Negro a university education, for there is no place for a Negro of such high attainments in the South. In Africa "every black child should have an opportunity to attain the highest standard of education, for there he should learn how best to rule himself and his nation; for there he has no white competitor." To train a Negro in the South to be a doctor, lawyer, or politician makes him discontented. And out of this class comes "the finished burglar, and bandit and trouble-maker. " In the South, the Negro ought to be taught to read and write and to be a hewer of the wood and drawer of the water. Then he will be satisfied. [70]

Although his sociological and historical facts are grievously inadequate, --that is, the South did not make university education available to Negroes in 1932, and Africa was ninety-eight percent imperialized--Hunter does articulate a significant, though brutal, political fact. Given the conscious objective of the South, which was to maintain a racial system of dominance and subservience, the development of the lower caste was obliged to be in selected areas to harmonize with the interests of the upper caste, and improvement in all areas of life had to be qualified and limited. Most discussions of "development" proceeded along this line.

J. B. Gambrell suggests that the upward road for the Negro "is not along the line of politics so much as industry, home making, education and religion. " He recommends, how-

ever, a qualified and limited political life for the Negro--
that he engage in intelligent nonpartisan voting, and that he
develop race consciousness. [71] Lewis A. Myers makes a
plea for equality in education for Negroes. He rejects the
contention that Negro teachers salaries ought to be lower
because the standard of living of the Negro is lower. "To
insist on that point of view is to insist that Negro standards
of living remain exactly where they are at present. "[72] The
Committee on Social Service and Civic Righteousness of the
North Carolina Baptist Convention recommends that more
Negroes be appointed to the state's employment roles in the
department of education, health and welfare for the purpose
of servicing Negroes. [73]

     The prevailing idea that the best that can be achieved
in race relations is a modus operandi in which friction is
lessened and cooperation increased is rejected by R. A. Helton. He contends that social intercourse between Negroes
and Whites ought to be on the same basis as social intercourse between Whites and Whites--conduct and character.
There is a Christian solution to the race problem. "The
exact pattern and degree of the solution for this problem has
[sic] not emerged yet. Nevertheless, Christians are obligated to give their utmost to reach a solution as soon as
possible. "[74] Although their positions are not as forthright
as that stated by Helton, the Inter-Racial Commission of the
North Carolina Baptist Convention in 1930[75] and that of the
Virginia Baptist Convention in 1941[76] committed themselves
to the furthering of justice and good-will between the races,
thus coming to moral terms with the system itself and departing from the pattern of mitigation conjoined with justification.

(7) Lynching and Lynch Bills

     During the period between the World Wars, the most
brutal and barbaric expression of racial conflict was the
lynching of Blacks by Whites. Southern Baptists generally
opposed lynching; but there was a goodly measure of sentiment which favored lynching.

     R. H. Pitt points to both these attitudes in expressing
amazement that even "a Governor of a great state should
openly applaud and approve such outbreaks of murderous
violence, " and in expressing his own unequivocal opposition
to lynching and the historical opposition of the Religious

Herald.

Pitt proceeds to say that lynchings in the South are
largely due to racial prejudice and hatred, but are due in
no small measure to a growing distrust of the courts of
justice, legal procedure and a general temper of lawlessness.[77] J. L. Williams puts greater emphasis on the distrust of the courts of justice and legal procedure. He calls
this "the cause" of lynching: "The CAUSE of lynching is the
failure of our executive officers--from Governor down--to
enforce our laws...."[78] The facts needed to support this
claim are not presented, perhaps because it is difficult to
find them. There has never been a failure to bring the full
force of the law into operation when crimes or even alleged
crimes are committed by Blacks against Whites in the South.

The climate of sentiment in favor of lynching is affirmed and deplored by Z. T. Cody in commenting on an
Aiken, South Carolina lynching:

> A large number of men planned and participated in
> this event. The officers of the law were overcome.
> The prisoners were rather easily taken. The coro-
> ner's jury can find no one who was responsible for
> the crime. The general expectation is that there
> will be no indictments, and if indictments come,
> that there will be no convictions, etc., and so on.
> As everyone knows such things point to a public
> feeling that is more or less in sympathy with the
> men who did the lynching. And let us repeat, what
> book place in Aiken can come in any county in
> South Carolina.[79]

Southern Baptist opposition to lynching is logically
followed by the idea that the full penalty of the law ought to
be brought against those who commit the crime. This is
fully implied in Z. T. Cody's statement above, and is explicitly stated elsewhere.[80] In 1931, the Social Service
Commission of the Southern Baptist Convention expressed
agreement with Will W. Alexander that lynch mobs ought to
be met by armed resistance.[81] And in its 1936 report the
Commission stated "that as a people we stand firmly for the
orderly processes of justice in all cases and give to all officers of the law our support and commendation in the performance of their duties."[82]

While the prevailing attitude among Southern Baptists

is one of opposition to lynching, in rare cases a partial justification of the deed is to be found, or to say the least, it
is explained away. T. F. Callaway rejects lynching as
wrong, but adds that "so long as the crime is committed
that produces lynching, the crime of lynching is going to
continue."[83] In reply to the Christian Century, Livingston
Johnson is even more explicit: "If there were as many un-
educated and vicious Negroes in the North as there are in
the South lynchings up there would be as frequent as they
are down here."[84]

     Although Southern Baptists generally opposed lynching
and supported law enforcement against lynchers, they insisted
that the laws be state and local in origin. During the 1920's
and 1930's, the anti-lynching forces of the nation strenuously
endeavored to achieve a Federal anti-lynching bill for the
very reason that the crime was consistently going unpunished
in the states and localities. As we have seen, Southern Baptists were aware of this, but their opposition to federal action continued.

     P. I. Lipsey expressed his opposition to the Dyer
Anti-Lynching Bill on three grounds. It is a political ma-
neuver; it is unconstitutional; and it is unreasonable in that
it singles out one crime from among many to be made a
federal offense.[85] J. S. Farmer opposes a federal anti-
lynch law on two grounds. First, the states have done and
are doing reasonably well in dealing with lynching. Statistics showing the decline of lynching over the years are used
to substantiate this contention, and state action as the cause
of the decline is assumed. Second, a federal law would be
a violation of states rights. It would hardly be supported
by public opinion, and might arouse animosity, thus aggra-
vating the evil that it was designed to remedy.[86]

     A departure from the prevailing view is voiced by
Livingston Johnson, who is convinced that the only way to
suppress lynching is for the federal government to take the
matter in hand. Federal courts have a greater prestige
than state courts, and in the former local influence is removed.[87]

(8) The South's Problem

     Closely akin to the Southern Baptist opposition to
federal lynch laws is the idea that the race problem in the

South is the South's problem anyway, and the South must be left to settle it in its own way.

Presenting statistics to show how the Negro is sharing in the educational progress of North Carolina, J. S. Farmer asserts that "the races are living together in harmony and good will, " and expresses uncertainty that "these good conditions would prevail had we not been left to ourselves to work out our own race problem. "[88] Reuben E. Alley affirms that adjustments between the races present different problems as between the northern and southern states of this country. "Race segregation is probably more complete in the large industrial areas of the North than anywhere else in America. " And few Negroes live in small towns and rural areas in the North. On the contrary,

> In the agricultural South Negroes are a part of community life. They are components of the social structure rather than a race apart. This more intimate relationship is a basis for better understanding between the two races but it also makes adjustments more difficult. ... "[89]

The "vicious intermeddling" in the southern race situation on the part of organizations usually with headquarters in New York or Boston, and especially those with "communistic and socialistic" orientations, is deplored by R. H. Pitt. Southern white people of influence, for many years, "have been steadily and earnestly seeking privately and publicly to promote the best relations between the white people of the South and their colored neighbors. " These organizations "make the task of the just and kindly Southern whites far more difficult by their unnecessary interference. "[90]

In accounting for the origin of race prejudice and conflict in the South, A. J. Holt attributes it entirely to the northern white man and the Negro, and limits it to the reconstruction context. There was a deep attachment between the Negroes of the old South and their former masters. But change came when ill-advised Northerners persuaded Negroes that southern white people were not their best friends, and taught Negroes to hate southern Whites. "In time this hatred resulted in strained relations between the races. " Negroes began to rape white women. And since the making and execution of laws were in the hands of Negroes, and there was little likelihood that a Negro rapist would be convicted, the white people felt compelled to take the law into their own

hands. [91] Thus Holt, in accounting for the existence of prejudice and conflict, disregards a long slave history, abolition,
decades of sectional conflict, and a long tradition of regard-
ing the Negro as sub-human.

T. F. Callaway does not believe that the race relations of the old South have been lost. The mutual understanding and genuine brotherliness which existed between
masters and slaves were still dominant in 1938. There are
of course extremes in both races. "But the best element of
both realizes that there is a community of comradeship, sympathy and purpose to pull together and work out the mutual
problems and highest destiny of each." Northerners find it
difficult to believe but "as a whole the friendly relations existing between the whites and the blacks of the South are not
to be surpassed, if equalled, by any other two different
races dwelling side by side in any other country on earth."[92]

Stating that the best friend the Negro has is the southern white man, Rufus W. Weaver describes the attitude of
both the Northerner and the Southerner to validate his position. The typical Northerner has sympathy for and appreciation of the Negro, but resents personal contact with the individual Negro. "The typical attitude of the Southerner is that
of a superior in the presence of an inferior race, but he
has for the loyal, honest, faithful Negro a genuine personal
affection...."[93]

Not only is the South qualified to handle its own "Negro problem" without northern interference; it is also qualified to help the North handle its "Negro problem," according to B. J. W. Graham. Recent migrations have created
a "Negro problem" in the North. To demonstrate that the
Negro is essentially a problem, Graham points out that the
Negroes who migrated North were not the most ignorant,
vicious and thriftless of their race; rather, they were the
opposite. Yet riots have broken out here and there, and
Northerners are embarrassed and humiliated because of
their previous criticisms of the South. [94]

> These criticisms were made by men and women
> who did not understand the Negro, nor did they
> know the best way to get along with him. Now
> that the Negroes are in the North in large num-
> bers, and that serious riots are breaking out, the
> white people are beginning to sympathize with the
> South, and wisely they are seeking our help that

they may be relieved from further humiliation. [95]

2.   After World War II

(1)   Supreme Court Decisions and
Civil Rights Legislation

The Supreme Court decision of 1954, outlawing segregation in public schools, fell upon segregationist circles like a thunderclap.   It came as a thunderclap because the majority of men are never able to discern that they are living at the end of an era when they are wedded to the patterns of the present and the past.   They are never prepared for an inevitable future because they are imprisoned in a present that is based on their own glorifications of the past.   To the majority, the Supreme Court decision was an aberration; it was a complete reversal of normal and "natural" direction; it could only be explained under such rubrics as "communist brainwashing. "

As a matter of fact, world events in general and Supreme Court decisions in particular since World War I had been moving toward the fulfillment of the promise of the rights of man to that large section of humanity who had never shared them, namely, people of color.   Ironically, it was the Supreme Court which nullified the efforts made to establish first class citizenship for Negroes in the nineteenth century.   The Supreme Court did not begin to reflect the idealism of the American Creed until 1915, when it declared unconstitutional the so-called "grandfather clause, " a voting qualification device used by Southern states to restrict Negro suffrage.   Since that date, there has been a succession of decisions, the cumulative impact of which has tended to implement first class citizenship for Negroes.   A landmark precursor to the Supreme Court decision of 1954 was the Gaines decision of 1938 in which the Court ruled that a state must admit Negroes to its law school or establish comparable separate facilities within its own boundaries.   This was the first decision which clearly put the emphasis on the element of equality in the "separate but equal" formula, the sociological principle that had guided race relations for decades, with the emphasis always on "separate. "   This decision made inevitable the future examination of the question, "is not segregation inherently discriminatory?"   The Supreme Court decision of 1954 gave a positive answer to this question.

The fact that this 1954 decision was inevitable is attested to by Reuben E. Alley, who identifies the progress and improved position of the Negro under segregated education, the situation of the United States in international affairs, and the demands of public welfare as causative factors. Alley also bears witness to the fact that the white majority in the South was unprepared for the decision, as people seldom are, "when a day of decision promises far-reaching and difficult adjustments." Unfortunately Alley himself was not prepared at the time to see the decision in its full dimension of moral depth. He affirmed that the opinion is "essentially... political though it carries moral implications."96

In response to the school desegregation decision, the discerning minority in the Southern Baptist Convention began to exercise its leadership at once. The Christian Life Commission of the Southern Baptist Convention recognized the decision as being "in harmony with the constitutional guarantee of equal freedom to all citizens, and with the Christian principles of equal justice and love for all men." The Commission urged the Southern Baptist constituency "and all Christians to conduct themselves in the period of adjustment in the spirit of Christ," that their thinking and attitudes may be subject to Him and their behavior loving and just. And the leaders and statesmen of Southern Baptist churches were urged

> to use their leadership in positive thought and planning to the end that this crisis in our national history shall not be made the occasion for new and bitter prejudices, but a movement toward a united nation embodying and proclaiming a democracy that will commend freedom to all peoples. 97

The Baptist General Association of Virginia followed the lead of the Southern Baptist Convention in calling for compliance on the part of its constituency, but the thrust toward renewal was greatly qualified by a lack of confidence in the spiritual and moral potential of the people. On the one hand, the Christian Life Committee of the Association urged the denominational leadership "to guide our communities through the adjustment period, ever seeking to advance the Kingdom of God with every action, recognizing that we must eliminate the causes of additional strife as far as is within our power." 98 On the other hand, the Committee accepted the Supreme Court decision as the supreme law of the

land and as in no way discordant with any cardinal Baptist
principle, "regardless of our own personal views"; and it
described the fulfillment of duty as a rigorous exercise in
moving against one's true feelings.   "As far as is humanly
possible we should try to submerge our own feelings for the
good of our nation and ultimately all mankind. "[99]

The Committee on Social Service and Temperance of
the Atlantic Baptist Association of North Carolina recommends the acceptance of the decision on both religious and
secular grounds:

> First, because God commands it in Romans 13: 1-
> 4.   Second, because the Constitution of our beloved
> state calls for such: 'Every citizen of this state
> owes paramount allegiance to the constitution of the
> United States and that no law or ordinance of the
> state in contravention or subversion thereof can
> have any abiding force. '[100]

In harmony with the spirit and outlook of the report
of the Christian Life Commission, adopted by the Southern
Baptist Convention in 1954, several writers make their appeal to the resources of the Christian faith and the essen-
tials of democracy.   Guy H. Ranson speaks of agape love
as the basic or general principle of race relations and asserts that when agape love is authentic, racial justice will
issue from it. [101]   Speaking directly to the matter of the Supreme Court ruling, he states that the minister's responsibility is to explain to the people the relevant Christian principles, to explain the ruling itself and its implications, and
to set forth the Christian response to a just law. [102]   John
G. Clark deplores the fact that Christians have so often
avoided and evaded the issues posed by the Supreme Court
decision.   He calls upon the individual Christian to seek the
mind of Christ and thus avoid the endeavor to twist the
Scriptures to fit his prejudices, to be a bridge builder instead of a builder of barriers, and to let his influence count
as one who is utterly fair, honest and Christian across racial lines. [103]   Writing in 1956, Edwin McNiell Poteat refers
to the two recent Supreme Court decisions as creating the
need to examine "certain basic propositions on which we
may all be thought to agree. "   These basic propositions are
designated as bases.   The first base is "the free democratic
society, " which presupposes equal rights for every man in
the sight of the law.   The second base is "the controlled
ethical society, " which presupposes equal dignity in the

sight of God, and accordingly freedom from discrimination
and full opportunity for self realization within the legal and
moral structure.   The third base is the distinctively Christian obligation of the ministry of reconciliation.   The Supreme Court decisions are just because they express and
point to these three bases. 104   Henry A. Buchanan addresses himself to the question of the relation of the church to
the Supreme Court's ruling.   The responsibility of the church
is two-fold.   It must "proclaim the undiluted truth of God
with a voice of conviction and authority, " avoiding any echo
of the confused voices of the people. 105   And it must apply
the truth proclaimed "in the spirit of Jesus Christ, to the
needs of all men. "106

The 1954 resolution of the Southern Baptist Convention concerning the Supreme Court decision did not win universal approval and agreement.   The presentation and adop-
tion of this resolution was called "the lowest point of the
whole Convention" by A. L. Goodrich, who criticizes it on
three grounds.   First, the resolution "is a political, not a
church matter. "   In presenting it, "the Christian Life Commission went out of its field to dip its finger in politics. "
Second, if the Commission had any justification for bringing
the school desegregation ruling to the Convention, by the
same token it should have brought other segregation questions, namely, the rulings of the Court that segregation in
public housing and on golf courses is unlawful.   Finally, in
dealing with a state matter, the action of the Convention
tends toward "a breakdown of the wall of separation between
church and state. "107

Finley Tinnin aims his fire at the Supreme Court itself, declaring the decision to be "ill advised" at this time.
Tinnin adds that great progress has been made in race relations during the past fifty years, and asserts that most
white people are "sincerely interested in the progress of the
Colored people. "   He also ventures to speak for Negroes in
the South by saying that most of them "feel that it would be
unwise to attempt to mix the races in the schools. "108

In 1945, New York passed the first state Fair Employment Practices law, and set up a state commission
against discrimination.   In 1947, the Committee on Civil
Rights, appointed by President Harry S Truman, made its
report in which it called for an end to all forms of segregation.   In response to the former of these events, Joseph E.
Brown rejects the idea of legislation as a weapon against

discrimination on the negative ground that a government
agency cannot probe men's motives, and on the positive
ground that men's motives must be changed from within by
a new birth in Christ. [109]   In response to the new Civil
Rights consciousness and discussion, partly generated by
the President's Civil Rights Committee, John J. Hurt, Jr.
charged President Truman with "seeking to obtain for the
negro new civil rights legislation when already the chief
objectives are being reached through the preaching and
practice of Christian rights. " To illustrate progress in
race relations, Hurt cites the reduction in lynchings, the
gains of the Negro toward equality in education, and erro-
neously claims that the Negro has won the right to vote.
He attributes these gains to the South's working in its own
way and the preaching and practice of "Christian rights. "
But "the South is not ready to give up its laws of segregation. " It must be left to move in its own way, "and it is
most familiar with the problem. "[110]   Hurt hints that legislation has been a factor in Negro suffrage, but he seems
wholly unaware of the importance of the constant threat of
a Federal Anti-Lynching Bill in the reduction of lynchings
and of much NAACP-sponsored litigation in the progress toward equality in education.   The recognition and knowledge
of these factors would, of course, tend to undermine his
argument against legislation.

        The idea that the race problem must be solved "by
the leaders of the two races in the South where they understand each other the best" is also advanced by the Social
Service Committee of the Florida Baptist Association.   The
Committee saw "real problems for both races" posed by two
recent Supreme Court decisions--the one declaring the Negro's right to vote in primary elections and the other making the segregation of the races on common interstate carriers invalid.   The Committee doubts that there is any final
solution to the race problem, but believes that Baptists who
love freedom and champion individual liberty "can distinguish
between the issue of social equality and that of political and
economic freedom and deal with the latter on its own merits
and in all good conscience.... "[111]

        Six years after the Supreme Court ruling on the de-
segregation of public schools, the Social Service Commission
of the Georgia Baptist Convention could still say that "federal law now stands in opposition to tradition, practice, and
religious convictions of Georgia Baptists. " Since their own
tradition, practice, and religious convictions were normative,

recommendations were based upon them, and it was impossible to indicate a clear course forward. Individuals and
local churches were advised to "give prayerful thought to the
matter of race relations in the light of the teachings of the
Bible." It was recommended that local churches "make an
attempt to repair the good will between the races which has
been damaged in recent years." This can only mean that
good-will existed under the undisturbed segregated system,
and Supreme Court decisions and the rulings of district
judges had damaged that good-will. Finally, the Commission
recommends that some third position between compliance and
noncompliance may be necessary and desirable:

> That Baptists of Georgia, as individuals, strive to
> harmonize their religious convictions with federal
> court rulings on the subject of race relations; and
> if the two be irreconcilable then to seek some al-
> ternative that will conform to faith and continues
> our position as law abiding citizens. 112

By 1963 the dialogue concerning a Civil Rights bill,
including a public accommodations section, had reached national proportions. The public accommodations issue attrac-
ted widespread attention and created much debate because it
impinged on one of the most celebrated values of American
culture--private property.

Entering into the debate on the side of the opponents
of the public accommodations section of President Kennedy's
Civil Rights program, E. S. James distinguishes between
integration by "the way of Christian love and respect for all
mankind" and integration by law. He opposes desegregation
by law because "the principle of free enterprise demands
that both the buyer and the seller must have freedom of
choice before the transaction can be rightly made."113

James develops his theme by comparing the business
and the home, as though the two were the same kind of private property. This is a fundamental error in the popular
definition of private property in America, and was used all
over the country as the main argument against public accommodations legislation. In the popular version, all private property is brought under the one defining concept of
"the man in his castle." The house is in fact private property oriented toward the person and his preservation, and it is
an environment into which outsiders enter by invitation. But
the business is private property oriented toward the public,
and it exists for the sole purpose of offering goods and/or

services to the public.   It holds a public franchise and enjoys the police protection of the state in order that it may
realize this purpose.   If the business man withholds his
goods and/or services from a segment of the public solely
because he does not like the way God created them, he is
violating the trust which has been vested in him in the form
of a public franchise.   He has a right to "pick and choose"
the people who come into his home, but his business is one
unit in a community of agencies designed to meet the common needs of the public within its reach.

Another matter in the Civil Rights legislation debates,
almost universally overlooked and overlooked by James, is
the fact that the Civil Rights forces did not choose their battle grounds.   Their battle grounds were chosen for them by
the segregationist forces, who were on the field first.   Anti-
Civil Rights and segregation have historically been imple-
mented by law and state constitutions.   It stands to reason
that once a Civil Rights impetus gained momentum, it would
have to deal with legislation and constitutionality.   And all
of those persons who claimed to be in favor of Civil Rights
but opposed to the legislative method were obliged in good
faith to demand that anti-Civil Rights laws be removed from
the statute books.   This obligation was consistently overlooked by churchmen who proclaimed that social patterns
can only be changed "by regeneration in Christ."

Against the background of an anti-Civil Rights tradition, supported by both the legal and moral sanctions of the
society, pro-Civil Rights legislation came as an aid to all
the forces who sincerely believed in democracy and first
class citizenship for all of the people.   This fact was recognized by James William McClendon, who testifies that by
and large Southern Baptist pastors have remained silent
about Civil Rights at the grass roots level.   But "passage
of the 1964 Civil Rights bill affords a fresh opportunity to
Southern Baptist pastors and church members to speak and
act on the side of fairness in community life."   Southern
Baptist leaders, whose consciences troubled them on the
race issue, were silent for three reasons--owing to the am-
biguity in the Civil Rights movement, the fear of the loss of
standing in the white community which forthrightness would
bring, and the conviction that speaking out was a futile exercise.   McClendon is convinced that the Civil Rights bill,
with the authority and prestige that stands behind it, has produced a "changed situation."[114]

Oddly enough, E. S. James, who opposes the legis-

lative method in desegregation, agrees in essence with this
position in the very article in which he opposes the legislative method. He points up the importance of pressures, judicial decision, and historical events in awakening a slum-
bering Christian conscience, and testifies that "Christian
people waited until the Supreme Court decision in 1954 before saying much about a Christian principle involved" because "we lived in a culture where segregation was practiced,
and we thought little about it until circumstances forced it
upon our attention. "115

The Christian Life Commission of the Southern Baptist Convention hailed the 1964 Civil Rights law as a turning
point in race relations. The Commission gave thanks to
God for the legal, sociological, and economic progress which
had been made in race relations during the previous year,
but reasserted its conviction "that the ultimate solution of
the racial problem lies on distinctively spiritual grounds. "
While in no sense minimizing the service of law and public
policy on behalf of justice, the Commission called upon the
Convention to go beyond the law by the transforming power
of the gospel of love. 116

(2)   Desegregation and the
Civil Rights Drive

The major instruments of the Civil Rights forces in
the 1940's were litigation and legislation. Even before these
instruments were having effect within the distinctively southern institutions, as well as thereafter, outcries concerning
the use of force and power and the need to leave the South
alone to work out its own problem were numerous.

In 1948, President Truman submitted a civil rights
program to Congress. Dr. C. Oscar Johnson, then president of the Baptist World Alliance, was quoted in a Religious
News Service story in such a way as to suggest that he
wholeheartedly supported President Truman's program.   Finley W. Tinnin attempting to set the record straight, excuses
Dr. Johnson for his ignorance of conditions, "and the thought
of the people of this section" on the ground that he "has been
out of the South for many years":

The difference between President Truman's and
Dr. Johnson's thinking on this explosive issue and
that of the majority of the people of the South is

> in the method of approach to it.... They would
> have the Federal government force upon the people
> of the South certain changes in their way of life;
> while Southern people would bring about these
> changes gradually.

Tinnin proceeds to "clarify" matters by making the following
claims: that coercion of the South is unfair to the white and
black people, that the southern white man is the Negro's
best friend and understands his aspirations and struggles,
that the South is rapidly approaching the day of equal opportunity, and that if left alone to work out its own problem the
South will achieve "the happiest concord between the white
and colored races. "[117]

        The themes of suasion instead of coercion and local
decision instead of Federal decision are consistently united.
S. L. Morgan, Sr. is convinced that "forced-integration
would prove a calamity" while "voluntary school integration
could succeed even in the deep South. " He suggests that "a
few wise leaders of both races" might agree to try out desegregation of a few students "in the lower grades as a be-
ginning--and as a pledge of good faith. " There is real hope
for settling the question "if the people of both races close
their ears to outside agitators and cultivate friendly relations
between the races on the local level. "[118] The Christian Life
Commission of the Alabama Baptist Convention accuses the
protagonists in the racial struggle in the South of merely
"trying to win legal points rather than do the most good for
the most people. " Declaring that "the advances of one group
must not inflict a penalty against another, " the Commission
asserts that "we can not see that it can be the will of God
to lower the standards of one great race in a hopeful gamble
that it lift the standards of another. "[119] The extreme integration viewpoint (a phrase that remains undefined), "with
all of its fuzzy idealism, " is declared to be unworkable in
the South "for a long time to come. "[120] Racial strife, says
Richard N. Owen, stems in large part from the fact that responsible groups in the communities involved are not being
permitted to offer solutions. "Problems cannot be solved
by outsiders. " Their solution "waits upon men of good will
of both races who can meet together sensibly and deal with
the matter on a just and spiritual basis. "[121] Testifying that
the main stream of life moves along happily in the South and
that disturbing outbursts are due to outside agitators, Leon
Macon gives assent to the position that the South will solve
the racial problem before the North does. On the one hand,

the majority of Southerners have no racial animosity; but, on
the other, outside agitators perform their activities with ul-
terior motives, and there is some communist influence
among them. [122]

The exponents of these views--that suasion alone is
the appropriate instrument of progress in race relations and
that the South and even the local community must be left
alone to accomplish the task--fail to speak out of the actual
context of race relations. Accordingly they overlook the importance of the very coercive factors which they decry as
agents of change. They also overlook the very significant
fact that during a quarter of a century of effective civil
rights action and states' rights complaints against federal
pressures, no southern legislative body presented a substitute civil rights bill of its own within its own domain.

The eyes of some Southern Baptists were always open
to the perception of these realities. Surveying the situation
as it stood in 1954, E. A. McDowell attributed the progress
in race relations to the Negro's own determination and
achievement, Supreme Court decisions and Executive Orders,
the shift in the Negro population out of the South, and Christian influence. [123] In 1969, Georgia confronted a new phase
in school desegregation, as did other parts of the South.
While admitting that few were happy with federal interven-
tion, Jack U. Harwell felt obliged to say:

> But if we are honest we must admit that without
> pressures from Washington, 'local control' and
> 'states rights' might continue to be camouflage
> words for 'white supremacy' in the South for dec-
> ades to come. Federal interference has come
> only because there was no other way. [124]

When it became evident that the desegregation process
would soon be extended beyond public schools, public libraries,
public parks, etc. to include the services of private business,
the argument that public institutions must be distinguished
from private businesses became a dominant theme. While
personally favoring the gradual desegregation of public institutions, Edwin L. McDonald states that he does not "agree
that the government should try to tell private businesses who
their employees or customers must be." McDonald gives no
reason for this position, but implies the "man in his castle"
view of private property by making the business decision
analogous to the decision concerning what neighborhood one

will live in "and who his neighbors shall be. "[125]

Jerrell Dee Gaddy gives an odd twist to the debate
by making the operations of private economic enterprises
identical with integration.   Gaddy is convinced that segregation is morally wrong because it means "enforced separation
of racial groups, " and is a form of suppression and control.
Desegregation is morally right because it removes the barriers and deprivations imposed by segregation.   But "to in-
tegrate means total mixing in all areas of life. " It comes
"through the process of individual and group selection. "[126]
Gaddy seems to be saying that an integrated community is
based on the positive and internal, spiritual connections between men.   Just how manufacturing, distributing, buying,
selling, advertising etc. are inherently expressions of such
a spiritual condition, if carried on by private groups, is not
made clear.

Beginning with the Montgomery bus boycott of 1955,
the Civil Rights Movement, which had depended on judicial
decisions, civil rights legislation in some northern states
and cities, Commission decrees and executive orders, added
the instrument of nonviolent direct action in the form of
marches, demonstrations, boycotts, freedom rides, sit-ins,
etc.

Southern Baptist reaction to these new strategies was
generally negative.   The March on Washington of 1963 was
viewed by Richard N. Owen as the work of "restive Negroes,"
who have "turned a deaf ear to counsel by some of their wis-
est leaders including men like Dr. Joseph Jackson, " president of the National Baptist Convention, USA.   In addition to
the turning away from "the wiser, saner leaders, " Owen
says the demonstration means "that Negro unrest is being
capitalized upon by certain elements. " Although the Communist party alone is identified among these "elements, "
Owen hastens to add that he is not saying that the March on
Washington, the freedom rides, sit-ins, etc. "have all been
Communist inspired. " But he is saying that "Communists
want to take over to use the Negro's discontent for their own
purposes, and it remains to be seen whether or not Negro
leaders will play into their hands. " The choice for Americans is whether they "are going to try to settle problems in
the streets by mass demonstrations or in deliberative assemblies by duly elected representatives. "[127]

Putting the stress on the idea that freedom means re-

sponsibility, James F. Cole accuses the freedom riders of
effecting a divorce between the two. He never states in
what respects this is true, but seems content with the gen-
eralization itself combined with a contrast between the thinking of "the average citizen today" and that of the founding
fathers. 128

        The extreme in vituperation is achieved by Leon Ma-
con, who runs the gamut in bringing charges against the Sel-
ma, Alabama demonstration. He calls it a "holocaust" and
a "filthily conducted demonstration. " He agrees with Governor George Wallace "that any qualified Negro in Alabama
has the right and opportunity to vote, " and denies that the
"disturbance" aims at voting rights alone. He insists that
there is strong Communist influence in the demonstration,
that demonstrators taunt the local police to create incidents,
that local citizens have also been harassed, that there is
drinking among the demonstrators, the use of vulgar language,
and even the use of the streets for toilets. 129

        In contrast to these sentiments, Gainer E. Bryan, Jr.
challenges Southern Baptist churches to identify with the Negro cause. He notes that "the major Christian and Jewish
bodies, except Southern Baptists, have shifted from paper
pronouncements to commitment and involvement, " and suggests that "the white man should be grateful that the tactic
in this phase of the struggle is nonviolence, for advocates
of violence lurk in the shadows. " The challenge to the
Christian conscience in the area of race does not come from
the Supreme Court, as those who justify the detachment of
the church contend. Rather, it comes from "the cry of the
oppressed" and "from the biblical demand for right dealing
with our fellow man as the acid test of a right relationship
with God. "130

        In the midst of the Louisville eating establishment de-
segregation crisis of 1961, C. R. Daley supported the sit-
ins, stand-ins, squat-ins, etc. Although he wrote in an atmosphere in which he felt he must belabor the point that he
was expressing a personal and not an official position, he
was obliged to testify that "as a Christian and a believer in
the New Testament concept of the dignity of man, I cannot
but espouse the cause of the Negroes. "131

        Any movement which achieves massive proportions
will inevitably spin off some aberrations. The aberrations
of the Civil Rights drive took the form of urban riots, ex-

cessive black power rhetoric and the James Foreman reparations demand.

Southern Baptist commentators on the riots generally
misunderstood them as products of relative justice and ex-
pectations of full justice. In reaction to the riots in Los
Angeles, Chicago, and Springfield, Massachusetts, Leon Macon states that, "the Federal government has gone entirely
too fast in granting what it thinks are rights due minority
groups...." This action is compared with giving an ignorant
country boy who has been brought to the city the false hope
that he can own the city by simply taking it. [132] Hudson
Baggett, Leon Macon's successor, echoes Macon's thinking
in 1966 when he says that "the recent riots and discontent
expressed in Northern cities is the harvest of false hopes
planted by the Federal Government and others in connection
with the Civil Rights movement. " Baggett also adds the
conspiratorial explanation. [133] The idea of a conspiracy,
even of the proportions of a central planning strategy, is
advanced by Richard N. Owen, who sees the Detroit riot
against the background of a greatly exaggerated view of Detroit as a model city. Owen claims that the city "had done
so much to improve race relations" and the churches of the
city "had done so much to alleviate the problems of the
city's more than 500, 000 Negroes. "[134] No less an authority
than the mayor of Detroit expressed regret that Detroit had
been referred to as a model city. He testified that only a
modicum had been done for the ghettos in a great sea of
need. But since this was more than other cities had done,
Detroit came to be referred to as "the model. "

As already suggested, the error in these commen-
taries is the assumption that the ghetto masses have experienced the relative justice of Civil Rights and are stimulated
by the potentialities of full justice. Actually the black masses have neither participated in nor been the beneficiaries
of the relative gains of Civil Rights. It is the black middle
class which has benefitted by Civil Rights. Civil rights
gains have been made in precisely those areas for which
the previous experiences of the black masses have not prepared them. Those Blacks who have benefitted by these
gains have been those who had already effected a cultural
and occupational breakthrough and the youngsters in colleges,
universties, and technical schools. These groups have been
making progress during the post-World War II period, while
the conditions of the black masses have been growing worse
under the impact of automation, unemployment, underemploy-

ment, urban renewal, inflation, and the ever present racial
victimization.   The riots of the ghettos must be understood
within this sociological framework.

     The black power concept has evoked little literary
response from Southern Baptists.   But the available interpretation of the concept is insightful and analytical.   In setting forth four elements in the meaning of black power, Daniel R. Grant carefully distinguishes between the legitimate
and the aberrant.   As a legitimate notion, black power is
the Negro's quest for self respect and self identity after
three hundred years of living under an image manipulated
by the white man.   And black power is legitimate political
power in a democracy as long as interests are ethnically
diversified.   But when black power means organized or un-
organized Negro violence and black separatism or nationalism, it is an aberrant notion. [135]

     The reparations demands of James Foreman evoked
warnings from Southern Baptist editors indicative of a clear
understanding of the tangential nature of the demands.   John
J. Hurt warned that the Negro race should no more be
blamed for James Foreman than the white race for the Ku
Klux Klan. [136]   Jack U. Harwell called Forman's demands
"outrageous" and the product of a "fanatical fringe. "[137]
James A. Lester states that "it should be said, in fairness,
that this apparently is not the posture of the majority of Negroes in the United States. "[138]   Each of these editors also
warned against the tendency to be detracted by the likes of
Foreman from the main business of Civil Rights and progress
in race relations.

     R. Stuart Grizzard rejects reparations because it is
not a Christian concept; but, in view of the racial history of
America, he seeks a substitute moral idea, settling on the
concept of restitution, combined with repentance and renewal. [139]   But since he gives restitution an individualistic and
person-to-person meaning, the concept is an inadequate answer to a massive, systematic and institutional problem.
No great social problem is amenable to privatized solutions
alone because the privatized approach cannot come to terms
with institutional concentrations of power and fixation of
policy.

(3) Segregation

As we have already seen, the racial caste system
was the ideal among Southern Baptists during the period
from World War I to the end of World War II.   Sentiment
in favor of segregation was so overwhelming that anyone who
believed the system to be unchristian was driven to silence. [140] With such a cultural tradition in the immediate
background, there is still much sentiment in favor of segregation.

In the post-World War II period, the defenders of
segregation take their stands on two grounds--theological and
Biblical, and practical.   Pseudo-science is minimal and, for
the most part, present only by implication.

The central theological theme is that God Himself ordained segregation and the favorite New Testament text is
Acts 17:26 in its second part: "God hath made of one blood
all nations of men for to dwell on all the face of the earth,
and hath determined the times before appointed, and the
bounds of their habitation. " Obedient response to the will
of God on the part of white Christian people means that they
will want Negroes to have equal institutions and facilities, if
possible, but there will be no mixing of the races in the
home, school and church. [141]

In an attack on the Southern Baptist Convention for
supporting the Supreme Court school desegregation decision
of 1954, T. J. Preston appeals to several Biblical teachings
and events to show that "the Bible teaches segregation. " In
addition to his citation of the Tower of Babel story in which
the languages and the bounds of habitation of the nations
were set, Preston asserts that the Lord through the Prophets
forbade the Jews to mix with other races and brought judgment upon them for disobedience; that the three sons of Noah
were the heads of three distinct races whose separation was
effectuated at Babel; that the New Testament teaches the
preaching of the gospel to all nations but not the mixing of
the races; and that Christ preached to the Samaritans but
lived with his own people, the Jews.   On the strength of
his reading of the Bible, Preston calls on his Baptist brethren to "preach the gospel to all but keep our races segregated.   That's the Bible way.   That should be our way. "[142]

Appalled by Henlee Barnette's article, "Southern Baptist Churches and Segregation, " which had recently appeared

in the Baptist and Reflector, L. J. McRae goes beyond Preston in appealing to the Divine word and action in favor of
segregation. "God segregated Adam by calling him away
from others that he might better train and develop a chosen
people. " (No information is given concerning who these
"others" were). The descendants of Abraham faithfully ad-
hered to the idea of segregation through the centuries.
"Leviticus 18 proclaims God as Lord, and his desire to
keep his chosen people pure by extreme caution in choosing
wives. " The displeasure of God is shown in Numbers 25
"by his ordering the slaying of thousands for their intimate
mixing with other tribes. " Christ chose twelve disciples
from his own race, "then he again segregated them by choosing three to be with him on a number of occasions. " After
he had trained his disciples, Christ sent them to carry the
message to his own race--"the lost sheep of the house of
Israel. " McRae contends that segregation does not mean
discrimination and Southern Baptists have "been true to the
Negro" in that they "have helped them build their churches,
schools and seminaries. "[143]

Although he endorses Acts 17:26 as a New Testament
witness to segregation as the Divine purpose, E. D. Solomon
adds a pseudo-scientific note as a warning against any breach
of the Divine will. "In amalgamation they (the races) par-
take of the vices of both and the virtues of neither. This
will never be a nation of Mullattos [sic]. Integration is
wrong and impossible. "[144] There is no anthropological or
historical evidence to support this claim concerning amalgamation, and, in asserting it, Solomon must make the un-
scientific assumption that culture and the life of the spirit
are carried in the genes.

> I am sure that every man knows that there is no
> difference in the souls of men regardless of his [sic]
> skin--that's spiritual. But what the Supreme Court
> passed was social and educational. I believe that
> every Christian believes in equal rights, but it is
> one thing to believe in equal rights and another
> thing to be unequally yoked. [145]

With these words the Augusta (Georgia) Baptist Association
defends segregation by resorting to a theological anthropology
which splits the psycho-physical being whom God has created.
If it is logically and consistently applied, this anthropology
has no more meaning for relations between races than within
them. But in the modern, colonial and racist societies, it

has been applied only to the "lower races" and has produced "the missionary attitude"--the claim of Christian love for people's souls while holding their bodies and the actual historic persons in social contempt. This view makes possible an alleged Christian brotherhood in "spiritual things" while all of the social distances and structures of oppressive power required by a secular society remain in force.

Efforts to justify segregation on practical grounds take two forms: the subjective, consisting in testimony that segregation is desired, and the objective, consisting in simple declarations concerning the objective situation without analysis.

Since segregation must be defended against the charge that it is an oppressive system, the most popular subjective defense is the testimony of the victim. All aristocratic systems claim to be operating on behalf of the victim and with his pleasure as well as approval.

In 1949, the Social Service Commission of the State Baptist Convention of South Carolina called upon the constituency to rid themselves of their fears of intermarriage and social equality, and "dismiss the bigoted and opinionated prejudices which have obscured their vision" by learning from the Negro himself "what it is that he is striving for." A group of Negroes, designated as "representative," had recently met in South Carolina and stated what they want: equal educational opportunities, but not desegregated schools and universties; the right to vote, "which has been denied him [the Negro] in far too many instances and States, to our shame"; a mitigation of economic pressures so that he will be able "to better his share-cropper status and become a property owner"; and "segregated churches and pastors." The "representative" Negro group is said to have had no interest in "mingling in social gatherings" and to have regarded segregated seating as not being segregation. [146]

In opposing the Supreme Court decision of 1954, Finley W. Tinnin appeals to the desires of southern Negroes. Even though he contends that "there are few instances today where the Negro does not receive fair treatment in business, in courts and educational opportunities," he proceeds to say that southern Negroes "know that the children of their races will suffer" from school desegregation because "white teachers naturally would favor white children."[147]

The technique of defending segregation through the
voice of the victim not only calls attention to his desires
but to the testimony of the prominent or allegedly prominent
leader. In its 1952 report, the Social Service Commission
of the Georgia Baptist Convention affirmed segregation and
quoted Booker T. Washington for support. [148] Finley W.
Tinnin hails the words of the Reverend C. C. Addison as
"a sane view on segregation." The Reverend Addison, identified as "a New York Negro leader," testifies that "we take
our segregation from the Bible" and integration is a sin. [149]
David M. Gardner commends an editorial by Davis Lee as
having "hit the nail squarely on the head and nailed the civil rights plank down in the right place." Lee had written in
his Newark, New Jersey publication, The Telegram, that
segregation is the economic salvation of the Negro in the
South, that the economic position of the Negro in the North
is unfavorable by comparison, and that the improvement of
the race from within would gain acceptance for the Negro on
his own terms.

As already suggested, the justifications of segregation
in terms of objective, practical realities consists of declara-
tive statements without the benefit of analysis. The Social
Service Commission of the Georgia Baptist Convention makes
the simple statement that "this practical solution to a complex social problem has helped an underprivileged race to
come a long way in a short time."[150] There is no analysis
of the elements which constitute segregation, the spiritual
motivations which prompt those who impose it, the tragic
spiritual effects upon them and their victims, and the economic and cultural losses for the society as a whole. There
is no consideration as to whether segregation is still needed,
even if it was once needed, no consideration as to whether
all Negroes need it, and whether it should characterize all
institutions. Oblivious to the fact that racial segregation
can only be based on intolerance, Charles F. Leek agrees
with Governor Sparks that "absolute segregation of Whites
and Negroes is essential," provided it is not based on the
intolerance of the powerful. [151]

The inability to analyze segregation as a spiritual,
moral, and psychological reality is seen in the claim of
Jack L. Gritz that "equal rights and opportunities do not
necessarily mean complete fellowship in home, club, and
church." The relevant question is, can this statement be
true if such fellowship is categorically and systematically
rejected? Gritz also is overcome by the fallacy of appealing

to the consequences of a bad system as a justification for
its continuance. He speaks of a "natural segregation," and
asserts that "usually those of the same race are happier and
better off together."[152] These allegedly empirical generalizations are situational; they are not universal. They are
drawn from an environment which has been guided in race
relations by racist sentiments and values without the effective competition of other values.

The defenders of segregation in the post-World War II
Southern Baptist world have not had the field entirely to
themselves. For the first time in Southern Baptist history,
their views are openly criticized. In rejecting the idea of
a Biblical basis for segregation, Edward A. McDowell cor-
rects the misinterpretation of the Old Testament which identifies Jewish religious exclusivism with racial exclusivism.
"The Jews were commanded to be separate and apart from
the people around them because their neighbors were idola-
ters."[153] McDowell might have added that in the ancient
world and even well into the modern period, separation
among religious groups was believed by all to be the only
way to prevent apostasy.

The classic case of Old Testament exegesis informed
by a racist ideology is the "Curse of Ham" doctrine, based
on Genesis 9:18-27. The essence of this doctrine is that
God placed a curse on Ham and his descendants, which involved their being turned black and the decree that hence-
forth they should be "the hewers of the wood and drawers
of the water." This doctrine was first used as a theological
defense of slavery, but after abolition it became the major
"Old Testament teachings" in support of segregation in its
subordinationist aspect. McDowell includes the "Curse of
Ham" doctrine among the "myths about race we must give
up," pointing out that the descendants of Canaan, enumerated
in Genesis 10:15-20, include several of the tribes whom the
Hebrews encountered in their conquest of the Promised
Land."[154]

Foy Valentine offers a corrective summary of the
distorted elements in the Biblical passage:

> Even a casual reading of the passage, Genesis 9:
> 18-27, reveals that (1) God places a curse on no
> one; (2) Noah did the cursing after having awakened
> from a drunken stupor; (3) there is no indication of
> God's having approved Noah's act or having imple-

mented it in any way, and (4) no reference is
made to anybody's having been turned any color
different from what he already was.

Furthermore, the reference to 'hewers of the wood
and drawers of the water' in Joshua 9 is Joshua's
pronouncement upon the Gibeonites, the inhabitants
of a city of Canaan who had deceived Israel into
making peace with them.   The Gibeonites would
have to be classified as Caucasians, like the Jews.
So it can readily be seen that this often quoted
passage does not justify white exploitation of colored help nor provide a Biblical basis for racial
prejudice. 155

In addition to rejecting the popular error that the
Hamites were Negroes, R. Lofton Hudson cites several teachings of the Bible which point up the unGodliness of segregation.   The unity of the human race is affirmed in the creation in the image of God and from one set of parents.   It is
also affirmed in Acts 17:26.   The brotherhood of all in
Christ is declared in Galations 3:28 where it is said, "There
is neither Jew nor Greek, there is neither male nor female:
for ye are all one in Christ Jesus. "   In Acts 10, there is
an application of this teaching, expressed in Peter's visit
with Cornelius and his announcement that "God hath shewed
me that I should not call any man common or unclean" (v.
28).   In this passage and in James 2:1-9, it is clearly
taught that "God is no respector of persons. "   In talking to
the woman of Samaria, "Jesus himself crossed the segregation line" (John 4).   Finally, segregation is sinful when
viewed in the perspective of the Golden Rule and the "universal, unchangeable, unconditional, personal, and active"
nature of Christian love. 156

Coming at the segregation issue under the alerting
force of the 1954 Supreme Court decision, the Baltimore
Baptist Pastors' Conference157 hails the decision as an application of "a biblical truth to political life. "   The Conference adds the judgment "that compulsory racial segregation
is discriminatory and is, therfore, a distortion of the biblical ideal as well as the constitutional principle of equality
of all men. "158

Henlee Barnett commends the church leaders for
speaking out increasingly on the racial problem but, noting
that little is said about the integration of the local church,

calls the leaders of the church to their responsibility along
this line. As "a people of the Book, " Southern Baptists
have a special responsibility to be responsive to its expressed teachings. "Jesus specifically states that His house
is the "house of prayer for all nations" (Mark 11:17). The
Holy Spirit at Pentecost created a common religious experience, thus making "it crystal clear... that there was to be
no segregated church" (Acts 2:1-12) and (Acts 2:46). Peter
learned that "God is no respecter of persons "(Acts 10).
The Epistle of James warns against all snobbery (2:1-7),
and Paul teaches "that all become one new humanity in
Christ" (Gal. 3:29; Eph. 2:11-22). 159

(4) The Renaissance in Christian Teaching
Concerning Race Relations

In 1947, the Southern Baptist Convention adopted a
"Charter of race relations. " The Charter contained six
fundamental doctrines and the principles of conduct which
issue from adherence to the doctrines. The doctrines are
belief in the Lordship of Christ and the love of all men
which His Lordship requires; belief in the Holy Spirit and
the unity of all men in the bond of peace which He inspires;
belief "in the Bible as the word of God" which summons
Christians "to practice justice towards all people of all
races"; belief "in the dignity and worth of the individual"
and the right of each man to fulfillment according to his
own God given capacity; belief in the fellowship of believers
regardless of race; and belief "in the principles of democracy in government" entailing the universalization of the
rights of citizens.

These doctrines which must commend themselves
to every conscience impel us to the observance of
the following principles of conduct:

1.   We shall think of the Negro as a person and
treat him accordingly.

2.   We shall continually strive as individuals to
conquer all prejudices and eliminate from our
speech terms of contempt and from our conduct
actions of ill will.

3.   We shall teach our children that prejudice is
un-Christian and that good will and helpful deeds

are the duty of every Christian toward all men of
all races.

4. We shall protest against injustice and indigni-
ties against Negroes, as we do in the case of people of our own race, whenever and wherever we
meet them.

5. We shall be willing for the Negro to enjoy the
rights granted to him under the Constitution of the
United States, including the right to vote, to serve
on juries, to receive justice in the courts, to be
free from mob violence, to secure a just share
of the benefits of educational and other funds, and
to receive equal service for equal treatment on
public carriers and conveniences.

6. We shall be just in our dealing with the Negro
as an individual. Whenever he is in our employ
we shall pay him an adequate wage and provide for
him healthful working conditions.

7. We shall strive to promote community goodwill
between the races in every way possible.

8. We shall actively cooperate with Negro Baptists
in the building up of their churches, the education
of their ministers, and the promotion of their missions and evangelistic programs. [160]

This Charter may be taken as the beginning of the
renaissance in Southern Baptist teaching concerning race relations. The limitation of the Charter is obvious. The
Committee failed to see or would not dare admit in 1947 that
the segregated society in which they lived was itself a violation of the dignity of man which was being proclaimed. The
Committee could not assert that segregation is a unilateral
thrust of hostile and contemptuous power, and being universal in institutional policies, denies the individual the opportunity to live out in fullness "the principles of conduct."
Despite this serious limitation, the Charter represented a
great thrust forward in the understanding of Christian responsibility.

It may be said to mark the beginning of a renaissance
in teaching also because its spirit was reflected in later pronouncements and statements on race. In the fall meetings of

the State Baptist Conventions following the spring assembly
of the Southern Baptist Convention, several state conventions
failed to endorse and recommend the charter, but a few did.
Admittedly, the beginnings were slow, and it is not possible
to know the degree of the persistence of old ideas.   But in
the 1960's, with the background of the Charter and the
stimulus of Civil Rights achievements, there has been a
crescendo of new voices articulating new ideas.

An outstanding feature of the new teaching is the confession of guilt. In response to the recently passed Civil
Rights Bill the Christian Life Committee of the North Carolina Baptist Convention regretfully acknowledged "complicity
in the patterns of life and culture that have served to keep
our brethren, the Negro in servitude--social, economic, political and religious"--and admitted that the present crisis
"springs directly from our unwillingness to speak or act in
accordance with the truths we hold dear."161   J. Marse
Grant warns Southern Baptists that they must share responsibility for the climate in which Martin Luther King, Jr. was
slain and much of the other anti-Civil Rights violence has
occurred, for they are the dominant religious body in the
states involved. 162   He also notes with sorrow the dual system of justice which exists in the courts in Southern Baptist
territory. 163   The Christian Life Committee of the State Convention of Virginia points up the falsehood in the racist ideology and testifies that it has decisively shaped American
history, having "been used by groups in power to hold in
subservience other groups who lack that power."164

Associated with this confession of guilt is an apparent
newness of perspective which can come only after confession
and repentance.   The Christian Life Committee of the Virginia Baptist Convention urges the constituency to help in the
implementation of Public Law 284 which concerns open housing.   "The privilege of owning a home and living in a certain neighborhood should be determined by one's desire and
ability to pay with no consideration as to skin color, religion,
or ethnic background."165   The Christian Life Committee of
the North Carolina Baptist Convention recommends an open-
door policy for worship and church membership and support
for the Civil Rights Law of 1964; it commends those who ac-
commodate all customers and practice fair employment; it
unequivocally opposes violence; and it encourages an open-
door policy in all of the institutions of the church. 166   Reflecting on his own experience at a recent Interracial Bible
Conference, R. Grady Snowden, Jr. stresses the importance

of the person-to-person encounter for the realization of mature human affection.   In the day-to-day process of sharing
common concerns he found that he was able to relate to a
black fellow conferee, not as another "black" preacher, but
as "Jim Jones, a fellow minister of the gospel who inciden-
tally happened to be black."167   Although he belongs to that
small minority of Southern Baptists whose public teaching
was the same a generation ago as it is today, the words of
Edward A. McDowell must be set down as the epitome of the
renaissance:

> And so I believe that the first obligation Southern
> Baptists must assume as they confront the race
> problem is to accept the fact that our commitment
> to the gospel demands a radically changed attitude
> and practice toward Negroes. We must repent of
> our sin of prejudice and our hypocrisy of profes-
> sion without practice and embrace the gospel of
> love in all of its demands. No longer can we
> claim to love the Negro 'in his place.' We must
> accept him as a person, a person who deserves
> the same rights and dignity that we grant to per-
> sons of our own race. 168

(5)   The Jew

Two attitudes toward the Jew are found among Southern Baptists.   There is anti-Semitism; and there is the notion that the Jews are peculiarly related to God and He is
guiding their historical destiny.   Anti-Semites usually deny
their anti-Semitism to the general public.   If the spokesmen here referred to as anti-Semitic are not, then it
must be said at least that they clearly express anti-Semitic
sentiments.

Although he condemns prejudice against and persecution of the Jews, Victor I. Masters nevertheless proceeds
to say that any spirit of prejudice in America against Jews
has been balanced by the sense of racial solidarity and exclusiveness of the Jews.   While denying that he is undertaking to balance the ledger, he proceeds to castigate the Jews,
affirming that the great mass of American Christians and
other Americans whose social and political outlook have been
moulded by Christian standards "are getting weary of those
Jews, who get themselves placed sympathetically before a
long-suffering public as interpreters-in-chief of tolerance,

by the urban press of America that profits largely by Jewish business advertisements--to tell American Christians
just what is religious prejudice and how they must avoid
it. "169   The Jew ought to acknowledge that he has gotten a
square deal in this country "and that he has made such
large use of it that it is in some quarters becoming a question of whether he shall be allowed to dominate the whole
American outlook and fashion the public mind to conform to
Jewish racial predilections. "170   The Jew must also learn
not to expect two or three times as much tolerance from
his non-Jew compatriots as the various elements of Jews
exhibit toward each other.   There is scarcely another race
which has such a hard time getting along with itself.   Furthermore, the Jewish interpretation of religious tolerance
as involving nonproselytizing of Jews by Christians is inconsistent with the age-long practice of the Jews themselves. 171

      Speaking specifically on the subject of Jewish permea-
tion of American life, Masters says "they are a mighty and
subtle force at work even now to pull America away from
its traditional moorings. "172   The retail trade in large
cities is primarily dominated by Jewish houses which "have
used the power of their advertising accounts to influence editorial and news results in the city press of this country. "
And the influence of Jews is great--probably determinative--
in the moving picture industry, which is debasing the minds
of American youth. 173

      Asserting that the Jews "have been puny dwarfs in
spiritual life" throughout their history, John D. Freeman
deplores their power and influence in American public life.
"It is a tragedy that the Jews of America should be so influential in politics just now, for the bulk of the stock of
liquor distilleries ('The Wrecking of the 18th Amendment')
and probably that of the breweries is owned by Jews. "
Freeman goes on to say that the Jews largely control the
movie industry; "they have always fought to destroy the
Christian Sabbath, " even when infidels in Judaism; and "if
there is a dollar to be earned, they somehow know how to
go about doing it. "   Five thousand years of "selective breed-
ing" among them has produced "a race of intellectual giants.
Only strong drink and night life have restrained them from
being even more titanic in creative genius. "174

      Charles L. Leek calls the Jews "one of the world's
chief problem children, " and explains this condition as due
to their perversion of their chosen status.   Leek makes no

distinction between the action of the Jews and their being
acted upon, and by implication assigns the burden of guilt
to them in both cases.

> Whether they are the pathetic victims of lie-in-
> spired programs as in Poland, or the rioters
> against their British benefactors, in Palestine,
> or the un-assimilated un-Christian citizens of the
> average American community, they are a problem
> to the civilized world and chiefly to themselves.
> They suffer not altogether innocently. Somehow
> since God chose them for His holy purpose they
> have missed the way. [175]

The old Christ-killer charge is revived by the editors
of The Word and Way, who also explain Nazi anti-Semitism
as rooted in this ground.

> The outburst of anti-Semitic feeling in Germany is
> but another demonstration of the feeling of resent-
> ment of the world for the attitude of these people
> toward Jesus Christ.

> ... For their superb ability the Jews might be the
> most respected and beloved race in all the world.
> Instead, they are the most disliked, and all be-
> cause of their treatment of Jesus Christ. [176]

The editors see the rejection of Christ as the turning
point in Jewish history, the transition being from glorious
attainment to inglorious failure, eventuating in suffering.
And they charge the Jews with having engendered envy and
hatred in the hearts of their gentile neighbors by practicing
exclusiveness, while at the same time claiming the fruits of
industry and commerce. While expressing regret at the use
of force by the Germans against the Jews, the editors express their appreciation of German awareness "of the impending danger of Russian Sovietism, led largely by Jews. "[177]

Charging the Jews with responsibility for the crucifixion, L. L. Gwaltney reflects on the twenty centuries of
Jewish persecution which culminated in the Nazi extermina-
tions of five- or six-million Jews. He concludes that this
long line of tragedy is incompatible with both the Christian
and the Jewish conscience, but adds "one cannot help but
wonder if there is a connection between the persecutions of
the Jews and responsibility for the 'blood' which the Jews

willfully involved upon themselves. "[178]

The idea that the Jews are peculiarly related to God
and He is guiding their destiny is the note most frequently
sounded concerning the Jews in Southern Baptist literature.
"The Jews are God's chosen people--whether obedient or
disobedient, " and persecution of the Jews brings the wrath
of God. [179] Although the scattering and persecution of the
Jews is a fulfillment of prophecy, God always deals with
those who mistreat His ancient people. [180] The Jews will
continue to be scattered until their times are fulfilled. Then
they will accept the Messiah and be a blessing to all nations. [181] To the logical mind, a strange mystery is involved in the inevitability of Jewish persecution and the certain punishment for the perpetrators of this evil.

Under the title, "The Jew in His Place, " E. D. Solomon sets forth what may be called a Jewish Christian Zion-
ism. The hope for the Jew lies, first of all, in the acceptance of Christ. When he does this God will make his enemies worship at his feet. But the Jew must also return to
Palestine. He no more belongs inside other nations than
Jonah belonged in the belly of the whale. "There is far
more than Hitler back of Jewish persecution in Germany.
The Jews had compromised their religion, intermarried
with Gentiles, despised their racial heritage, and ridiculed
their ancient land. " Germany is only the beginning of the
troubles. "God means for His ancient people to return to
their native land which He has marvelously preserved and
miraculously delivered. " Not until they return to their
rightful place will things ever be settled. [182]

On the surface, the absence of criticisms of anti-
Semitic tendencies among Southern Baptists in the literature
of the ecumenically minded is surprising. But, on second
thought, it is understandable for two reasons. First, anti-
Semitism does not appear on as large a scale as anti-Ne-
groism. And second, the preoccupation with this very anti-
Negroism has consumed the attention of the ecumenically
minded. One voice must be noted, however, who rejects
the Christ-killer charge, directed at the Jews alone. O. W.
Taylor turns to the Scriptures for the testimony that the
world princes, the Jews, the Gentiles, and "all of us"
killed Jesus. "All of us" did not do it, historically, but
we did it redemptively. "That is to say, our sins made
the death of Christ necessary and redemptively nailed Him
to the cross. "[183] Taylor might have changed the form of

the verb from the past to the present tense and pointed to
anti-Semitism as a prime example of the slaying of the
Christ with whom we are contemporaneous.

Notes

1. In the South, the "race question" means the color ques-
    tion.
2. Beall, Noble Y. , "Educating the Negro Baptist Preach-
    er, " Religious Herald, CIX (June 11, 1936), p. 17.
3. Ibid.
4. Breland, R. L. , "The Children of Ham, " The Baptist
    Record, XXXII (June 5, 1930), p. 9.
5. Ibid.
6. In the division of the world, as set forth by Breland,
    Japheth was assigned the eastern part of Asia. How
    people who are the descendants of Europeans became
    the sons and daughters of Japheth, he does not indi-
    cate.
7. Ibid.
8. Pitt, R. H. , "Foolish and Criminal Chatter" (Editorial),
    Religious Herald, XCI (December 5, 1918), p. 11.
9. Ibid.
10. Pitt, R. H. , "Good People--White and Colored" (Edi-
    torial), Religious Herald, CI (May 17, 1928), p. 15.
11. Masters, Victor I. , "Southern Christians and the Negro
    Problem" (Editorial), Western Recorder, CIX (No-
    vember 28, 1935), p. 7.
12. Farmer, J. S. , "The World Alliance, " Biblical Re-
    corder, XCIV (July 11, 1928), p. 7.
13. Lipsey, P. I. , "Editorial Comment, " The Baptist
    Record, XXI (August 7, 1919), p. 1.
14. Lipsey, P. I. , "The Anti-Lynching Bill" (Editorial),
    The Baptist Record, XXIV (January 19, 1922), p. 4.
15. Porter, J. W. , "The Negro Problem North and South
    (Editorial) Western Recorder, 93rd Year (June 29,
    1918), p. 8.
16. Report of the Racial Commission, Minutes of the Co-
    lumbia Baptist Association of Alabama, (1944), p. 9.
17. McDowell, E. A. , "The Color Line, " Biblical Recorder,
    CVII (April 2, 1941), p. 6.
18. Ibid.
19. "Caste, as distinguished from class, consists of such
    drastic restrictions of free competition in the various
    spheres of life that the individual in a lower caste
    cannot, by any means, change his status, except by

a secret and illegitimate 'passing,' which is possible only to the few who have the physical appearance of members of the upper caste"--Gunnar Myrdal, An American Dilemma (New York, Harper and Brothers, 1944), I, pp. 674-675.

20. "An Urgent Need and an Open Door," Report of the Committee on Temperance and Social Service of the Southern Baptist Convention, Annual of the Southern Baptist Convention (Nashville, 1920), p. 97.

21. Cody, Z. T., "Living with People of Other Races," (Sunday School Lesson), The Baptist Courier, LXIV (December 1, 1932), pp. 10-11.

22. Lipsey, P. I., "Righteousness Among Races" (Editorial) The Baptist Record, XXII (September 9, 1920), p. 4.

23. Barbour was at that time editor of the National Baptist Voice, organ of the National Baptist Convention, U.S.A.

24. Allen, W. C., "Unwise Negro Leadership" (Editorial), The Baptist Courier, LXX (June 30, 1938), p. 2.

25. Masters, Victor I., "As to Unwise Negro Leadership" (Editorial), Western Recorder, CXII (July 7, 1938), p. 8.

26. Masters, Victor, I., "Friendship and Social Apartness of Races in the South" (Editorial) Western Recorder, CXII (July 14, 1938), p. 6.

27. Lide, R. W., "Concerning Unwise Leadership," The Baptist Courier, LXX (July 14, 1938), p. 4.

28. Gambrell, J. B., "Some New Phases of the Race Question in America," Baptist Standard, XXXIII (February 24, 1921), p. 6.

29. Johnson, Livingston, "The Crumbling Color Line" (Editorial), Biblical Recorder, XCV (August 14, 1929), p. 7.

30. Ibid.

31. Paschal, George W., "Another Phase of the Race Problem" (Editorial), Biblical Recorder, CIV (July 20, 1938), p. 7.

32. Tinnin, Finley W., "Racial Prejudice Bugaboo Again" (Editorial) Baptist Message, XLIX (July 30, 1942), p. 2.

33. McDowell, E. A., "The Social Gospel of the New Testament," The Baptist Courier, LXVI (December 13, 1934), p. 8.

34. Ibid.

35. Cody, Z. T., "Philip and the Ethiopean Treasurer" (Sunday School Lesson) The Baptist Courier, LVI (May 7, 1925), p. 6.

36. Moore, J. D., "Interracial Problems" (Editorial) Bap-
    tist and Reflector, LXXXVIII (January 5, 1922), p. 2.
37. Ibid.
38. Johnson, Livingston, "The Negro in Politics," Biblical
    Recorder, XCIV (November 14, 1928), p. 7.
39. Reported by Z. T. Cody, The Baptist Courier, L (May
    22, 1919), p. 6.
40. McGlothlin, W. J., "The 75 Million Campaign and Ne-
    gro Education," The Baptist Courier, L (October 9,
    1919), p. 2.
41. Ibid.
42. Allen, W. C., "A Better View Concerning the Race
    Issue" (Editorial), The Baptist Courier, LXX (Sep-
    tember 15, 1938), p. 2.
43. "Resolutions--Concerning Lynching and Race Relations,"
    Annual of the Southern Baptist Convention (Nashville,
    1939), p. 141.
44. Leathers, W. W., "Ways to Aid the Negro," The Bap-
    tist Courier, LXIII (September 3, 1931), p. 6.
45. Ibid.
46. Ibid., p. 7.
47. Ibid.
48. Morgan, David, "Alongside Us Caucasians," Biblical
    Recorder, CVI (November 6, 1949), p. 9.
49. Ibid., p. 10.
50. Tinnin, Finley W., "Effects of Dangerous Negro Leader-
    ship" (Editorial) Baptist Message, LV (July 21, 1938),
    p. 2.
51. Wicker, J. J., "Chips--Great Negroes," Religious
    Herald, CXI (March 24, 1938), p. 9.
52. Ibid.
53. "'Old Joe'--Keeper of the Keys" (Anonymous), The
    Baptist Courier, LII (November 21, 1949), p. 12.
54. Gilbert, O. P., "Black But White, Poor But Rich
    (Editorial), The Christian Index, CXIX (December
    21, 1939), p. 9.
55. Tinnin, Finley W., "Wild-eyed Social Equality, Vapor-
    ings" (Editorial), Baptist Message, LX (April 29,
    1943), p. 2.
56. Johnson, Livingston, "Different Views Among Negroes,"
    Biblical Recorder, LXXXV (January 28, 1920), p. 7.
57. Johnson, Livingston, "Two Types of Negroes," Biblical
    Recorder, XCV (July 10, 1929), p. 7.
58. Masters, Victor I., "Lynching and the Negro Problem,"
    Biblical Recorder, LXXXVI (September 15, 1920),
    p. 5.
59. "Inequalities and Injustice," Report of the Annual of

the Southern Baptist Convention, Report of the Social
Service Commission of the Southern Baptist Convention, (Nashville, 1949), pp. 84-85.

60. Ibid., p. 85.
61. Ibid.
62. Ibid.
63. "Race," Report of the Social Service Commission of
the Southern Baptist Convention, Annual of the Southern Baptist Convention (Nashville, 1943), p. 107.
64. Knight, Ryland, "The Historic Baptist Principle in Race
Relations," Religious Herald, CIX (July 23, 1936),
p. 4.
65. Leek, Charles L., "Too Fast in the Right Direction,"
The Alabama Baptist, CVIII (August 12, 1943), p. 4.
66. Gwaltney, L. L., "Race Relations" (Editorial) The
Alabama Baptist, XCVIII (July 20, 1933), p. 3.
67. Ibid.
68. Hunter, R. M., "Treating the Negro Wrong," The
Alabama Baptist, 96th year (July 28, 1932), p. 9.
69. Ibid.
70. Ibid.
71. Gambrell, J. B., "The Negro in Politics," Western
Recorder, 96th year (March 17, 1921), p. 14.
72. Myers, Lewis A., "Equal Education for Negroes" (Editorial), The Arkansas Baptist, XLI (March 5, 1942),
p. 3.
73. "Assistance to the Negro," Report of the Committee on
Social Service and Civic Righteousness of the North
Carolina Baptist Convention, North Carolina Baptist
Annual, (1942), p. 44.
74. Helton, R. A. "The Christian and the Race Problem"
(Sunday School Lesson), Religious Herald, CXVII
(October 26, 1944), p. 17.
75. Report of the Inter-Racial Commission of the North
Carolina Baptist Convention, Annual of the Baptist
State Convention of North Carolina (1930), p. 35-36.
76. Report of the Inter-Racial Relations Committee of the
Virginia Baptist Convention, Virginia Baptist Annual
(1941), pp. 128 ff.
77. Pitt, R. H., "Recent Lynching" (Editorial), Religious
Herald, CVI (December 14, 1933), p. 11.
78. Williams, J. L., "Brookhaven on Lynching," The Baptist Record, XXX (August 16, 1928), p. 10.
79. Cody, Z. T., "The Aiken Lynching" (Editorial), The
Baptist Courier, LVII (October 21, 1926), p. 6.
80. Cody, Z. T. and Keys, J. C., "It Was an Abominable
Deed" (Editorial), The Baptist Courier, LI (April

26, 1920), p. 5.

81.   "Mob Murders, " Report of the Social Service Commis-
       sion of the Southern Baptist Convention, Annual of
       the Southern Baptist Convention (Nashville, 1931),
       p. 122.

82.   "Recommendations... Lynchings and Mob Violence, " Re-
       port of the Social Service Commission of the South-
       ern Baptist Convention, Annual of the Southern Bap-
       tist Convention (Nashville, 1936), p. 34.

83.   Callaway, T. F. , "The Old South and the Negro Slaves,"
       The Christian Index, CXVIII (August 18, 1938), p. 4.

84.   Johnson, Livingston, "Churches on Lynching, " Biblical
       Recorder, XCVI (November 5, 1930), p. 7.

85.   Lipsey, P. I. , "The Anti-Lynching Bill" (Editorial),
       The Baptist Record, XXIV (January 19, 1922), p. 4.

86.   Farmer, J. S. , "A National Anti-Lynching Law, "
       Biblical Recorder, XCIX (March 14, 1934), p. 7.

87.   Johnson, Livingston, "Lynch Law, " Biblical Recorder,
       LXXXIV (May 14, 1919), p. 3.

88.   Farmer, J. S. , "Negro Education in North Carolina, "
       Biblical Recorder, C (March 25, 1936), p. 7.

89.   Alley, Reuben E. , "A Good Omen" (Editorial), Re-
       ligious Herald, CXVI (April 15, 1943), p. 10.

90.   Pitt, R. H. , "Vicious Intermeddling" (Editorial), Re-
       ligious Herald, CVI (May 4, 1933), p. 10.

91.   Holt, A. J. , "The Baptists of the South and the Negro"
       (Editorial), Florida Baptist Witness, XXX (August
       2, 1917), p. 6.

92.   Callaway, T. F. , "The Old South and the Negro Slaves, "
       The Christian Index, CXVIII (August 18, 1938), p. 3.

93.   Weaver, Rufus W. , "The Salvation of the White Races, "
       The Christian Index, CI (June 16, 1921), p. 8.

94.   Graham, B. J. W. , "The Negro Problem of the North"
       (Editorial) The Christian Index, XCIX (August 7,
       1919), p. 2.

95.   Ibid.

96.   Alley, Reuben E. , "End of Segregation" (Editorial) Re-
       ligious Herald, CXXVII (May 27, 1954), p. 10.

97.   "Recommendations No. 3--Concerning the Supreme Court
       Decision on Public Education, " Report of the Chris-
       tian Life Commission of the Southern Baptist Conven-
       tion, Annual of the Southern Baptist Convention (Nash-
       ville, 1954), p. 407.

98.   "Supreme Court School Decision, " Report of the Chris-
       tian Life Committee of the Baptist General Associa-
       tion of Virginia, Virginia Baptist Annual (November,
       1954), p. 89.

99. Ibid., p. 88.
100. "Race Relations," Report of the Committee on Social
     Service and Temperance, Minutes of the Atlantic
     Baptist Association (November, 1956), p. 19.
101. Ranson, Guy H., "The Minister and the Supreme Court
     Ruling," Review and Expositor, LI (October, 1954),
     pp. 529-532.
102. Ibid., p. 534.
103. Clark, John G., "Segregation and the Christian Con-
     science," Religious Herald, CXXVII (November 11,
     1954), pp. 4-5.
104. Poteat, Edwin McNiell, "Current Perspectives on the
     Race Problem," Biblical Recorder, 122 (February
     4, 1956), pp. 2-3. Published posthumously by the
     Editor.
105. Buchanan, Henry A., "The Church and Desegregation,"
     The Review and Expositor, LII (October, 1955), p.
     475.
106. Ibid., p. 477.
107. Goodrich, A. L., "The SBC Convention," (Editorial)
     The Baptist Record, 66 (June 10, 1954), p. 3.
108. Tinnin, Finley, "Non-Segregation" (Editorial) Baptist
     Message, 71 (June 3, 1954), p. 2.
109. Brown, Joseph E., "Fair Employment Practices
     Legislation," The Word and Way, 83 (August 2,
     1945), p. 2.
110. Hurt, John J., Jr., "Christian Rights" (Editorial),
     Christian Index, 128 (March 4, 1948), p. 6.
111. "The Race Problem," Report of the Social Service
     Committee of the Florida Baptist Association,
     Minutes of the Florida Baptist Association, (Oc-
     tober, 1946), pp. 29-30.
112. "Race Issue," Report of the Social Service Commission
     of the Georgia Baptist Convention, Minutes of the
     Baptist Convention of the State of Georgia (Novem-
     ber, 1960), p. 105.
113. James, E. S., "Desegregation, Yes - by Legislation,
     No," (Editorial) Baptist Standard, 75 (July 24,
     1963), p. 3.
114. McClendon, James William "The Civil Rights Bill: A
     New Opportunity for Baptists"? Baptist and Re-
     flector, 130 (August 6, 1964), p. 8.
115. James, E. S., op. cit.
116. "The Racial Crisis," Report of the Christian Life
     Commission of the Southern Baptist Convention,
     Annual of the Southern Baptist Convention (1965),
     pp. 246-257.

117. Tinnin, Finley W., "World Alliance President and
         Civil Rights" (Editorial), Baptist Message, 65
         (March 18, 1948), p. 2.
118. Morgan, S. L., Sr., "Beware of Forced School Inte-
         gration," Western Recorder, 130 (May 17, 1956),
         p. 7.
119. "Race Relations," Report of the Christian Life Com-
         mission of the Alabama State Baptist Convention,
         Annual of the Alabama Baptist State Convention
         (1959), p. 126.
120. Ibid., p. 127.
121. Owen, Richard N., "Racial Strife" (Editorial) Baptist
         and Reflector, 129 (May 30, 1963), p. 4.
122. Macon, Leon, "The South Will Solve Its Problems,"
         (Editorial) The Alabama Baptist, 128 (February 14,
         1963), p. 3.
123. McDowell, E. A., "What About Race Relations in the
         South Today"? Religious Herald, CXXVII (January
         14, 1954), pp. 4-5.
124. Harwell, Jack U., "Prayer, Patience Needed in
         School Integration" (Editorial) The Christian Index,
         148 (July 24, 1969), p. 6.
125. McDonald, Edwin L., "One Word More" (Editorial),
         Arkansas Baptist, 62 (September 26, 1963), p. 3.
126. Gaddy, Jerrel Dee, "Desegregation Versus Integration,"
         Baptist Standard, 75 (October 16, 1963), pp. 6-7.
127. Owen, Richard N., "America Must Decide" (Editorial),
         Baptist and Reflector, 129 (September 5, 1963),
         p. 4.
128. Cole, James F., "Freedom Riders" (Editorial), The
         Baptist Message, 78 (June 29, 1961), p. 2.
129. Macon, Leon, "Things Not Generally Known" (Edi-
         torial) The Alabama Baptist, 130 (April 1, 1965),
         p. 3.
130. Bryan, Gainer E., Jr., "Southern Baptists Should
         Identify with Negro Cause" (Editorial), The Mary-
         land Baptist, XLVIII (May 13, 1965), p. 8.
131. Daley, C. R., "A Personal Conviction" (Editorial),
         Western Recorder, 135 (May 4, 1961), p. 4.
132. Macon, Leon, "A National Problem" (Editorial), The
         Alabama Baptist, 130 (August 26, 1965), p. 3.
133. Baggett, Hudson, "Recent Riots" The Harvest of
         False Hopes" (Editorial), The Alabama Baptist,
         131 (August 11, 1966), p. 2.
134. Owen, Richard N., "Criminal Revolt" (Editorial),
         Baptist and Reflector 133 (August 10, 1967), p. 4.

135. Grant, Daniel R., "Black Power's Many Faces," The Alabama Baptist, 133 (October 10, 1968), p. 7.

136. Hurt, John J., "Don't Blame Them All" (Editorial), Baptist Standard, 81 (May 28, 1969), p. 6.

137. Harwell, Jack U., "Keep Racial Demands in Historical Perspective" (Editorial), The Christian Index 148 (May 29, 1969), p. 6.

138. Lester, James A., "The Black Manifesto" (Editorial), Baptist and Reflector, 135 (June 12, 1969), p. 6.

139. Grizzard, R. Stuart, "Reparations, Restitutiona and Repentance," Religious Herald, CXLII (November 6, 1969), pp. 12-13.

140. It must be observed that American Christianity as a whole failed to challenge segregation until the mid-1940's. No Protestant church body ever presented a Christian criticism of segregation until 1946 when the Federal Council of Churches called for a desegregated church in a desegregated society.

141. Sullivan, H. T., "The Christian Concept of Race Relations," The Baptist Message, 74 (October 10, 1957), pp. 1, 4.

142. Preston, T. J., "Baptists and Segregation" (a letter to the editor), Christian Index, 134 (January 6, 1955), p. 8.

143. McRae, L. J., "...Disturbed Over Barnette's Article" (a letter to the editor) Baptist and Reflector, 130 (March 26, 1964), pp. 2-3.

144. Soloman, E. D., Editorial, Florida Baptist Witness, LIX (February 28, 1946), p. 4.

145. "Race Relations," Report to the Augusta (Georgia) Association of Baptist Churches, Inc., Minutes of the Augusta Association of Baptist Churches (October, 1957), p. 51.

146. "Race Relations," Report of the Social Service Commission of the State Convention of the Baptist Denomination in South Carolina, Annual of the State Convention of the Baptist Denomination in South Carolina (November, 1949), pp. 138-139.

147. Tinnin, Finley W., "Non-Segregation," (Editorial) Baptist Message, 71 (June 3, 1954), p. 2.

148. "Human Relationships," Report of the Social Service Commission of the Baptist Convention of the State of Georgia, Minutes of the Baptist Convention of the State of Georgia (November, 1952), p. 55.

149. Tinnin, Finley W., "A Sane View of Segregation," (Editorial), Baptist Message, 73 (September 37, 1956), p. 2.

150. "Race Issue, " Report of the Social Service Commission
      of the Baptist Convention of the State of Georgia,
      Minutes of the Baptist Convention of the State of
      Georgia (November, 1960), p. 105.
151. Leek, Charles F. , "Segregation or Subjugation, " The
      Alabama Baptist, 111 (November 28, 1946), p. 4.
152. Gritz, Jack L. , "What About Integration?" (Editorial)
      The Baptist Messenger, 45 (March 8, 1956), p. 2.
153. McDowell, Edward A. , "Myths About Race We Must
      Give Up, " Baptist and Reflector, 134 (July 18,
      1968), p. 9.
154. Ibid.
155. Valentine, Foy, "The Curse of Ham, " Baptist Stand-
      ard, 66 (August 12, 1954), p. 3.
156. Hudson, R. Lofton, "Is Segregation Christian?" Bap-
      tist and Reflector, 120 (August 5, 1954), p. 4.
157. Sixteen pastors voted for the statement, seven against,
      and several abstained.
158. "Pastors Adopt Statement on 'Human Equality, ' The
      Maryland Baptist, XLI (November 15, 1958), p.
      14.
159. Barnett, Henlee, "Southern Baptist Churches and
      Segregation, " Baptist Standard, 76 (February 12,
      1964), p. 7.
160. Report of the Committee on Race Relations, Annual of
      the Southern Baptist Convention (Nashville, 1947),
      pp. 342-343.
161. "Race Relations, " Report of the Christian Life Com-
      mittee of the Baptist State Convention of North
      Carolina, Annual of the Baptist State Convention
      of North Carolina (November, 1964), p. 151.
162. Grant, J. Marse, "Southern Baptist Convention Must
      Share Responsibility for Climate in South, " (Edi-
      torial) Biblical Recorder, 134 (April 13, 1968),
      p. 3.
163. Grant, J. Marse, "Is Christian Conscience Insensitive
      to Injustice?" (Editorial), Biblical Recorder, 131
      (May 15, 1965), p. 3.
164. "Racism, " Report of the Christian Life Committee of
      the Baptist General Association of Virginia, The
      Virginia Baptist Annual (November, 1968), p. 65.
165. Ibid. , p. 66.
166. "Race Relations, " Report of the Christian Life Com-
      mittee of the Baptist State Convention of North
      Carolina, Annual of the Baptist State Convention
      of North Carolina, (November, 1964), pp. 151-
      152.

167. Snowden, R. Grady, Jr., "An Appraisal of the Inter-
        racial Bible Conference," Florida Baptist Witness
        86 (November 20, 1969), p. 10.
168. McDowell, Edward A., "The Race Problem and the
        Gospel," Baptist and Reflector, 134 (June 27,
        1968), p. 5.
169. Masters, Victor I., "The Jew and the Persecution
        Complex" (Editorial), Western Recorder, CVIII
        (April 26, 1934), p. 8.
170. Ibid., p. 9.
171. Ibid.
172. Masters, Victor I., "Consider the Jew" (Editorial)
        Western Recorder, CVIII (August 2, 1934), p. 9.
173. Masters, Victor I., "The Jew and Public Opinion"
        (Editorial) Western Recorder, CVIII (November 22,
        1934), p. 7.
174. Freeman, John D., "Will Jewry Be Warned?" (Edi-
        torial) Western Recorder, 119 (February 22, 1945),
        p. 8.
175. Leek, Charles L., "A Pervarsion of Jewish Destiny,"
        The Alabama Baptist, 111 (July 18, 1946), p. 4.
176. Brown, S. M. and Brown, Joseph E., "The Jews and
        Germany" (Editorial) The Word and the Way, LXX
        (April 6, 1933), p. 2.
177. Ibid.
178. Gwaltney, L. L., "The Jews and the Crucifixion"
        (Editorial), The Alabama Baptist, 113 (April 1,
        1948), p. 3.
179. Masters, Victor I., "The Wickedness of Persecuting
        the Jews" (Editorial) Western Recorder, CVIII
        (November 8, 1934), p. 8.
180. McConnell, F. M., "Germany and the Jews" (Edi-
        torial), Baptist Standard, XLV (April 6, 1933),
        p. 3.
181. McConnell, F. M., "The Destiny of the Jews," (Edi-
        torial), Baptist Standard, L (December 1, 1938),
        p. 3.
182. Solomon, E. D., "The Jew in His Place" (Editorial),
        Florida Baptist Witness, XLVII (July 19, 1934),
        p. 6.
183. Taylor, O. W., "The Gospel Not Anti-Semitic" (Edi-
        torial), Baptist and Reflector, 115 (July 7, 1949),
        p. 2.

INDEX

as active agent of war, 104-105
as immanent in man, 105-106
Government
duty of rulers, 90, 91
limits of authority, 66
source of authority, 61ff.

Harmony
racial, 208ff.
Home
nature of, 162
relations in, 162-164
Husband
relation to children, 163-164
relation to wife, 163

Idleness, 194-195
Integration, 241
Intermarriage, 214-215

Jew, 254ff.

Kennedy, John F., 20, 21, 22

Labor
rights, demands, and duties of, 195-198
Law
and ideas, 69-71
and morals, 66-69
enforcement, 64-65
League of Nations
opposition to, 119-120
support for, 118, 119, 120
Leisure, 194
Liquor
evils of,
biological, 135
economic, 135-136
moral, 134-135
Locke, 62-63, 89
Luther, 60, 98
Lynching, 226ff.
bills, 228